TWO TITANS, ONE CITY

JOSEPH CHAMBERLAIN AND GEORGE CADBURY

Andrew Reekes

Published by West Midlands History Limited

Minerva Mill Innovation Centre, Alcester, Warwickshire, UK.

© 2017 West Midlands History Limited.

© All images are copyright as credited.

ISBN:

Caric Press Limited, Merthyr Tydfil, Wales.

To Patrick Derham, historian and friend.

ACKNOWLEDGEMENTS

I am grateful to Malcolm Dick for his perceptive advice in the writing of this book, and to Mike Gibbs for his enthusiasm and support for the project; indeed, it was he who first challenged me to compare these two Birmingham figures. Jenni Butterworth has been a wise and insightful editor, making innumerable valuable suggestions to improve this work. The entire West Midlands team: Alison Davies, David Beattie and Janet Sullivan have been a privilege to work with, David being a rigorous and relentless proofreader and the latter sourcing many excellent images to illuminate the text.

I have learnt much from talking and listening to Peter Marsh, that doyen of Chamberlain studies whose work is so influential that to try to write anything on Joseph Chamberlain seems an impertinence. I am also grateful to the archivists at the *Cadbury* Research Archive: Special Collections, the University of Birmingham, whose enthusiastic willingness to help has made researching there a joy. I am grateful, too, to Sarah Foden at the *Cadbury* Archive at Bournville for her unfailing helpfulness and for the bonus of supplementary chocolates for the flagging researcher. The archivists at the Library of Birmingham have had to survive near-death by a thousand cuts, but in their reduced circumstances have remained cheerful and very constructive.

The encouragement of friends like Patrick Derham and Alison Goodfellow has been inestimable; above all I am grateful to Lynne for tolerating two insistent cuckoos in the household as the author's preoccupation with Cadbury and Chamberlain deepened.

Contents

2   Author's Note

3   Introduction

10   Chapter One
Birmingham Businessmen

20   Chapter Two
A Zeal for Education

32   Chapter Three
Projecting Values in Brick and Stone

44   Chapter Four
Social Preoccupations

63   Chapter Five
Differences over Party and Politics

73   Chapter Six
Three Dividing Lines

84   Chapter Seven
Scandal

95   Chapter Eight
Private Passions

114   Chapter Nine
Family and Dynasty

126   Timeline of Events

130   Notes

140   Index

Author's note

Until the death of Richard Cadbury in 1899 the family chocolate firm was known as *Cadbury Bros*. So, when writing of the firm in the nineteenth century I have called it *Cadbury Bros*. Thereafter it is referred to as *Cadbury*, its subsequent trade name.

Joseph Chamberlain was a director of *Nettlefold and Chamberlain* until 1874. After he left the firm it became known as *Nettlefolds* before merging with *Guest and Keen* to become *GKN* in 1902.

Whilst Joseph Chamberlain continues to attract historians, being the subject of a number of excellent recent biographies, George Cadbury does not.[1] The most recent full-length study, that of his friend A.G. Gardiner, was published nearly a century ago in 1924. This new book then attempts to be a modern appreciation of the life and work of George Cadbury, whilst at the same time doing something that has not been done before – drawing a comparison between two Birmingham contemporaries with significant national reputations. Such a study offers a fresh perspective and throws into sharp relief the extent and character of the achievement of each.

INTRODUCTION

The 'one city' of the title refers to Birmingham, which by the end of the nineteenth century had established itself as Britain's leading provincial city. During the course of the nineteenth century its population had increased exponentially from around 70,000 to 500,000. Its prosperity was located in the thousands of small workshops specialising in metal-working, with products ranging from jewellery to toys and cutlery, from locks to guns. With justification it has been dubbed 'The First Manufacturing Town in the World'.[2]

Birmingham experienced in the early nineteenth century a growing and palpable sense of exclusion from the country's decision-making structures centred on Westminster. That resentment against political and social ostracisation was fanned by Birmingham Nonconformists who encountered an Anglican establishment which effectively barred schools, universities and some high offices to other denominations. Nonconformists in Birmingham were leaders of a municipal and political revolution, and they were at the heart of the Radicalism which characterised the city throughout the nineteenth century. At the top of their agenda for much of that time was the campaign to persuade Parliament to concede equitable representation to burgeoning industrial centres like Birmingham. Reflecting this, Thomas Attwood's Birmingham Political Union led the national charge for parliamentary reform, which culminated in the Great Reform Act of 1832. It was in Birmingham that Chartism's demand for universal manhood suffrage, a vote for every man, was launched in 1838 by men disillusioned by the failure of the Great Reform Act to loosen the grip of the traditional classes on power. Again Birmingham was the venue for John Bright, its Radical MP, to revive the call for parliamentary reform in October 1857.[3] Finally, leading Birmingham Nonconformists and businessmen also formulated and propagated a highly influential philosophy of municipal governance, the civic gospel; the city became a model of enlightened administration for imitators within and beyond Britain.

Within this 'one city', there were of course several significant figures who, at various times, impacted on its history, but this book argues that Joseph Chamberlain (1836-1914) and George Cadbury (1839-1922) tower over all others as Birmingham's two historic titans. Their names still resonate powerfully in Birmingham and more widely, partly because their families continued for many years, in their own ways, to carry on the work of the paterfamilias, in so doing consolidating the family name in the local consciousness.

What is significant about these two men? Joseph Chamberlain was arguably the first great middle-class statesman in modern British political history. He had been a very successful businessman. His mayoral term between 1873 and 1876 then established Birmingham as the model for the application of the civic gospel and for good government. Once at Westminster he consolidated a reputation as the foremost Radical of the age, an articulate and imaginative visionary campaigning to improve the working and domestic lives of the labouring classes. He led the way on local government reform, on winning free elementary education for all, on workers' compensation, land reform, Old Age Pensions, job creation for the unemployed, and graduated taxation. He was a dynamic force in party politics for thirty years, his speaking tours of the country being a feature of election campaigns from 1892 to 1906. Such was his organisational ability and personal charisma that he created a political fortress (his Duchy) consisting of eleven impregnable seats in the West Midlands, a unique phenomenon in modern British history. Peel, Gladstone, Disraeli, Lloyd George and Churchill never achieved a geographical power base like this, let alone one that lasted nearly seventy years.

Yet as much as he sought to be constructive with his social reforms, he was a destructive force too, the only man to have split two parties (the Liberals in 1886 and the Unionists in 1903). He was also a leading author of the Boer War in 1899 which became known as 'Joe's War'; whilst for a number of years that association with popular jingoism made him a hero for millions, the war's final reckoning in men and money knocked the gloss off his reputation. Nevertheless, right through to 1939, and long after his death, the Chamberlain Effect kept Birmingham and its immediate surrounds loyal to the Unionist party cause.

George Cadbury was one of the foremost English philanthropists of his age. When the Convocation of the Church set out to investigate the (unfair) distribution of wealth in Britain in 1906 it was to George Cadbury that they turned for advice. He had made his fortune building up his family firm *Cadbury Bros.* into a market leader in confectionery. He became renowned as a model employer, and in that regard his significance lay in the pioneering work he did in introducing welfare schemes, pensions and leisure activities for his workforce. His concern for the working classes broadened out to embrace their housing needs and indeed, the quality of the whole environment in which they lived. Again he was a pioneer – in Bournville Village he was the first Garden City disciple to implement his vision of a generously planned and imaginatively built settlement. Bournville Village attracted international attention, and brought the King and Queen to Selly Oak to see for themselves in 1919.

George Cadbury achieved much else besides. He is a significant part of Quaker history in his establishment of five Selly Oak Colleges intended to train Quakers and representatives of other Christian denominations in theology, missionary and teaching work. He did much to bring the Free Churches together. He organised and funded successful national campaigns to win Old Age Pensions for all, and to abolish the worst evils of sweated labour. Finally, he was a party figure but his political activity was channelled through the Press, for he was important in funding the only metropolitan daily paper, the *Daily News*, to stand out against delirious nationalism during the Boer War.

Birmingham celebrated their achievements while they lived. There have been few occasions to rival the junketings of tens of thousands who saw a victorious Joseph Chamberlain depart to tour conquered South Africa in 1902 or the commemoration of his 70th birthday in 1906. Bournville factory and village hosted huge gatherings for the King and Queen in 1919, which were as much a tribute to their founder as to the royal visitors.

The city continues to memorialise the work of the two titans, in bricks and mortar. Joseph Chamberlain's great improvement scheme from 1875 resulted in the range of impressive Venetian Gothic buildings on Corporation Street, while his mayoralty set down a lasting legacy in the municipal buildings of the Council House and the City Museum and Art Gallery. His time as Chairman of the Birmingham School Board is still commemorated by a host of surviving red brick and terracotta school buildings, characterised by their steep roofs, generous windows and lofty towers. In a more directly personal way, the memorial fountain which until recently stood in Chamberlain Square with its gothic spire, its mosaics and its portrait medallion of Joseph Chamberlain, and the Jewellery Quarter Clock, celebrate the man and remind fresh generations of his importance.[4] Above all, the great campanile at the University of Birmingham is a memorial clock tower, paying tribute in 1905 to the educational vision of its founder. Said to be the tallest free-standing clock tower in the world, it is a very visible reminder for miles around of Joseph Chamberlain's towering presence in the city.

The architectural impact of George Cadbury's Birmingham legacy is less ostentatious, even if the noticeboards welcoming drivers to Bournville bear large photographs of its founding father. The scale of Bournville, the variety of its hundreds of Arts and Crafts houses built in a Worcestershire/Warwickshire cottage vernacular, the sense of space and of green, make it refreshingly different from almost every other suburban development in the country. George Cadbury's original intention of creating a settlement which mixed the classes in a cohesive community with institutes, places of worship, shops and schools, all in a style indigenous to the counties around, has been honoured in that the community remains unspoilt. Indeed, so attractive is it that in 2003 the *Rowntree Foundation* judged it probably the happiest community in Britain in which to live.[5] George Cadbury's physical mark on Birmingham extends to embrace the surviving Victorian Bournville factory itself, Woodbrooke where he developed his former residence into an institution, and several of the Selly Oak Colleges, as well as Meeting Houses or Institutes in Stirchley, Selly Oak and Cotteridge.

When taken together, George Cadbury and Joseph Chamberlain illuminate and personify some of the central trends and preoccupations of their generation. At their outset as Nonconformist businessmen they both illustrate how commerce and industry was a well-trodden path for many Nonconformists denied conventional routes to advancement by an Anglican Establishment (Chapter 1). Success in business was in any case taken as a sign of divine approbation. They both had to wrestle with a workforce used to a pre-Industrial Revolution freedom about the hours they chose to work. Businessmen like them, now employing unforgiving factory machinery, demanded a new discipline – in hours and in sobriety.

Familiarity with their workers led both to respond in similar ways, to seek to be enlightened employers, looking after the welfare of their employees, to aim to pay well and provide opportunities for constructive (rather than alcoholic) recreation. Both rapidly came to realise how important education was to improving life chances (Chapter 2). They taught in Adult Classes, and each realised the imperative to do a great deal more for the education of the children who fell through the net of voluntary (that is, church) provision. Education was a central concern for many sentient Victorians, terrified by the prospect of illiterate voters, of an unschooled workforce and of growing signs of a failure to compete abroad.

Coincidentally, both concluded at around the same time that education and culture would be impossible luxuries for homes where disease flourished, where clean water and sanitation were lacking, and where housing was such that privacy was impossible and immorality was rife (Chapter 3). Again, they reflect a national preoccupation with decent sanitation and with slum clearance. In their different ways both would be converted to the importance of town planning, and would come to realise that inequitable land ownership was the key obstacle to a comprehensive solution. It is interesting that their sons – Neville Chamberlain and George Cadbury junior – should each perpetuate their father's commitment to properly planned settlement.

What terrified the propertied middle class about millions of uneducated workers was the prospect of violent revolution – Chamberlain and Cadbury were children while the Chartists protested, and occasionally rioted, through the 1840s and would have absorbed the apprehension the middle and upper classes felt. Allied to concern about ignorance and alienation from the political system, Victorians worried about drink, its ready availability, and the amount consumed. Drink emboldened the rioter, and did great damage to many families. So, unsurprisingly, our two subjects agreed that something needed to be done, and expended much energy in that cause (Chapter 4).

Both independently concluded that while drink contributed to poverty, at least as pressing was the need to do something about pensions for the aged. Their interest chimed in with the contemporary work of social reformers like Charles Booth, Joseph Rowntree and Maud Pember Reeves, all of whom contributed to creating a collective consciousness and resolution in the first years of the twentieth century that reform was imperative – and both our subjects were significant actors in the fulfilment of the demand for a state pension for the aged.[6]

Across their lifetimes a British Empire emerged, expanding and gaining coherence. George Cadbury and Joseph Chamberlain as businessmen experienced it initially as a marketplace; later, each came to respond to popular enthusiasm (jingoism) and to ideas of consolidation and augmentation in their different ways. Each in time represented an important strand of argument about Imperialism, and as such they illuminate something of the dilemmas facing policy-makers in the late Victorian era (Chapter 6).

All the foregoing suggests that to a degree they were alike. Their Nonconformist backgrounds – although they represented different denominations, Unitarian and Quaker – established in them similar values. Both treasured education; both felt a deep urge to improve and to reform the lot of ordinary working people. Neither of them sought or accepted honours, preferring yeoman simplicity to baronial elevation. Although, as we will see, they were very different people, they nevertheless shared an important characteristic: the impulse to control. Joseph Chamberlain's domineering personality was evident from his dictatorial leadership of the Education League, and expressed itself through the subsequent decades as he broke and created new parties and organisations, imposing his will at every turn. George Cadbury – to all intents a saintly quietist – was equally controlling, closely stipulating the behavioural norms of his workers and tenants in Bournville. Finally, in their home lives to the south-west of ever-expanding Birmingham, most especially in the contentment of their marriages and their love of gardening and their absorption in their estates and their model farms, they typified the fashions and mores of the prosperous middle class (Chapter 8).

For all that they had in common, for the most part they were radically different from each other. Whilst both, as successful men, were ambitious, Joseph Chamberlain achieved his goals through an overt drive and ruthlessness, and through a willingness to use all political means at his disposal. From early in his career he relished a high-profile public role. He mastered the wiles of electoral politics, and enjoyed campaigning and speechmaking, at which he became his generation's acknowledged star. A veteran of a decade in municipal politics, which overlapped with thirty years at Westminster, he revelled in intrigue and gossip, loved vigorous argument and confrontation, and proved adept at the conspiracies and schemings which are meat and drink to the true political animal. His energy and relentlessness when engaged on a campaign were formidable and irrepressible qualities.

George Cadbury shunned the limelight, even if he did make the occasional speech, usually in a virtuous or charitable cause. Not for him political tub-thumping, vehement debate or the dissimulations and deceits which necessarily characterised politicking; he did not enjoy electioneering or public office, being a councillor for just a year and rejecting every subsequent Liberal blandishment to stand for Parliament. Although he supported Chamberlain's mayoral reforms, he came to dislike his methods. He engaged with politics on particular defined campaigns – like sweated labour and pensions – and through trying to educate the wider public through his newspapers. He was happier operating below the radar, and where Chamberlain's life came to be dominated by high office and by red boxes, or by national crusades like Home Rule or Protection, Cadbury thought religious and charitable work far more worthy of his attention.

Although both men were moved to improve the working and domestic lives of ordinary people, they differed sharply about how this could be best effected. George Cadbury was a Quaker and deeply religious; in a complete contrast to Chamberlain, his life was dominated by his Christian faith, and by a conviction that his personal mission was to evangelise the Gospel message (Chapter 8). In practice, living out the Word, he believed in private charity, the philanthropy of those who had the means to be able to give. It should be directed, he thought, to pragmatic projects. The Bournville factory, showcasing enlightened employment and welfare practices, and Bournville Village, a model of good housing and a clean, healthy environment, were his response to the national crisis in the working and living conditions of the labouring classes. Faced with evidence of nationally undereducated working classes, of their tendency to drink, of their lack of clean air and water, his response was to create an area of influence in South-West Birmingham as sharply delineated as was Chamberlain's Duchy. His aim was that it be a model for others, and Joseph Rowntree for one followed him (Chapter 3).

Joseph Chamberlain grew up a Unitarian, but wore his faith lightly, while he had it. He was to lose it after the death of his second wife, Florence, in 1875. He was brought up on the Unitarian's rational wing, believing in hard-headed reformative action, rather than Christian redemption, to transform the lives of the poor in Britain. For him, individual philanthropy was insufficient, for it could not address the scale of the social problem; his visits to Birmingham's slum streets when researching educational provision in 1869 were formative (Chapter 3). He concluded that only municipal effort, and beyond that, national legislation, could begin to deal with the social issues of illiteracy, health and housing that he discerned. Cadbury did seek Parliamentary action occasionally; but he remained convinced by the efficacy of personal charitable work, where Chamberlain committed himself to a life of political action to legislate for the necessary reforms himself.

These contrasts are reflected in the type of source material used in this book. The Special Collections at the University of Birmingham hold voluminous materials on Joseph Chamberlain. Decades of correspondence, years of official papers, notebooks and scrapbooks of published articles, and records of published speeches, all help the historian to flesh out a tale of political motivation and achievement, as well as providing insights into Chamberlain's interior and family world. Council records at the Library of Birmingham illuminate his energy, drive and imagination in carrying a civic revolution in the 1870s. The diaries of Beatrice Webb, a spirited and perceptive observer of the Chamberlain household in the 1880s while she still had hopes of marriage to its head, flesh out his character and his attraction.

George Cadbury was barely interested in political intrigue and speculation, and remained a businessman to the end, so that the *Cadbury* Archive at the factory in Bournville which curates minute books of Directors' meetings, works magazines, and personal reminiscences of early workers in the factory is invaluable for constructing a narrative of George Cadbury's stewardship of the company. It is supplemented by the University of Birmingham's Special Collections archive of papers covering the São Tomé and Príncipe slave-grown cocoa saga; these comprehensively relate the delays and indecision characterising *Cadbury* actions in this controversial area. Bournville Village Trust materials, and the local press, record the inception and fruition of *Cadbury's* unique community vision in Birmingham. In the absence of the sort of daily correspondence Chamberlain generated, a picture of George Cadbury has been assembled from the letters and day journals of his wife Elizabeth Taylor Cadbury in the Library of Birmingham; from the writings of George Gardiner, his friend and biographer; and from the *Daily News*, his national newspaper. More especially with Cadbury the historian has to be aware of a hagiographical strain in the writings of family, friends and co-religionists.

If they differed in character and in how to transform Victorian Britain, they also found themselves on opposite sides of the political divide. While they both started out as Liberals, the events of 1886 when Gladstone committed himself to Home Rule drove the two men apart as it fractured the entire party (Chapter 5). Chamberlain's belief that Irish Home Rule threatened the integrity of the British Empire coloured his subsequent enthusiasm for Imperial Preference, and for consolidating South Africa under British rule. Cadbury steadily moved in the opposite direction, his chocolate products no longer by 1900 packaged with Imperial images, and his unfashionable opposition to the Boer War and its accompanying jingoism becoming ever more entrenched. He believed, too, in Free Trade, with all its connotations of international trust and peace; so, he was fundamentally opposed to Chamberlain's Tariff Reform policy from 1903 onwards (Chapter 6). In Chamberlain's last years before a stroke ended his active life in 1906, the two differed sharply over the ways to fund Old Age Pensions and over Balfour's Education Act which abolished Board schools and put Anglican schools on the rates.

There were several reasons why these differences do not appear to have made the two personal enemies. Joseph Chamberlain's political life was indeed marked by a number of animosities, for example towards John Morley, the Gladstonian Liberal, and David Lloyd George, a bitter anti-Boer War foe, but in truth George Cadbury, who was not an MP or national political figure, did not register as an appropriate potential target for Chamberlain. For his part George

Cadbury was temperamentally and religiously averse to the passionate and often vitriolic discourse of political rivalry. Although they lived within a few miles of each other on the borders of South-West Birmingham their social circles barely overlapped, Cadbury's being largely Quaker in its constitution, and Chamberlain's centring much more on society and national political connections. In fact, for some years, Chamberlain had more to do with George's brother, Richard, from neighbouring Uffculme, than he did with George. A further factor is that for several decades the careers of our two titans were not synchronised, and so antagonism was avoided. Joseph Chamberlain's contribution to the municipal transformation of Birmingham was largely completed by 1876, when he was elected to Parliament, and thereafter his stage was a national one, as was the focus of his radical political programme. George Cadbury, it is true, did sit for a year on the Birmingham Council in 1878, and Chamberlain was still involved on a number of committees. They did not cross swords there.

Whilst they were to find themselves on either side of the Liberal divide over Home Rule from 1886, Cadbury was not a significant player in the Gladstonian camp and kept his head down while Chamberlain directed his attack against those who refused to follow him into the Unionist camp. Ireland apart, there was a congruity of interest between them over the nature of the social reform that was necessary to tackle working-class poverty and deprivation. While George Cadbury got on in the 1890s and made real his visions of better planning and housing in Bournville, Chamberlain was preoccupied with national politics and ministerial responsibilities. So it was only in the last seven years of Chamberlain's political career that there was a major divergence between them, in Cadbury's deeply committed opposition to Chamberlain's South African War. Even then, that division did not become personal. Chamberlain's fire was drawn to other more vociferous parliamentary opponents. Cadbury's opposition was expressed by proxy, through the editorials and articles of others in his newspaper, the *Daily News*. Beyond occasional speeches to his tenants in Bournville, he was no platform orator and his opposition to war remained largely indirect and so avoided provoking a Chamberlainite broadside. The fact that their personal relationship had been unsullied by sharp differences on the merits of war can be seen by their combining to work together to save the Rowton House scheme to provide a hostel for working men in Birmingham at the height of the Boer War.

Cadbury undoubtedly disapproved of Chamberlain's methods but saw the value of many of his reforms; Chamberlain saw Cadbury as a rich philanthropic local worthy with whom it was important to remain civil, especially after 1897 with a university to fund and build.

It is these parallels and contrasts between George Cadbury and Joseph Chamberlain which are the subject of the ensuing chapters in this book. In addition, it considers the nature of the scandals which engulfed them both, and examines the ways in which strong-willed fathers determined the careers of their children and, as husbands, the roles they wanted their wives to play (Chapters 7 and 9). These two titans created dynasties which for decades preserved the influence of two extraordinary men in the city to which they dedicated their lives. To this day the names of Cadbury and Chamberlain are universally recognised there, more readily associated with Birmingham than any other.

BIRMINGHAM BUSINESSMEN

Temperamentally and politically George Cadbury and Joseph Chamberlain were markedly different. Still, in one regard, they shared an important experience and a common background. They were both successful businessmen, taking extant but undeveloped companies and transforming them into market leaders. The wealth they generated enabled each to pursue their differing political and socially reformative interests beyond the factory gates. George Cadbury presided over the growth of the Bournville cocoa and chocolate factory in Birmingham and the establishment of the *Cadbury* brand world-wide. Chamberlain so energised a newly mechanised wood-screw company in Birmingham that it came to achieve national dominance and considerable international significance before being subsumed in the industrial giant *GKN*.

These comparisons need some qualification. Joseph Chamberlain's career at *Nettlefold and Chamberlain* spanned the years from 1854 to 1874, at which point he sold out, making a small fortune in the process; he was then to be Birmingham's greatest mayor, the architect of a civic revolution, before spending over 30 years at the heart of national politics. By 1874 the transformatory move of *Cadbury Bros.* (as it was then called, before its twentieth-century incarnation as *Cadbury*) from the confined inner-Birmingham Bridge Street site to a new factory, Bournville, in the surrounding countryside had yet to happen. George Cadbury was to stay involved in the firm, as partner, managing director or company chairman, from the early 1860s to 1922, by which time both the business environment and the post-war world were dramatically different from the Victorian hey-day when Chamberlain retired. In addition, to be strictly accurate, the credit for the first decades of success at *Cadbury Bros.* must be shared with his brother, Richard Cadbury, every bit as central a figure in the day-to-day management and decision-making at the factory as George, until his untimely death in the Holy Land in 1899.[7]

Both Joseph Chamberlain and George Cadbury went into a family business. This was not uncommon in nineteenth-century manufacturing concerns. For example, another confectionery magnate, Joseph Rowntree, took over and expanded a family cocoa and chocolate manufacturing factory in York at around the same time.[8] In Joseph Chamberlain's case, on leaving University College School in North London in 1854, he was dispatched by his father to Birmingham, to supervise the investment he had made in the wood-screw business of John Sutton Nettlefold, his brother-in-law.[9] Joseph's ambition and drive established him as the pre-eminent influence in the management of the business, the firm's chief accountant commenting that 'money was made quickly after Master Joseph came'.[10]

George and Richard Cadbury inherited the struggling cocoa business at Bridge Street from their father John in 1861, when they were twenty-two and twenty-five respectively. They, like the Chamberlains, were Nonconformists. The Cadbury brothers were Quakers, while Joseph Chamberlain was a Unitarian. Quakers and Unitarians, although comprising barely 5% of worshippers in Birmingham at the time of the 1851 census, had a disproportionate influence in the city, from the time of Joseph Priestley, philosopher, scientist and Unitarian onwards at the end of the eighteenth century; and John Bright, the country's most prominent Quaker, was a Birmingham MP for a quarter of a century from 1858. For long barred from the ancient universities and from public office, Nonconformists had compensated by making a success of business enterprise, where they could use their talents unhindered and where their prosperity might signify divine approbation for their efforts.[11]

Both George Cadbury and Joseph Chamberlain's enterprises flourished in their respective fields. In Richard's last years to 1899, and then with George at the helm with a board of directors, exports of Cadbury chocolate and cocoa surged, increasing seven-fold from 1891 up to the start of the First World War. New lines – *Cadbury's Dairy Milk* and *Bournville Cocoa* – introduced in the Edwardian years became rapidly and enduringly successful. *Cadbury* in these years became the dominant chocolate producer for Empire markets: Australia, New Zealand, South Africa and India.[12]

In the twenty years that Joseph Chamberlain was involved in *Nettlefold and Chamberlain*, the firm had diversified to produce 730 varieties of iron screw and others in copper or brass, and nuts, bolts, rivets, hooks, eyes, washers and rivets. The business was exporting screws through agents or directly to Russia, USA, Italy, Poland, Spain, France, India, New Zealand, Japan, Germany, Switzerland, Belgium, Canada and Austria. The catalogue of the firm's products was published in French with a distinctive salmon pink cover, with weights quoted in decimals, and in Spanish. Rivals had been seen off, and arrangements negotiated so that the firm was paid to stay out of the US market where it had been too successful for the domestic producers.[13]

George Cadbury and Joseph Chamberlain were advocates of the factory system, although their differing justifications for a move from the glorified workshops that had hitherto comprised the working environment reveal something of their contrasting dispositions. Chamberlain had arrived in Birmingham just as John Nettlefold opened a new factory on the borders of Birmingham and Smethwick, hard by the canal and close to the Soho railway station, built to accommodate innovatory machinery; he became an instant convert to the rationale of the new arrangements. He articulated his reasoning in a chapter entitled 'Manufacture of Iron Wood Screws' which he contributed to Samuel Timmins's *Birmingham and Midland Hardware District* in 1866. He wrote: 'A revolution is taking place in the principal hardware trades, which is assimilating the town to the great seats of manufacturing in the North and depriving it of its special characteristic, viz., the number of its small manufacturers.' 'Factories have grown with extraordinary rapidity', he continued, and – anticipating the Cadburys' move out to Bournville over a decade later – he said: '... businesses have enlarged and the owners have moved out of town'. Technological changes – the introduction of machinery and steam power – had led to 'the introduction of large capital and the construction of large mills'. At any event, he concluded, 'the following advantages will spring from its consummation – healthier work-places, regularity of hours, economy of labour, increased demand, lower prices and higher wages'.[14]

In a Report of the Royal Commission on Children's Employment in 1864, commissioners commented on how the best factory conditions were found in the most recently established trades, especially those that had purpose-built factories. They observed that *Nettlefold and Chamberlain* was one such and was 'well-ventilated and clean', a 'better workshop could not be imagined'. It seems that Chamberlain's actions were as good as his words on the superiority of the factory environment.[15]

For Chamberlain, the business imperative dictated that the factory system be adopted wherever suitable. And this reasoning certainly weighed heavily when the Cadbury brothers determined to move out of central Birmingham, but it was matched by an equally persuasive human case. Helen Cadbury Alexander, in her filial memorial of her father Richard, quotes the brothers rationalising the Bournville move: 'We consider that our people spend the greatest part of their lives at their work, and we wish it less irksome by environing them with pleasant and wholesome sights, sounds and conditions.'[16] A.G. Gardiner, in his equally pious biography of George Cadbury, dwells at length on this philanthropic dimension.

'The congestion of industry in towns he saw to be physically and morally degrading.'... 'Why could not industry be allied with natural conditions?'... 'He saw that the disregard with which industry used its instruments was not only ruinous to the moral (*sic*) of the people but deplorably wasteful. It was not necessary that a factory should be in a town and that its workers should be in a slum.' He went on to add: 'From his first association with business in Birmingham he had been disquieted by the degradation of human life which resulted from the pitiless condition of modern industry – long hours, low wages, ruthless dismissals, loss of health, loss of morals. It was this disquiet which had largely prompted the removal into the country.' He wanted the factory to 'become a positive benefit, a centre of hygiene and intellectual activity'.[17]

All this illustrates a characteristic social and human dimension to *Cadbury Bros.*' decision-making which, as we will see, is a world away from Joseph Chamberlain's business priorities. Still, George and Richard Cadbury would not have made their fortune and presided over a growing business empire if they had not made hard-headed decisions. George Cadbury linked the personnel and the business case in replies to an enquiry on the responsibilities of wealth from the Upper House of Convocation in 1906. 'What', they asked,' is your theory of giving?' 'As far as you have the means, give the people space', he replied, 'this was our main object in removing from Birmingham to the country. It was morally right and proved financially to be a success.'[18]

The official centenary history of *Cadbury* by Iolo Williams, funded by the firm and a largely uncritical purveyor of the familial orthodoxy, concedes that part of the rationale for the move from Bridge Street was commercial, for around it 'the solid belt was growing every year, a less suitable locality for a food factory to which clean air and surroundings are so valuable'. Moreover, 'they knew that supposing they enlarged the existing premises... it might not be long before they were faced once more with an overcrowded factory'.[19]

For Cadbury and Chamberlain other subsidiary factories would follow, and here the business case was all. It was a matter of securing reliable, good-quality and cost-effective supplies. The instant popularity of *Cadbury's Dairy Milk Chocolate* created a demand for factories to handle the milk condensing process. From 1911 new factories at Knighton in Shropshire and later at Frampton-on-Severn took the condensing process into the heartland of dairy farming. Indeed, at Frampton, over 600 farms supplied the new plant, these cows and dairies subject to Cadbury's stringent inspection regime.[20]

As demand for wood screws grew, *Nettlefold and Chamberlain* determined to control the supply of wire, firstly buying Gibson's Ashtree works at the Cape, Smethwick in 1869, re-christening the new supplier the *Imperial Wire Company*. Even then a young Joseph Chamberlain was signalling the importance to him of Imperial markets, long before his conversion to Imperial preference, when he was Colonial Secretary at the end of the century. Later they bought land at Hadley Castle, near Wellington in Shropshire, for their own iron works, erecting a blast furnace, puddling furnaces and rolling mills to convert bar iron into coil of a quality and consistency to meet their exacting standards for wire used in the making of their wood screws. The firm also bought a defunct wire drawing mill whose premises were opposite the *Nettlefold and Chamberlain* factory on Heath Street.[21]

Decisions to expand factory space and to diversify into subsidiary processes – extending even into making the boxes and wrappings in which their products were packed – were part of a broader open-mindedness towards new ideas demonstrated by both Cadbury and Chamberlain. When the latter arrived at the new Heath Street factory in the mid-1850s, John Sutton Nettlefold had already made the decision to purchase the American Sloan patent for the manufacture by automatic machinery of wood screws with gimlet points, which he had seen at the Great Exhibition in 1851. A hitherto arduous and skilled process of 'screw grinding', which yielded a handcrafted product, could be replaced by a mass-produced item. Chamberlain maximised its potential. By the time he sold up there were 2000 machines in the factory producing 7.2 million screws per annum, where the pre-automation figure was a small fraction of that.[22]

Chamberlain encouraged workers' suggestions for technological solutions and improvements to the manufacturing process. It saved having to rely on, and pay, the Sloan engineers from the USA. 'Being actively involved in the assembly and maintenance of these machines encouraged technical innovations, and new designs were generated in the firm, rather than the acquisition of patents from overseas', writes *GKN*'s official historian. One employee, a Mr Wakefield, patented a forging machine that earned him a bag of money every quarter, which he showed off round the factory, a very public affirmation of his value to the company.[23]

George Cadbury and his other family directors too would see the value of tapping into the experience and common sense of his workers. From 1902 Suggestions Committees were founded for men and for women, with Edward Cadbury arguing that the suggestions would have pecuniary value, and would help to develop the employees' mental and creative faculties. A glance at the *Bournville Works Magazine* first published in 1902, 'to foster comradeship and fellowship', reveals detailed lists of suggestions, some of which were very much aimed at improving the manufacturing process, including covering tables with slate slabs, lining the trolley floors with zinc, introducing uniform labelling of boxes, and providing the girls with new and better sweeping brooms. It seems small fry, but over the years many of the suggestions improved the hygiene, the cleanliness and the efficiency of the Bournville plant.[24]

In an altogether more fundamental and transformative way George and Richard Cadbury, and their sons after 1899, showed a keen and prompt awareness of the potential gain to be made from innovatory machinery. At the start of the 1870s George Cadbury had bought and introduced

Dutch patented methods for pressing out cocoa butter from the cocoa beans, permitting the firm to promote its products as uncorrupted, neatly coinciding with government legislation on adulterated foodstuffs. Indeed, George Cadbury, having seen the light, wanted others to be compelled into virtue, thereafter campaigning for government inspection. Within a short time the 'comforting gruel', which had characterised the original cocoa products with their sago and potato starch additives to counter the bitterness of the cocoa butter, was abandoned.[25] *Cadbury Bros.* was over fifteen years in advance of Joseph Rowntree in adopting the Dutch machinery to make unadulterated cocoa.[26]

Soon after *Cadbury* became a limited company in 1899 under George's chairmanship, son George junior was dispatched to the Continent and there saw the fondant-making machines of *Lehmans*, the Dresden confectioners, influencing investment in sweet-filling machinery. Prompted by *Bakers*, a London firm, *Cadbury* purchased plant for making milk chocolate and *Dairy Milk Chocolate* in 1904 was the result, almost on its own transforming *Cadbury* into an international byword for milk chocolate.[27] An historian of the cocoa and chocolate industry, J. Othick, observes that 'both the Rowntrees and the Cadburys were assiduous visitors to international exhibitions and trade fairs in various parts of Europe.... We are dealing here with imitators rather than innovators.'[28] Indeed, in 1905 *Cadbury* bought machinery from abroad to create alkalised cocoa, yielding a smoother better-dissolving product; *Bournville Cocoa* was the result. This too was to become an iconic product.

Under George's aegis *Cadbury* proved alert to the possibility of new departures and was quick to invest in new machinery; the contrast with an altogether more hesitant and cautious Joseph Rowntree is apparent in the period between 1870 and 1900. Rowntree was to translate his factory from central York to Earswick, on the city's outskirts, a decade after Cadbury brothers made their move, and lagged fifteen years in investing in the machinery to make a pure cocoa product. The comparison only serves to highlight the extent of George Cadbury's commercial acumen. But it must also be said that he would only adopt what had already been proved to work; he did not take extravagant risks.[29]

His keen apprehension of the lessons that could be learnt from abroad applied to other areas too. So, *Cadbury* imitated the employees' baths, dining facilities and library of *Stollwerck Bros.* in Hamburg and Cologne. The *Menier* factory at Noisiel influenced George Cadbury with its solid brick houses built in the 1870s for employees to rent. *The National Cash Register Company* in the United States, visited by George junior in 1902, inspired the suggestion and complaints schemes, and the creation of a works magazine, innovations to which we have already alluded.[30] Like Joseph Chamberlain, George Cadbury proved a quick learner and with sensitive antennae to locate possibilities for improving the business.

Both had responsibility for sales at their respective firms. It was George who early in the 1880s despatched a senior employee, Thomas Edwards, to establish an Australian base, from which a network of Antipodean and Far Eastern contacts and depots arose.[31] His gift for copywriting can be seen in the enduring influence of the phrase 'Absolutely Pure' which was applied to *Cadbury's* cocoa and chocolate for many years. Even the creation of Bournville Village around the new factory was artful, with an eye to the product's image – health-giving, pure, clean like the air and the rural simplicity that environed the Bournville works. The name was chosen to evoke a Gallic echo, for France was the acknowledged home of sophisticated chocolate. His brother Richard's homespun paintings of girls, kittens, Swiss mountain scenery, Swiss flowers – gentians, Alpine roses and cyclamen – decorated the chocolate boxes and reinforced the association of the product with simple goodness.

Chamberlain approached the management of *Nettlefold's* sales with typical professionalism. He employed a French speaker to converse with him over breakfast, and a new facility with the language enabled him to take advantage of the turmoil in France during the Franco-Prussian war in 1870; Chamberlain secured hundreds of new customers. He adapted the firm's packaging for the new market; the French preferred their screws packed in blue (not *Nettlefold* green) and liked the contents enumerated by hand on the outside of the packet (unlike the Scots who liked them typed). Weights and measures were calculated in decimals. He also understood how to build a network of middlemen and agents, attracted by a range of discounting arrangements.[32] He later explained his painstaking approach: 'No work is worth doing badly and he that puts his best into every task that comes to him will surely outstrip the man who waits for a great opportunity before he condescends to exert himself.'[33]

Chamberlain's dynamism and innate competitiveness, betrayed by his reflections on the attributes of a successful businessman, explain why the attitudes to competition of our two subjects varied considerably. George Cadbury worked closely with the other leading confectionery firms during his lifetime. He had learnt his trade in the Rowntree pavement grocery store in York in his teens. He had absorbed from the Frys of Bristol (a rival Quaker chocolate manufacturing family) the value of the morning service for all employees. At the end of the nineteenth century *Cadbury* and *Frys* merged in a commercial partnership. The Cadburys bought cocoa in Southern Nigeria with the Rowntrees and the Frys. The three companies also formed an agreement in June 1899 that 'no gifts be given to customers in terms of cash, kind, goods, bonuses or special discounts,' to try and establish ground rules for local agents who were pressing rival products on shops, kiosks, and railway waiting rooms in an increasingly unseemly skirmish, which sometimes involved the tearing down or defacing of rivals' advertisements.[34]

Overwhelmingly, the heads of the three companies were friends and allies. Their faith, and political sympathies, held them together. All three signed up to a collective (critical and pacific) position on the Boer War, supporting a circular sent to all their travellers to explain *The Quaker position on the War*.[35] Joseph Rowntree seems to have been profoundly influenced by George Cadbury, imitating his initiatives in building a model village, introducing doctors and dentists to the factory, and buying a newspaper, first *The Northern Echo*, then *The Nation* just as Cadbury had taken a majority share in the *Daily News*. In the end, Rowntree and Cadbury, dubbed the Cocoa Press, acquired an interest as partners in the *Morning Leader* and the *Star* in 1910.[36]

So, the competition was, for George Cadbury, to be treated with civility, for he and his rivals could reach understandings about respective geographical and product specialisms. Joseph Chamberlain was altogether more confrontational. The screw-making firms of James and Amery, and of John Hawkins, were dangerous rivals, and Chamberlain saw them off with an aggressive price-cutting campaign, before pouncing to buy and absorb them both. An even greater threat was posed by a new prospective rival, the *Birmingham Screw Company*, which was planned in 1870-71. He met that challenge head-on to smash the new company. This he duly did in a number of ways.

He convinced his business partners that *Nettlefold and Chamberlain* should hike prices by as much as 50% during the period in which the rival company tooled up for production. While prices were high the profits would be banked before a really aggressive slashing of prices was initiated to undermine the new company. He also stepped in to snatch the plant at which Josiah Mason of the *Birmingham Screw Company* had intended to initiate production, buying it from under his nose. He made it clear to his workmen: any who left for his rival would never be re-employed by *Nettlefold and Chamberlain*. He was helped that this relentless campaign coincided with the outbreak of the Franco-Prussian war, cutting the *Birmingham Screw Company* off from the supply of French screws it had contrived to use as seed corn for its start-up.[37] In sum the *Birmingham Screw Company* was 'damaged permanently by Chamberlain's unyielding strategy', in the words of *GKN*'s historian.[38]

It is inconceivable that George Cadbury would have behaved like this, or have been dogged by the sort of accusations of sharp practice which led the vicar of Rugeley to conduct his own very public enquiries into Chamberlain's methods a decade later. He was, however, quite unable to find evidence of those rumoured questionable dodges, such as for example the circulation of threatening pamphlets to small screw manufacturers whom he was supposed to have ruined.[39]

As for all Victorian businessmen who owned factories, Cadbury and Chamberlain sought to inculcate the values of punctuality, discipline and hard work, and to develop in their workers the virtue of time thrift, which were all necessary in an environment where the machinery dictated the rhythms of production. Both successfully overcame a deeply engrained working-class devotion for Saint Monday; in many industries, while the women and children might attend work, their menfolk often spent a good part of the day drinking their earnings from the previous week with predictably damaging results for family life as well as for industrial productivity.[40] George Cadbury recognised 'that the factory economy required the simultaneous presence of a large number of employees', wrote his biographer; 'it was worth granting a Saturday half-holiday if Monday's working hours could be preserved.' He claimed that *Cadbury* was the first firm in Birmingham to introduce that half-holiday.[41] Observing the havoc resulting from drunken indulgence unquestionably influenced the Cadburys, their father John included, in a conviction of the rightness of teetotalism for themselves and for their workers.

Joseph Chamberlain approached the question of working hours in his usual analytical, scientific way. He observed the symbiotic relationship between hours worked in his factory and the productivity of each unit of labour, concluding that 'productivity lessened as the working day lengthened.'[42] In the light of this, *Nettlefold and Chamberlain* reduced the working day to nine hours; the productivity of the workforce was improved. He did not, however, introduce the Saturday half-holiday, persisting with the six-day week. Still, labour leaders judged that he was enlightened and could be trusted to give them a fair deal. As a result, he was employed frequently in the arbitration of industrial disputes.

It was wholly characteristic that he should seek to apply his insights more widely through support of legislation, anticipating his own translation from capitalist to a national politician in a position to influence policy. So he persuaded Birmingham's Chamber of Commerce to abandon its obstructionist position towards the Factory Acts and implement them in the late 1860s; so, too, as a councillor on the Birmingham Council he led the campaign in 1870 to ensure the Workshop Act was adopted in the town. He strongly endorsed the Act's objectives of limiting working hours, improving workplace sanitation and providing for the education of young employees. These were to be prominent themes in Chamberlain's politics over the subsequent few years. They also show the limits to which Chamberlain thought manufacturers should go.

George Cadbury took a much more holistic view of an employer's responsibilities. He and his brother were industrial paternalists. The collected reminiscences of employees from the pioneering days of Bridge Street and the move to Bournville highlight the same impressions. They talk of the personal interest shown by both brothers in everything concerning the work people, their physical and their spiritual welfare; of every applicant to *Cadbury Bros.* being personally interviewed; and of how daily assemblies of the entire workforce (until it became too large and unwieldy in 1911) generated an *esprit de corps* as well as a profoundly spiritual atmosphere. They mention the little personal touches: of Richard stopping to help a girl carry heavy boxes; of George halting work to get the men into the grounds for a quick and vigorous game of football, or giving the girls fresh air and recreation through an afternoon's hay-making at his Woodbrooke home; of George, worried about the effect of odd working hours on his night-workers, providing them with hot drinks; of both founders sending men out with lanterns on dark winter mornings to see women workers safe from the station to the factory; and many accounts dwell on the Christmas parties, where all employees and sales representatives were handsomely fed, entertained, and departed with goody bags of fruit, nuts and biscuits.[43]

Iolo Williams explained the firm's unquestionable paternalism thus: 'Is there anyone who will deny the advantage that a business has in employing healthy, contented, intelligent and prosperous workpeople? The value of anything that will associate the factory not with drudgery only but with things pleasant and interesting is obviously very great.'[44] George Cadbury, writes Gardiner, 'understood that behind all the athletics, dentistry, doctoring, swimming baths and arrangements for meals lies a supreme commercial objective – speed of hand coupled with accuracy of eye. These are the qualities that make the business pay.'[45]

A whole range of welfare initiatives was implemented to achieve a happy, clean, healthy and productive workforce. Temperance dining facilities (prompted by the need to attract workers from lunchtimes at the local public houses) were introduced in the mid-1880s; changing rooms then swimming baths followed. By the turn of the century the firm was funding and organising sports clubs for employees of both sexes and founding musical and choral societies. A model village, a third of whose houses were occupied by employees, sought to shape the physical environment in which workers lived. Classes were being conducted for boys and for girls with widely different curricula. A sick club, and sick pay funded by the firm, was followed by a pension scheme which anticipated that developed by the Liberal government in 1908.

Although in many ways beneficent, George Cadbury could in a different perspective be viewed as controlling and interfering. There seems a compulsion to organise, and bring order to, sporting and musical events in the belief that the firm could do things better. It has been argued that the Bournville Athletic Club, with accompanying playing fields and splendid pavilion, was a response by the Cadburys to evidence of unregulated physical horseplay, men with office stool-jumping and girls hanging from a bar on the ceiling in the office workroom. Such spontaneity needed channelling. The Board of Directors was even represented on the Executive Committee of the Bournville Athletic Club, presiding over enquiries into incidents of sporting indiscipline.

The Cadburys' Quaker beliefs and personal adherence to temperance percolated into the business. Workers were recruited to the Blue Ribbon Temperance campaign and backsliders into drink were identified. 'They could see the utility of a temperate workforce which was mentally and physically healthy.'[46] Equally, George and his directors worried about the vice of gambling. The Directors issued a notice to foremen in August 1903 saying that: 'We know the practice of gambling has taken a considerable hold on our employees. Mention the names of all you know engaged in the practice.'[47] The threat of disciplinary action was implicit. The overt faith of the Founders manifested itself at the assemblies, in the calls to attend Sunday schools and Friends' meeting houses, in George's house visits made to prospective converts, and finally in favouring the appointment to management positions of Quakers – in 1900 only total abstainers could be clerks and they formed the majority of foremen.

George Cadbury had very particular views on family issues too, which coloured the lives of workers at Bournville. He told his biographer that 'he will never take the mothers away from their homes and their children. He said when he had allowed married women to work for him he found that their husbands were quite content to loaf about doing nothing, living on the wages of their wives. The poor things invariably come back after childbearing to work long before they were fit to work.' The policy of not employing married women was justified on grounds that it helped staff turnover; it delayed the marriage of young girls till they were really ready, and it made the putative loafers more responsible men.[48]

Good rates of pay, generous welfare benefits, pensions and the abandonment of a fines system for tardiness and ill-discipline in 1898, contributed to a largely amenable workforce. Only the introduction of piece work by Edward Cadbury, one of the directors before the First World War, threatened the harmony. 'The extension of piece work wherever possible will greatly promote the efficiency of the factory', wrote the head of the Works Organisation department – a Quaker. It made sense for the business but placed pressure on the individual worker to perform, and trade unions disliked it, with the threat of the first strike in *Cadbury's* history barely averted in 1913. In George's last years *Cadbury* reasserted its reputation for looking after the interests of its workers, being one of the first firms to introduce Works Councils of employers and employees in 1918.[49]

Joseph Chamberlain certainly took pride in the fact that his employees had meaningful work and were well remunerated.[50] He did encourage the foundation of a club for working men in Smethwick close to the Heath Street mill, joined by some employees and other local men.[51] But that is as far as he thought an employer should go. In an article in the *Birmingham Mail* on his retirement in 1874 he wrote that 'the firm had never engaged in any particular work of philanthropy in connection with the works'. He went on to claim that the working class 'did not want charity, but they desire they may be treated fairly'.[52] For Chamberlain the solution lay not at the level of the business but on an altogether, more ambitious national plane – Radical reform through parliamentary action was needed to transform the lot of the working man.

Both men were extremely successful in expanding and establishing nationally significant businesses. They implemented innovative thinking in mass production. But in the treatment of their workforces Chamberlain and Cadbury differed sharply, a reflection perhaps of religious faith but more likely of temperament and personality. They both certainly understood the importance of decent pay and conditions, but Chamberlain had little interest in the kind of philanthropic welfare that George Cadbury applied to his workforce. Where Cadbury made his business his life's work, Chamberlain sold out and moved on, when still a relatively young man as if business, for him, was but a chapter – albeit lucrative – and a prelude to other more important work yet to come.

A Zeal for Education

For George Cadbury and for Joseph Chamberlain it was entirely natural that they should both become involved early in teaching in Adult Sunday Schools – their Nonconformist background encouraged them. Each in his different way reflected the widely held Victorian faith in the transformative possibilities of education.[53] George Cadbury felt more keenly than Joseph Chamberlain what others of his denomination believed to be the challenge for schools, that they should become breeding grounds for a moral reformation to counter the ill effects of a prevailing working-class culture. His teaching emphasised 'the spiritual aspect'.[54]

Chamberlain as ever highlighted the pragmatic. He told the Mutual Improvement Society of the Church of the Messiah that 'education was the first step to a remedy for the condition of the working classes, as it would lead to a reduction of pauperism and crime, better homes, better lives and temperate recreation'.[55] Ever the businessman he understood the need for secular instruction to enable students to read fluently, write competently and make out a simple bill or invoice.[56] But although for each in his way education would continue to be an abiding interest through his life, the truth is that for both of them involvement in schools, absorption in the issues that arose there, was but the start. It induced comparable dramatic revelations, with each subsequently broadening their work to engage with fundamental social reform.

So, their early involvement in education followed parallel lines. Joseph Chamberlain started teaching at the age of sixteen or so in the Sunday School run by the Carter Lane Chapel in London, the congregation 'displaying in a marked degree the zeal for education which so honourably distinguished the Unitarian'.[57] He carried on that teaching when he moved to Birmingham in 1854, and became attached to the Church of the Messiah. A former pupil of Chamberlain's Sunday School class later reminisced about him, painting a picture of a strict disciplinarian with an occasionally acid tongue, once chiding them that 'you are without exception the most ignorant set of fellows I have ever come across'. At first blush he seemed austere, invariably punctual, keeping his hat and coat on as he walked around the room, teaching all the while. Yet there was a kindly streak – he knew the boys were often weary and once when one snoozed in front of him he said: 'Goodnight Jones. I don't mind your going to sleep, but please don't snore.'

He prepared his teaching materials as methodically as he prepared his business accounts. He compiled a synopsis of events in British history from Caesar to the Hanoverians the better to teach the boys, he made abstracts from English Literature for them, and he revealed what would become a life-long interest in horticulture when he brought beautiful flowers into the lessons to deepen their botanical understanding. In his inclusion of both History and Science in his class curriculum he shows the influence of that founding father of Unitarianism, the Birmingham philosopher and scientist, Joseph Priestley. For Priestley and his Lunar Society colleagues a rational education imparting practical knowledge, rather than the backward-looking classical curriculum of the public schools, was essential for aspiring dissenters and for the middle classes in the future.[58]

Beyond the academic curriculum Chamberlain sought to impress on the boys some guidelines for conducting themselves, frequently reminding them of the importance of a sense of responsibility in life, and telling them that for himself: 'My religion consists in doing my duty to my fellow man and in alleviating the lot of the poor.'[59] For all that he could be stern and dry, his earliest biographer Garvin concluded that 'from many boys whom he had helped he earned lasting respect'. He also pointed out that his impact on the working men to whom he taught French, at the Smethwick Working Men's Institute which he founded, was somewhat different, revealing that force of personality so beguiling to political audiences: 'The room buzzed with life always when he was there, being so smart and vivacious, not bothered with nerves,' recorded one old man later.[60]

George Cadbury joined the Severn Street School in Birmingham in 1859, a flourishing Adult Sunday School founded by a fellow Quaker, Joseph Sturge, over a decade earlier to gather up men from the slums who were sometimes barely literate and instruct them in the rudiments of learning.[61] They would read and write half the day and have a lesson of scripture for the other half, with the ultimate hope that 'the lives of the scholars might be diverted into better channels of new interests and higher aims, i.e. thrift and independence'.[62] In 1863 Cadbury was placed in charge of his own class – class XIV – and he continued to run it for over fifty years.

Where Joseph Chamberlain would leave behind his adult classes to develop his interest in education on a municipal and national stage, George Cadbury preferred – to the end – to make his contribution at the grass-roots level. His brother Richard was engaged in the same work, and his biographer gives a flavour of the challenges and the satisfaction involved, when she quotes from an observer of the Adult School commenting on: 'These great rugged-face men with their hands stiffened by their daily toil, earnestly labouring over the letters they are putting together in their copybooks. They are all cleanly and respectably dressed. If they come the worse for drink' –the visitor is told – 'we let them sit down with the rest, we do our best for them, but we have to use great care and patience.'[63] That vignette well illustrates both the skill and empathy that teachers like the Cadbury brothers possessed, but also the sincere quest for learning which characterised many members of the working class in the nineteenth century, contributing to a generation of autodidacts.[64]

George Cadbury was evidently an inspirational teacher with a wide range of interests and able to deliver a disquisition on politics, history or religion. At the heart of his teaching, aside from the basic literacy skills, was the Bible lesson. Richard Cadbury had always argued that 'the object of our classes is to induce an earnest study of the Scriptures', and for George that 'spiritual aspect' was very important.[65] No doubt this betrays a strong Quaker missionary impulse. It is in marked contrast to Joseph Chamberlain; a former pupil was quite clear that the Bible was never used as a class book, and that Mr Chamberlain always confined himself to secular subjects.[66] The biblical emphasis does not appear to have had any deleterious impact for George Cadbury's pastoral gifts won for him enduring popularity; he understood how to build an *esprit de corps*, entertaining hundreds of his pupils at his home for the annual summer party; many of his pupils went out and recruited others, some ex-convicts, some habitual drinkers, for their teacher saw the role of the class as more than academically educative but as genuinely redemptive too.[67]

Although we have no evidence that they communicated with each other on the issue, it is interesting that both George Cadbury and Joseph Chamberlain should independently conclude that their work in their Adult Schools was somehow insufficient, that more needed to be done. Chamberlain observed his workers' need of opportunities for recreation and so established the Smethwick Working Men's Club, encouraging friends and relations to give professional advice and provide the wherewithal to build the clubhouse.[68] With what Garvin called 'his blazing interest in education', he himself taught and attended on the club's varied activities.[69] By 1867 the lamentable state of primary education in Birmingham had borne in on him and on fellow members of the Church of the Messiah the conviction that radical action was needed. Most especially they were conscious of the revolution brought about by the 1867 Second Reform Act enfranchising many workingmen in the cities. The cautionary words of the MP Robert Lowe echoed beyond the House of Commons: 'We need to compel our future masters to learn their letters.'[70]

In the years before the 1870 Forster Education Act when education in England was largely provided by voluntary organisations – the religious denominations – this Unitarian church agreed to set up separate primary schools for boys and girls, with the aim of making inroads into the shamefully large number of unschooled, unlettered, Birmingham children. Head teachers were secured for the schools, money raised among the congregation, fees were set, Chamberlain was appointed treasurer, and within a year 109 boys, and 112 girls had commenced a non-denominational education there.[71] The two schools had a chequered few years, coming firstly under local School Board control with their funding re-directed to Home Mission work, and then resuming as the venue for night classes for the thirteen- to sixteen-year-olds for whom there was no state provision, even after the passing of the Forster Act in 1870.[72] Where George Cadbury would continue involved with individual schools into the next century, this venture of the Church of the Messiah was to be Joseph Chamberlain's last intimate involvement with a particular school, although he did play an active role in the foundation of Edgbaston High School in 1871.

Yet, like Chamberlain, George Cadbury had learnt much from his teaching, which brought him profound new insights. Gardiner wrote that 'undoubtedly his association with the Adult School movement gave impetus to his thought, and direction to his social enterprise. It brought him into direct contact with the poor.'[73] Cadbury, too, saw that men must have recreations; for want of any other provider, it would fall to the voluntary Adult School movement. So he founded the Selly Oak Institute in 1894, as Chamberlain had done at Smethwick. Convinced that Class XIV should reach out to men in their slums, he set out to create satellite 'habitations' of his class, in places with which those men were familiar; he therefore purchased the Coppersmith's Arms in troubled Rea Street, banishing the drinking culture of beer and skittles, introducing coffee and bagatelle, and regenerating the workshop as a classroom for Sunday morning classes, with adjacent rooms refurbished for writing instruction, and furthermore, with a small library. Perhaps even more ground-breaking was that the facilities were used for Sunday afternoon classes for women.

Steadily George Cadbury was being drawn to a much more holistic approach. Class XIV might indeed change over the years as the government ensured basic literacy for the young, but it would continue into the twentieth century as a forum for debates, bible study, and lectures on a range of topics. Beyond that he had come to realise that 'it is not enough to talk to a man about ideals.

How can he cultivate ideals when his home is a slum and his only possible place of recreation is a public house?'[74] And so, George Cadbury came to see the central importance of working-class housing and of a healthful environment in which to live and work.

Joseph Chamberlain's views on education evolved rapidly from 1867 onwards. Several events crystallised his thinking. He had become aware of the contemporaneous teaching of George Dawson, renowned preacher at the Church of the Saviour, on the responsibility of prominent local citizens to lead a civic reformation of both public utilities and educational provision. His own prominence at the Church of the Messiah, and as a successful local businessman, had seen him invited to join a group of influential Birmingham figures assembled at his home in February 1867 by the town's new mayor, George Dixon. Its purpose was to found the Birmingham Education Society, committed to doing something about the semi-barbaric state of public education in an otherwise wealthy society. From its antecedent in Manchester (the Manchester and Salford Education Aid Society) Birmingham's activists learnt that 'no private or voluntary effort can reach the depth of this evil'; only a public rate could meet the financial demands.[75]

The Society developed as it went along, refining its programme in light of evidence, and the changed circumstances of a newly enfranchised urban working-class electorate. It sponsored a bill in Parliament incorporating its views, though that failed with Parliament's dissolution in 1868; it aimed to raise funds to pay for school fees for 5,000 poor children in Birmingham. Within a year it was clear that it had sufficient funds for only 2,000 children. Chamberlain and his peers set out to establish the facts; the Society visited over '700 shabby streets' (his own words) to see how the children lived, to assess the quality of the schools that did exist, and calculate the projected shortfall of places were all children to attend school. It found that schools in Birmingham had space for only 8% of the school population; even so those institutions were not full.[76]

Involvement in this survey had a profound effect on Chamberlain. He was radicalised. He realised that the voluntary efforts of the churches (of which he had been a part) – hitherto almost the only providers of schooling in Britain, dame schools apart – were totally inadequate. In Garvin's words, 'he became convinced that without national legislation the problem was hopeless'.[77] He was also converted to a belief in compulsion; parents must be forced to send their children to school. As a first step he and other members of the Society got themselves elected to the Town Council (November 1869), in the belief that any legislation establishing national schooling would be executed locally by the councils. It is safe to say that his involvement with the Society and educational reform projected him on the path to a national political career – compared with the worthy but paltry efforts of individual benefactors, he recognised that only the power of the state could really effect radical change.

The first step on that journey was his memorandum: 'A National Society for promotion of Compulsory Education' in which he asserted that 'it is as much the duty of the state to see that children are educated as to see that they are fed'.[78] Influenced by a new friend Jesse Collings, who called for national, secular, compulsory, rate-funded, state-aided, state-inspected, and locally managed education, Chamberlain, Dixon and other Society members launched the National Education League in early 1869 to pursue Collings' aims, and to replicate the campaign of the Anti-Corn Law League decades earlier.

Chamberlain was prominent from the start; with Dixon elected to Parliament and so translated to London, he became chairman of the executive committee in Birmingham. Members of the Chamberlain and Nettlefold families gave significant sums of money for the League's start-up funding. Birmingham men colonised all the important positions in the organisation; they were subject to the chairman. He exploited his position to obtain virtual control over the whole organisation, through the force of his intellect, his political acumen, his personality and his sheer ambition. He effectively became sole dictator, for he demanded unquestioning obedience from the one hundred or so provincial branches of the League which he established.[79] In other words, the National Education League enabled Chamberlain to channel into a political context those qualities of dynamism, energy, supreme competence, and yet also of ruthlessness, which he had already revealed in his business career.

Gladstone's government did not meekly adopt the League's prescriptions. W.E. Forster, vice-president of Education, was responsible for the passage of the Act that bore his name in 1870. It aimed to ensure an education for all children of elementary school age. By its very existence it articulated what had been a national epiphany, a recognition that voluntary schools had evidently failed in their self-appointed mission to teach the country's children. Yet in nearly all other regards it was deeply disappointing to League supporters, overwhelmingly to their Nonconformist members.

Far from stipulating a wholesale reform of educational provision, Forster concluded that the voluntary schools (most of them Church of England) should be supplemented not replaced – a policy known as 'filling the gaps' in voluntary provision. Local areas with insufficient voluntary provision could elect School Boards – they would be elected, contrary to the policy favoured by the League, by all ratepayers, and not nominated by local councillors. Those School Boards could build new schools. Fees would be charged. Still, at least, the passage of the Cowper-Temple clause ensured that – rather than be subject to Anglican teaching – the new board schools would have no denominational teaching at all. Chamberlain was content with that concession.

However, he and all Nonconformist supporters were enraged by the unheralded infiltration of a minor clause to the Act, clause 25, which in areas where there were insufficient grounds for building a board school permitted the payment of church school fees out of the local rates. Thus Nonconformists would in certain parts of the country – where numbers were unfeasibly small – be subsidising the Established Church's schools. For Chamberlain the battle against that clause was elevated from simply one of religion into a much more generalised assault on all privilege.

The Education League fought to overturn the iniquities of Forster's policy from the outset. Garvin sketches in one purple passage that almost demonic energy of its effective leader, Joseph Chamberlain:

> All his qualities as a man of action, and the defects of his qualities, now came out – swift and punctual in dispatch; prompt in decision; fibrous in tenacity; over sanguine; full of venture; but full of resource; too blistering in attack and retort; but never fumbling nor shrinking, he is for fighting to the last.[80]

He it was who led the deputation of over 400 Nonconformists and 46 MPs to 10 Downing Street to meet the Prime Minister and Forster in March 1870; and as a witness later wrote: 'The manner in which he secured the earnest and rapt attention of Mr Gladstone, whilst purposely ruffling the temper of Mr Forster was not easily forgotten.'[81]

Chamberlain's dash and aggression, as well as a touch of menace, come through in his letters to George Dixon, now a Birmingham MP: 'We have sent out an inflammatory circular to all our branches urging large delegations and public meetings (of protest)' ... (and) 'If Forster forces the bill through the house there will be a tremendous revival of agitation for the Disestablishment of the Established Church.'[82] His dynamism can be seen as he took the campaign to the country, bombarding newly established branches with pamphlets and publicity, encouraging them to contest the new School Board elections and to resist the imposition of clause 25. Oddly, the one area in which he and his experienced team failed was in Birmingham's first School Board elections in 1870 where through an overambitious strategy the Nonconformists were beaten by a more focused campaign of the Anglican and Catholic candidates. It never happened again.

He led the fight against the Conservative-dominated School Board's policy of implementing clause 25 in Birmingham, resisting every attempt of the law, including the threat of distraining of his goods, to make him pay rates which would be directed to supporting the town's voluntary schools.[83] Only the election of a Liberal majority in the School Board election of 1873 lifted the threat of legal action. Chamberlain became the Board's new chairman. He became a formidable builder of schools, which were spacious, notable for their separate classrooms and large playgrounds on continental models. He quadrupled the rate of construction.[84]

His own personal notebooks about the School Board held in the University of Birmingham's Special Collections reveal so much about the skills and qualities making him a formidable political operator. In his immaculate handwriting, page after page records the attendance figures in every board school; the income and the fees paid; the salaries and identities of the heads; the teachers' names; the work books recommended in each subject. The eye for detail, the gathering of a battery of facts, while he was extricating himself from the *Nettlefold and Chamberlain* business and preparing to take over as Mayor of Birmingham, during the period when he was also still running the League's campaign, show his immense capacity for hard work, his ability to master the minutiae, and an impressive, earnest diligence.[85]

That fight against the Act was taken out to the country. Those notebooks also contain extracts gathered from provincial news reports all over the country, showing the lengths the denominations would go to resist school boards. The Church party at Luton issued a handbill, *Vote Against A School Board*, which sought to persuade locals to resist this innovation:

> If you don't want your children taken from you by compulsion; If you don't want your home taken from you because you can't pay a fine; If you don't want your wages reduced because your employer would have to pay heavier rates.

In the face of this hysterical hostility Chamberlain met fire with fire. He devised an electoral strategy whereby Nonconformists would withdraw support for any Liberal by-election candidates who supported Forster's hated Act, and refined it to suggest putting up League candidates to split the Liberal vote.[86] For the first time, but not for the last, Chamberlain was seeking to do real damage to his Liberal party leader, Gladstone. He himself came to believe that Gladstone's defeat in the 1874 General Election was largely because the Prime Minister had alienated his Nonconformist base.

The process of researching constituencies for the implementation of this electoral strategy was very important in Chamberlain's political apprenticeship. He began to develop that deep understanding of the country's electoral profile which would continue to mark him out as exceptional among contemporary politicians right up to the campaigns of the Tariff Reform League at the start of the next century. In the case of the National Education League, all this effort did not ultimately bear fruit. By the end of 1873, its parlous finances drove Chamberlain to conclude that it should draw in its horns and wind down its activities; the coincidental elevation of the Radical John Bright to Gladstone's cabinet allowed Chamberlain to argue that Gladstone was now clearly listening and that revision of the hated Forster Act was imminent. For Chamberlain had other preoccupations now.

He had learnt so much from his immersion in the education issue. The wounding recognition for a Liberal that it was a Liberal government that had introduced that detestable Education Act and the realisation that his pressure group, the National Education League, had failed to amend it convinced him of the need to create an altogether different organisation, the National Liberal Federation, which he launched in 1877. As he himself put it: 'I don't think the League will do.'[87] His new NLF would represent grass-root Liberal thinking and force party leaders to adopt its policies; it would ensure 'errors' like the Forster Act were avoided. It would be run from Birmingham using the techniques he and his team, Harris, Schnadhorst, Collings and others had previously employed. Now he had a national profile, this Federation would be the means to entrenching policies in the Liberal Party country-wide, ones in which he and his Radical colleagues believed.[88]

Furthermore, the education issue had drawn him into municipal politics, prompting him to become a town councillor in 1869, and then – as he learnt more – leading him inexorably to an understanding of the need for related social reforms. In a speech at the Annual General Meeting of Severn Street Adult School in 1874 (which we may suppose was attended by one of its most prominent teachers, George Cadbury) Chamberlain, now town mayor, revealed the logical process by which he had come to a new conviction:

> You must have found that your educational and other work is hindered by the obstacles which the existing sanitary condition of the town interposes. It seems to me that education must be a perfect farce when the instruction at the school is contradicted by the experience of the home. It seems to me absurd to preach morality to people who are herded together in conditions in which common decency is impossible. It seems to me ridiculous to talk of temperance to men who have every reason to leave their homes and are driven thereby to the public house. It seems to me monstrous to preach thrift to those whose whole lives are wasted in a perpetual struggle with disease and death.[89]

The sentiment and the conclusion would have resonated with the George Cadbury who had asked how it was possible for a man 'to cultivate ideals when his home is a slum?' What Chamberlain said to the Adult School movement was his impetus to action through the

Birmingham Council; the gas and water socialism of the civic gospel it would enact sprang from the realisation that schooling and libraries were not enough until the physical environment was transformed for the working man.

The contrast between Chamberlain and Cadbury in these years is instructive. On one hand for Chamberlain, education opened new horizons and new prospects, bearing him away from his own teaching, and soon enough when his term as Chairman of the Birmingham School Board was served, away from Birmingham education altogether. Cadbury, however, remained dedicated to making his mark, to affecting and improving lives, in that part of Birmingham where he lived, worked and gave employment. Not for him, sitting on councils (with one brief exception) or in Parliament, pursuing aggressive political campaigns or involvement in the cut and thrust of electoral rivalry. He was not prominent in the Education League; nor was he sufficiently exercised by the decision of its leadership, to support unsectarian religious teaching in the Board schools, to join more vociferous Nonconformist protesters in its ranks. Although we are told by Gardiner that 'he gave enthusiastic support' to Chamberlain's cause of 'enlightened local government' in the mid-1870s the local satirical paper, *The Dart*, wrote of George Cadbury:

> What we hear,
>
> That Cadbury has been the working-man's friend
>
> That Cadbury is not a slavish follower of Mr Chamberlain,
>
> That neither is the Dart.[90]

One can surmise that for Cadbury, Chamberlain's ends did not justify the means, and that those feelings of his were widely known. While Chamberlain rose to Cabinet rank, and then in 1886 rebelled against his leader, Gladstone, with devastating results for the Liberal Party, George Cadbury's interest in the education of the people of Bournville and the surrounding outcrops of Birmingham continued. In a short period between 1890 and 1894 he founded his Institutes at Stirchley, Selly Oak and Northfield both for Quaker Meetings and for Adult School classes in which, as we have seen, he retained a strong personal commitment.[91]

He and Elizabeth, his wife, made themselves responsible for the provision of schools for the village of Bournville, furnishing them with 'double clock tower, spacious playgrounds, abundant classrooms, laboratories, library and handicraft shops, (a) model of school architecture and equipment which will not be paralleled in any village community in the country', as Gardiner proudly avowed. He goes on to point out that Bournville was the first example in the country of the day-continuation school where employees were given (paid) time off to attend classes. Cadbury evidently had decided views on educational provision; in working with the local authority (King's Norton Education Committee) he was challenged on the size of classrooms in his Bournville schools, which he had devised to accommodate a maximum of forty-five children, somewhat below the fifty-five deemed appropriate by an economically minded Committee. He won but only after taking his case to the Board of Education; small class sizes, he divined, aided learning.[92] George and Elizabeth Cadbury's urge to educate went beyond this; in 1909 they equipped a house in Thorn Road to teach housewifery skills for girl employees in the conviction that education precedes responsibility, and that girls need to be prepared for their ultimate destiny, when they would leave *Cadburys* to become housewives and mothers.[93]

It would be too neat to draw a contrast with Cadbury by suggesting that Chamberlain completely abandoned an interest in education once the League had been wound up in the mid-1870s, once he had surrendered the chairmanship of the School Board and once he had moved on to mayoral and parliamentary responsibilities. That would be to ignore an important sequence of events in his career as a national politician. For aspects of the conflict over the 1870 Act continued to resonate with him. He did not forget the League's commitment to free elementary education.

When in 1885 he launched his Radical Unauthorised Programme, seeking to attract the rural working-class householders enfranchised in the Third Reform Act of the previous year, this was in his mind. Chamberlain addressed the Birmingham Artisans Association in January 1885 in what would be forever after known as the 'Ransom' speech, because at one stage he seemed to threaten violence on the landed aristocracy and gentry: 'What ransom will property pay for the security it enjoys?' 'There is a doctrine in many men's mouths that property has obligations as well as rights.' And to our purpose, that incendiary speech ended with this: 'You must look for a cure in legislation that will give a free education to every child in the land and which will enable everyone, even the poorest to make the best use of the faculties which he must have.'[94] He therefore ensured the issue remained in the public eye.

Paradoxically it was the propertied party which Chamberlain had so violently castigated that proved much more amenable on the subject of elementary education. The Conservative Prime Minister Lord Salisbury was beginning to see the advantages of working more closely with the Liberal Unionist rebels who had helped him bring down Prime Minister Gladstone in 1886 over his Home Rule proposals. Chamberlain's radical ideas about local government and education might add a progressive tincture to his government. Fearing that the Liberals were likely to win the imminent General Election, Salisbury bid for the working-man's vote, arguing that once the state had forced a man to educate his children: 'You are bound to make it as easy for him as you can… and very greatly to relieve the difficulties of the working man in that respect.'[95] So it was that with the 1891 Education Act he adopted Chamberlain's long-standing policy of free elementary education for all, ensuring that schools were compensated for the loss of fees by extending increased Treasury grants to them.

In 1891 Salisbury had very deliberately tip-toed round the fraught matter of rate aid to voluntary schools, which the Church of England and many of his party members were demanding at the time as a logical way of ensuring that cash-strapped voluntary schools received a transfusion of funding. He knew it would alienate those Liberal Unionists led by Chamberlain, many of whom were Nonconformists, for whom it was an article of faith that they would not support the Established Church. In 1896 his government returned again to the issue. The financial struggles of the church schools were increasing and pressure from the Church of England was applied because of a growing feeling that children should have a religious education, not the studiedly non-denominational offering of the Board schools; many churchmen felt it to be their sacred duty to provide Anglican instruction.

A strong case was developing too against the proliferation of *ad hoc* local government committees of which School Boards were one example, their byzantine elections defying logic.[96]

John Gorst MP was entrusted with preparing a bill; in a diplomatic fudge he proposed creating Local Education Authorities (LEAs) alongside School Boards. He also suggested diluting the Cowper-Temple clause of 1870, which proscribed denominational instruction in school. Chamberlain, now a senior member of Salisbury's cabinet as Colonial Secretary, opposed it, especially disliking the growing pretensions of Anglican clergymen. He made his views plain, for 'nothing was more regular than his absence from the Treasury Bench'.[97] That displeasure, and the internal contradictions in Gorst's bill, saw it defeated. Voluntary schools were temporarily bailed out by increased treasury grants. Chamberlain had acted as a conservative brake, ensuring the preservation of the 1870 status quo and the integrity of the Forster Act's School Boards.

Only six years later in 1902 matters turned out very differently. Now an expensive war (the Boer War) compelled the Treasury to return to the idea of funding voluntary schools from local rates. Arthur Balfour, who in 1902 succeeded his uncle Lord Salisbury as Prime Minister, was determined comprehensively to resolve the issues of funding, of declining standards in cash-strapped voluntary schools, and of a lack of structure for secondary education in England and Wales. His bill proposed the abolition of the School Boards, the creation of LEAs, rate funding for schools, comprehensive inspection, and contained a clause instructing LEAs to survey local secondary education needs, and then meet them. It infuriated Nonconformists, for whom the use of public monies – especially local rates – to support Anglican and Catholic schools was an abomination.[98] George Cadbury was evidently one of them. In his newly acquired newspaper, the *Daily News*, he gave considerable space to a series of passionate articles by the outspoken Nonconformist critic of the Bill, John Clifford.

The Bill was extremely awkward for Chamberlain. On one hand he understood the financial position of the government, which had had to fund an expensive war (of which he was the author) of over three years' duration. He now felt a strong loyalty to his Conservative Unionist allies who had stood by him in the difficult years of fluctuating fortunes while the war was being fought. And a man who had built a reputation as a social reformer could hardly oppose a social reform of this importance, sponsored by his own government. He of all people sympathised with the compelling case for an efficient education system to avoid the waste of human potential in the struggling voluntary schools, and at secondary level. Furthermore, his patience with Nonconformists was wearing thin. He believed them to be 'more fanatical, more bitter, more selfish and more unscrupulous than I have ever known champions of the Church to be'.[99]

On the other hand, he felt a strong residual loyalty to the Board Schools of which he had at one time been a manager. He and the National Education League had fought tooth and nail in 1870 to ensure voluntary schools were not supported by the rates; he could see the validity of the charges of hypocrisy that would be levelled against him by Nonconformists. Indeed, the most pertinent argument for him against the Bill was political. That is why he argued strongly for the inclusion of a clause giving a 'local option' whereby rate aid for voluntary schools could only be given after negotiations between local authorities and school managers. Balfour accepted it for a while to assist his Liberal Unionist colleague, who he knew faced fierce criticism in his own party, but the clause was removed at the committee stage in the House, and the Act passed into law.

Chamberlain was indeed well aware of the potential for damage in his own Liberal Unionist party. He wrote to Lord Selborne, a prominent Liberal Unionist and First Lord of the Admiralty, also an enthusiast for root and branch education reform: 'If you were to promote a Bill giving rate aid to denominational schools I think you would lose Birmingham and the Birmingham influence. You may be unaware of the strong feeling of the other sections of our party.'[100] In fact, Chamberlain would go on to hold Birmingham, although only after a personal appeal to the Birmingham Liberal Unionist Association where a mix of compelling advocacy, remorseless logic and flattering blandishments saw him overturn an earlier motion condemning Balfour's Bill.[101]

His prognostication of collapse in the country at large as outlined in a letter to the Duke of Devonshire, co-author of the Bill but also leader of the Liberal Unionists, was much more accurate: 'The greatest blow struck at Liberal Unionist influence has been, as I warned it would be, the introduction of the Education Act for which you were in a special degree responsible – which has driven from our ranks many of our most energetic Nonconformist supporters.'[102] Chamberlain had already witnessed the revival in the country of both Nonconformists and of the Liberal Party, which – after its divisions over how to respond to Chamberlain's war – now had an issue around which all could rally. Education would be a key component in the Liberal landslide of 1906, an election which saw George Cadbury actively opposing Joseph Chamberlain.

On one aspect of education the two could agree: the importance of extending university provision. Chamberlain understood that 'the most important function of the universities will always be their indirect influence on the whole education of the country'.[103] He was acutely conscious of Britain's provision compared with that of its trading and diplomatic rival Germany, which had twice the number of universities, and where the government subsidised 70% of the cost.[104] He believed that the influence of a university on the surrounding city was profound; it could 'elevate the whole mass (of the industrial population) to higher aims and higher intellectual ambitions'. For him a specialist technological college like the financially insecure Mason College in Birmingham, founded by the steel pen manufacturer Josiah Mason in 1880, was insufficient because its curriculum was too narrow; a university was defined by the presence of the liberal arts in its curriculum.

In 1897 he set out to create the University of Birmingham, taking over and absorbing Mason College, and fundraising to establish a secure financial base of £250,000 to pay for the professorial chairs. He understood the psychology of competitive charitable giving, encouraging wealthy steel magnates Lord Strathcona and Andrew Carnegie to vie with each other in levels of generosity. He persuaded the Calthorpe estate to give a 25-acre site on the Bournbrook estate for an Engineering and Metallurgy faculty; indeed, he raised money throughout Birmingham for his enterprise and by 1902 had exceeded his target. This was especially impressive given the demands of the South African War on his time and his emotions and the saga over the Balfour Education Act. Just before Richard Cadbury died Chamberlain wrote to him saying he 'would like to have an opportunity of talking about the new University to which your brother has been a magnificent contributor'.[105]

George Cadbury had indeed been one of the earliest supporters of the university. But it is possible to detect a change in his attitude, coloured no doubt from 1899 to 1906 by his growing detestation of both Chamberlain's adventurous foreign policy and his damaging assaults on Free Trade, the latter an article of belief for Cadbury. In July 1909 the King and Queen came to open the new buildings at the university, a royal imprimatur for Chamberlain's achievement, even if he was now crippled with the stroke that ended his political career. George Cadbury was invited to accept an honorary degree of LLD. He declined it, confiding to Gardiner that 'such honours should be reserved for those who have been distinguished in science, literature or original research, or for special effort on behalf of the university'.[106] To his biographer this was an expression of the self-effacement, and hatred of titles and decorations, of a plain and simple Quaker. Cadbury's wife Elizabeth wrote in her day journal that day when they were invited as guests: 'I had thought I had persuaded George to come with us and he got all ready, but at the last moment said he could not stand the idea of two hours waiting.'[107] So was it modesty or impatience, or do these fragments betray a real reluctance to be seen giving any approbation to an opponent of whom he had come deeply to disapprove?

George Cadbury had his own higher education project in the very same years as Chamberlain's vision reached fruition. Far from the universal curriculum of the new University of Birmingham, his foundation of Woodbrooke in Selly Oak was specifically for the Society of Friends, providing them with 'an opportunity for more fully qualifying themselves spiritually, intellectually and experimentally for the work to which they have felt called by the Holy Spirit'.[108] It proved a considerable success; students came from all over the world, and the college drew on surrounding Birmingham to train them in social service. It also spawned other similar institutions, at West Hill, Kingsmead and Carey Hill, to specialise in Sunday school teaching and missionary work. In sum these colleges aggregated to what Gardiner called 'a new university of a new type, predominantly religious in character, a place where men and women can be prepared for social service of many kinds'.[109]

Whatever else divided George Cadbury and Joseph Chamberlain it is clear that at least in this, their passionate advocacy of the value of education and training, for children and for adults, they shared a common goal and a common vision. This permeated their attitudes to social reform throughout their lives. In Birmingham their educational legacies were similar. Both have left schools – Cadbury's Bournville buildings remain handsome and striking, as are Chamberlain's School Board schools. Both have bequeathed important Higher Education campuses, even if Chamberlain's Aston Webb architecture at the University of Birmingham is the more imposing. The philosophy underpinning each has not changed from the time of their foundation. Chamberlain's aim to elevate the thinking and the intellectual ambition of the manufacturing classes of the Midlands by creating a great civic university has been realised, as has Cadbury's vision of Christian colleges to promote inquiry and faith for people in Britain and internationally. Chamberlain's legacy, however, encompasses national policy too – his determination and his campaigning brought to fruition the policy of free elementary education for all.

PROJECTING VALUES IN BRICK AND STONE

The conscientious propertied classes were dogged by a question insistently posed from the 1840s onwards – 'What was to be done about the living and working conditions of the working classes?' It was first eloquently addressed by Frederick Engels in his classic work, *The Condition of the Working Class in England*, based on his experience of Manchester in the early 1840s.[110] Joseph Chamberlain and George Cadbury were more significant than almost any of their contemporaries amongst wealthy Englishmen in the contribution they made to finding an answer to improving the lot of the poorest of their fellow countrymen.

For Chamberlain insights into the living conditions of his workers came when he was a businessman; as we have seen, his foundation and funding of the Smethwick Institute when a young man was an attempt to improve the quality of recreation and education available to his employees. Garvin, his earliest biographer, wrote: 'The more he studied social conditions the more he believed them to be a disgrace to nineteenth-century civilisation.'[111] Those fact-finding trips he undertook in some of the town's run-down streets in 1869, to establish the true nature of working-class education in Birmingham for George Dixon's Education Society, were shocking; he discovered just how squalid and filthy were the tenements and alleys many children called home.[112] At the same time he joined the Town Council. His education was then rapidly broadened, for all Birmingham councillors had to take responsibility for the town's execrable sanitary record, which had rendered it recently subject to a suit in Chancery. This compelled the Council to find solutions to the seemingly intractable problem of disposing of the town's waste.[113]

The months and years he spent on the education issue wrought in him a transformation. So, in a speech in 1874 in the Unitarian Chapel in Birmingham, he argued that the two causes of misery and vice in Birmingham were firstly 'from the ignorance of the masses. In the second place from the horrible, shameful homes in which the poor are forced to live.'[114] His horror at the slums he had seen led him to organise a sanitary conference in the city for January 1875 and in his keynote, introductory speech (his first to a large national audience of 700 to 800 delegates) he memorably articulated the gravity of the situation with such effect that he can be credited with influencing the new Conservative Government of Benjamin Disraeli to draft and pass the Artisans' and Labourers' Dwellings Act.

> I do not believe the ordinary public is at all aware of the enormous waste of life which is going on in our midst and of the frightful consequences, sanitary, moral, pecuniary and otherwise which result from it. ... (The insanitary conditions) are the fruitful occasion of misery, pauperism, intemperance and crime. ... All this disease is produced by filthy, ill-ventilated, uncomfortable homes. Those homes drive the people to public houses and worse places. What folly it is to talk about the moral and intellectual elevation of the masses when the conditions of life are such as to render the elevation impossible. ... We find bad air, polluted water, crowded and filthy homes and ill-ventilated courts everywhere prevailing in the midst of our boasted wealth, luxury and civilisation. ... Even the air they have is contaminated by unmentionable impurities and

filth. Hardly a gleam of sunshine ever comes into the dark and dreary courts. All reverence is blotted out and common decency is an empty name.[115]

Chamberlain ended this powerful speech with a call to action: 'Of one thing I am certain; we cannot afford any longer to sit still or stand with folded arms in the presence of so great an evil.' It was an evil which George Cadbury had himself identified, and one which impelled the Cadburys' move from Bridge Street in the heart of Birmingham out to Stirchley and Selly Oak. His second wife, Elizabeth, wrote of it in rather cloying terms in a paper celebrating the fiftieth anniversary of the Bournville move: 'He had resolved to move their factory from the smoky surrounds to fresh fields and blue skies, amongst trees where the birds sang and the rooks raised their plaintive friendly voice, and where even trout swam in a nearby little brook.'[116]

If the attractions of the countryside are here highlighted rather more than the awfulness of the slums, Iolo Williams, *Cadbury's* official historian was blunter:

> For years George Cadbury was in touch with many of those living in the poorest and most squalid parts of Birmingham (from his work with the Adult School in Severn Street). As years went on he became more and more deeply impressed by the ill effects of slum conditions, and of the ever-increasing areas of badly and closely built houses, upon both health and character.[117]

George Gardiner, who knew his subject well, started his biography in 1922 with the assertion that, like the Victorian critic John Ruskin, George Cadbury thought 'the only true wealth of a nation was in the life of its people, and if that life was perishing in sunless slums and fetid hovels (then) the country was doomed'.[118]

George Cadbury articulated his vision in responding to Birmingham's housing crisis, when he set out the objects of his charity, the Bournville Village Trust in 1900:

> The object of the charity is to be the amelioration of the condition of the working-class and labouring population in and around Birmingham and elsewhere in Great Britain by the provision of improved dwellings with gardens and open spaces to be enjoyed herewith...[119]

Birmingham bricks and mortar still stand as cynosures for the radically different ways that Joseph Chamberlain and George Cadbury reacted to the social and environmental challenge of their generation. Cadbury's legacy is an aesthetically harmonious village, influenced by the vernacular architecture and materials of rural Worcestershire and Warwickshire cottages. Back to back terraces were eschewed for brick houses in pairs or fours, occupying spacious gardens, set back from the road; rather than useless ornament on the houses as was the wont of contemporary jerry-builders, the emphasis was on quality and restraint.

The cottages reflected George Cadbury's concern for a wholesome family life, for privacy and for the healthy pastime of spade husbandry, gardening. The lay-out of the village allowed for ample open spaces, including a village green, children's playgrounds, girls' and youths' gardens, a public park, well-wooded recreation grounds and allotments; it would soon have well-appointed schools, an institute and places for worship. Although subsequently engulfed by the expansion of the city, Bournville remains the harmonious, green, well-maintained community its founder first envisaged.[120]

Chamberlain's contribution, on the other hand, was on a different scale and had an equally noble intention: the Venetian Gothic red brick and terracotta of Birmingham's public buildings, its Council House (1874-79), the City Museum and Art Gallery (1881-1885) and a number of shops and offices in Corporation Street are all, in a phrase made memorable by David Cannadine, 'the projection of values into space and stone'. Those values were of the civic gospel; the buildings were designed to dignify corporate life, promoting 'a municipal life nobler, fuller, richer than any the world has ever seen', argued J.T. Bunce, the editor of the *Birmingham Daily Post*.[121] Bunce was a friend and ally of Chamberlain. He might have added that Corporation Street was planned by Chamberlain at least partly as a solution to the deplorable slum conditions in the heart of Birmingham. So these municipal buildings neatly symbolise Chamberlain's collective approach to social action.

The contrast then was of the municipal with the homely scale. The practical response, making a difference locally with concrete measures to show others how it was done, was very much Cadbury's way. As Gardiner writes: 'His aim was to solve the whole problem of housing and town-planning, and... he made it his chief task to supervise the experiment and control the main lines of development.'[122] The close interest he paid to every detail of the Bournville Estate, from the standards of behaviour expected of its inhabitants, to the planting in the gardens, and the horticultural training of the young men bespeaks a controlling character, however munificent and kindly he was. His canvas was limited, regional, though profoundly influential for all that. It reflected his distaste for public life and for public display, a degree of shy reluctance about leading national political campaigns. He – after all – remained a successful businessman, a director of an expanding national brand into old age.

Thus was the Bournville Estate's character determined by its founder. The architecture of its vernacular housing, its parks and open land, its community facilities, and its productive gardens were all, it seems, designed to promote Bournville as a bucolic idyll which channelled contemporaneous yearning for a golden pastoral age, 'Merrie England'. Cadbury was not alone in seeking to mitigate unfettered industrialisation's impact on workers. John Richardson at Saltaire and Lord Leverhulme at Port Sunlight preceded him and had developed good-quality housing for their workers; by contrast barely 50% of Bournville's occupants would actually work in the Bournville factory.[123]

Cadbury was also influenced by Ebenezer Howard, later creator of Letchworth, who wrote an influential text on the *Garden Cities of Tomorrow*, advocating new suburban towns of limited size, surrounded by green belt, with land owned by trustees.[124] Birmingham Council also unintentionally proved a spur. In 1889 it decided that since unsubsidised houses were not economically feasible, none should be built by the Council at all. Flats were thought to be the answer though Cadbury did not believe working men would be happy with that proposal.[125] If the Council would not act, then he could show the way. And if the solution had to be private building then Bournville was also conceived as an economic proposition, to show speculative builders that construction of housing was a profitable undertaking.[126] It was to be educative in another way: 'although small in itself', George Cadbury recorded that he intended Bournville 'may do something to open people's eyes to the cruelty of overcrowding in towns'.[127] A stream of visitors, and imitators, demonstrated the compelling attraction of his creation.

On the other hand, the way that Chamberlain would make a difference was through political action; he had an irrepressible urge to act, to speak up, to get involved in campaigns on big and national issues which seized him; he found in himself qualities of leadership, and – in time, and with hard work – of oratory. He was intensely combative, determined and energetic. There was a remorseless logic to the way he progressed in the 1860s from an interest in education to election to the Council and to School Board chairmanship, and then on to the mayoralty in 1873, where he felt empowered to tackle the social ills which had so impressed him in the few years earlier. For the answers for Chamberlain were to be found in political activity. On one occasion he told the Town Council that 'all private effort, all individual philanthropy sinks into insignificance compared to the organised power of a great representative assembly such as this'. For him the Corporation was 'engaged in a great struggle to promote the welfare, health and happiness of the population over which it rules'.[128] Later he said: 'If a man is a philanthropist, where else (apart from the Council) can he expect to be influential in saving the lives of thousands of persons and in bringing health to tens of thousands of homes.'[129] Clearly, then, the scale of the problems he confronted demanded municipal, later national, action; however admirable and exceptional the Bournville social experiment, that private, personal philanthropy was never enough for Chamberlain.

He was greatly influenced by George Dawson, minister of the Church of the Saviour in Birmingham, who preached consistently from the late 1840s on the importance of developing public virtue, of recruiting Birmingham's talented entrepreneurs to 'sacrifice themselves for the good of the town' and to 'prefer before (their) own prosperity and well-being that of the town and country to which (they) belong'.[130] Dawson had a dim view of those contemporary councillors who ran Birmingham from the beery atmosphere of the Woodman pub, for he thought their limited outlook was reflected in the squalor of parts of the town.[131]

By the end of 1873 the education issue which had hitherto dominated Chamberlain's thinking was to cede second place in his mind to the challenges of reforming Birmingham's environment. As Mayor he was then to preside over a civic revolution. Whilst it is true that individual aspects of his reform prospectus had been anticipated elsewhere, in Glasgow, Leeds and Manchester for example, what was startlingly innovatory, and what established Birmingham as the template and foremost proponent of the civic gospel, was the new coherent and empowering vision of the function and nature of the Corporation and its Mayor.[132]

The Birmingham Council Proceedings, the minute book of the Council, preserved in the Library of Birmingham Archives, tell the story of a municipal revolution. Financial prudence and a paralysing inertia characterised the outlook of most of Chamberlain's predecessors, many of whom were collectively dubbed the 'Economy Party'. Its leaders like John Sadler and William Brinsley, representing a libertarian and economical brand of Birmingham Liberalism, carried on the fight against Chamberlain's type of interventionist Liberalism throughout Chamberlain's time on the Council.[133] We can get a sense of the way constraints hampered the work of purifying and improving Birmingham from the report of the Medical Officer of Health, Alfred Hill, months before Chamberlain became Mayor. He wrote in August 1873: 'The water supply constantly engages my attention and, whenever it is found impure, I recommend its abandonment but, there is no legal power to enforce the recommendation and for want of proper sewerage some parts of the town are in a very dangerous state.' [134]

Sitting on the Council since 1869 Chamberlain was well aware of the tainted state of the wells which supplied half the town's dwellings with water; he also observed how the town's waterworks seemed financially impregnable and resistant to any prospect of a take-over at a price the Council might be able to afford. But from the outset of his mayoralty the *Proceedings* record a new determination to grasp the nettle. Immediately, by-laws were passed to regulate the conditions prevailing in private lodging houses; builders were required to ensure that new houses had at least one privy shared with a second. New sewage tanks were initiated at Saltley to try and satisfy the resolutions of Chancery, which demanded that the nuisance of the town's sewage deposits dumped at Gravelly Hill be tackled. [135]

Yet the most important initiative was unquestionably Chamberlain's decision to municipalise gas supplies. He recognised that radical sanitary reform was required to transform the health and the environment of Birmingham's working classes; only he envisioned how a municipalised gas supply could be made to yield the profits for reinvestment in a publicly owned water company. The minutes in March 1874 chronicle Chamberlain's reasoning: 'The Committee find that the sale of Gas continually and steadily increases year by year, and the Corporation will derive from such increased sales a profit...'. So, the Council borrowed £2 million (for Chamberlain had taken advantage of favourable terms available to municipal corporations) and within a short period was indeed making handsome profits and was able to reduce the price of gas to the customers.

Chamberlain's motivation was firstly to provide the funds for future plans. This the take-over did handsomely, with £241,000 passing to the Borough Improvement Fund by 1884 and with money found for the Municipal Museum and Art Gallery in 1880, the fulfilment of a civic dream for Chamberlain. [136] Secondly it was to build up public opinion, impatiently looking for the next step, for the acquisition of the water works. [137] Underpinning it was that conviction he shared with his colleagues on the Council: 'All monopolies, regulated monopolies sustained by the state in the interests of the inhabitants generally, should be controlled by the representatives of the people, and should not be left in the hands of private speculators.' [138] He was deeply suspicious of such individual action, greatly preferring the almost socialistic powers of municipality and state.

In the cause of reforming sanitation the Council continued to act to further prescribe the conditions of all lodging houses in Birmingham, detailing how they should be registered, repaired, cleansed, swept, and provided with privies and with bedsteads. [139] Still, the biggest reform came in December 1874 when, utilising the new powers available under the Public Health Act of 1872, Chamberlain moved the bill to promote the compulsory purchase of the town's water infrastructure. No councillor voted against it. He argued that many of the town's wells were vilely contaminated, that it was outrageous to have to criminalise people for stealing that which was one of the necessities of life, that water should never be the source of profit and he promised that all profits would go into the reduction of the price of water. No single policy in nineteenth-century Birmingham did more for the health of its inhabitants; it was a truly significant piece of social reform.

The third part of the trilogy of mayoral reforms was that of the improvement of the centre of Birmingham with a scheme in late 1875 which was very much his own. At the dinner given to him to mark his retirement from the mayoralty in November 1876 he boasted of 'the great scheme of improvement which will change the face of a large part of the town and which we are confident will conduce to higher morality, greater happiness, better health in very many of the poorest and most unfortunate of the population'.[140] By a neat circularity he was availing himself of the very Artisans' Dwellings Act his Sanitation Conference had inspired twenty months earlier. It permitted local authorities in large towns to buy up property, without paying additional compensation for compulsory purchase, in order to tear down slums and let land to builders to construct good working-class housing.[141] As Peter Marsh notes, the Medical Officer's report on Birmingham's unhealthy areas might have been framed by Chamberlain himself: 'No scheme for the improvement of dwellings can be considered satisfactory which does not provide for ample accommodation by means of wide, well-arranged thoroughfares, combining full capacity for traffic, with power of admitting free currents of air and sufficiency of sunlight.'[142]

Here he elides the twin factors which Chamberlain and his newly constituted Improvement Committee identified for their scheme for rebuilding the centre of Birmingham. First was that concern for the sanitary conditions, the health of the inhabitants in the worst slum areas of the town. Secondly, there was a desire to transform the 'mean huddle' at the heart of a town which aspired to be a new Venice, a model of civic government. So, fine shops and offices, distinguished public buildings, and a broad *boulevard*, as Chamberlain himself put it (for he was unquestionably influenced by Haussmann's Paris), would characterise this rival to the great city-states of the Renaissance and Antiquity.[143] The Improvement Scheme was enacted, the slums were cleared, the slum families removed themselves where they could, and New Street and Corporation Streets were laid out, with new shops and offices eventually established along their length.

Right to the end of his time as mayor, Chamberlain showed his concern for reforming and managing the built environment, pushing through by-laws to regulate back to back houses, improving over 100 miles of pavements in the town, supporting the establishment of public parks and the building of new Council offices to allow for more efficient civic government.

Those three years of his pre-eminence were transformatory for Birmingham. He wrought the reformation by the force of his personality. From the outset he had grasped that only a crusade would capture the imagination of colleagues and of Birmingham people. He had the ability to articulate the task and to inspire others to follow with rhetoric flights and invigorating prose. Sometimes, as with his attempt to impose a higher rate at a ratepayers meeting about his gas proposals in 1875, he failed and had to retreat to find another way of raising money. But his drive and advocacy overrode opposition to the water and improvement schemes, both locally and when he acted as counsel at a Local Government Board enquiry into the improvement proposals. He proved comfortable and persuasive in arguing his case with Westminster politicians like Home Secretary Richard Cross, a taste for him of national politics he would not forget.

Throughout his time he showed a grasp of the detail, and a financial acumen and creativity, which ensured he could out-argue critics and opponents and could see solutions to problems that had perplexed others. His energy was relentless; the sheer number of special meetings of Council he instituted illustrate that impatience to get on with the task of reformation, while he involved himself in the work of Council sub-committees to ensure he could see that things happened. He understood, too, the need for administrative oversight; he ensured that Birmingham had a full-time Medical Officer, and the lieutenants he needed to supervise the sanitation reforms the town instituted. His chairmanship was brisk and brooked no obstruction; he immodestly described one meeting in a letter in 1876 to his friend and ally Jesse Collings.

> I carried a stringent set of by-laws about back to back houses in the teeth of the timid ones. I took the matter in hand myself, and begged the Council to pass the by-laws without discussion of the details. This they did. And the whole set were printed, distributed and approved before the opposition had time to turn around.[144]

Unquestionably his contribution to the lives of ordinary citizens was immense; the place was immeasurably cleaner and healthier, its centre rebuilt to make it more fitting for its reputation as a leading provincial city. Still, a few points need to be made by way of a corrective. The achievement was not his alone. He had a team of supporters like Jesse Collings who helped push through reforms. Nor was he the sole initiator of reform; Thomas Avery, a councillor, and mayor in the 1860s, had developed financial controls, and set about improving the town's drainage and widening the streets, even if he was held back by worries about increasing the Council's expenditure.[145]

The most important caveat concerns the slum clearance scheme. When Chamberlain addressed the Council's new Improvement Committee he outlined the housing provision 'that the Committee would probably make for the poor' – lodging houses, flats and houses of different sizes and suited to persons of different means – it was just a flight of fancy.[146] In fact, by the terms of the Artisans' Dwellings Act, the Council itself was not permitted to do the building without specific permission from the Local Government Board. Instead it should make the former slum land available to private developers. The high cost of that land, and the onset of a deep recession, meant that only 62 houses were built to replace the 600 which had been destroyed in clearing the centre. The displaced poor colonised other parts of the town. Only a decade or so later was some housing built by the Council, 22 two-storey cottages in Ryder Street.[147] It by no means compensated for all the units of housing which had been lost through the Improvement Scheme. So, the Chamberlain mayoralty disappointed many with regard to the housing of the poor.

Yet housing continued to exercise him when he launched his Radical Programme in Birmingham in 1885. His new focus was on the agricultural labourer:

> Should agricultural labourers be entirely divorced from the soil they till and so be driven into the towns to compete for work? Alike in town and country, the labouring population (is) huddled into dwellings unfit for man or beast, where the conditions of decency are impossible and where they lead directly to disease, intemperance and crime.[148]

Better housing and allotments ('three acres and a cow') was the prescription he proposed to stop the drift to overcrowded cities, and to help provide the country's poorest workers with decent living conditions. He elaborated in Warrington later in the year: 'We purpose that the local authority in every district shall have power to let land for labourers' allotments, for artisans' dwellings and for small holdings.'[149] For him, local authority and government action remained the solution to housing reform. Ten years on he still held to that conviction. Once again speaking in Birmingham in 1894, he posed the rhetorical question: 'What is the best security and guarantee that the home of the working man shall be comfortable, shall be healthy? A man shall be the owner of his dwelling...and (I propose) a House Purchase Act. My proposal is that the state shall do for you what it has done for Irish tenants.'[150]

George Cadbury did not see the solution to poor housing as one the state itself could satisfactorily provide. Furthermore, he was very obviously uncomfortable with public office. *The Dart* in August 1878 identified that want of enthusiasm when it welcomed the victor of the municipal election in the Rotton Park ward: 'Mr George Cadbury had his municipal honours thrust upon him. He was pushed and carried into the Council, showing (as) much reluctance to enter the Chamber.... He would have preferred continuing his useful work by stealth.'[151]

He sat with Chamberlain on the Council, who though he was no longer mayor was still an alderman and member of the Gas, Improvement and Health Committees. But his dynamism in municipal matters was not Cadbury's style even if the latter 'gave him enthusiastic support', according to Gardiner.[152] He chose instead to join the Baths and Parks Committee; the *Proceedings* do not minute any particular contribution to the work of this committee in the brief year or so that Cadbury was a councillor, before the Bournville move proved a bigger counter-attraction. For the forty-five years remaining to him he never again sat on the Council or sought election to Westminster.

That contrast between Chamberlain's very visible activity and George Cadbury's stealth explains why Cadbury was happiest to make his contribution to ameliorating the lot of the working classes through private and personal initiatives. Yet both were evidently men who liked control, Chamberlain driving a reform agenda through committees or Parliament and organising national political campaigns; Cadbury in the development of the Bournville factory (chapter 1) and in the fulfilment of his vision of urban housing in south Birmingham. That vision was intensely personal, shaped by his happy childhood in the family house in Edgbaston. He deduced from that experience a guiding principle: 'the more wholesome life of his childhood bred a type of citizen healthy in body and independent in spirit. He saw how the life of the town was purified by the cleansing contact with the primal sanities of nature. He realised how profoundly environment affected character,' wrote Gardiner.[153] Cadbury watched Birmingham's green spaces disappear with the rapid and inexorable expansion of the city and determined to act.

In 1895 he started the purchase of land, appointed the architect, Alexander Harvey, and proceeded to build – first 143 houses, sold at cost price on 999-year leases, then by his death in 1922 over 1,400 more, for rent at levels which were affordable to Birmingham's hard-working artisans. The urge to act was not just that revulsion at the living conditions in the back to back houses which affected the health, the growth and the life expectancy of working people in the city centre. It was also motivated by a very real fear that the land surrounding the works might fall into the hands of jerry-builders and so 'those very slum conditions from which in Birmingham the firm had escaped would grow up around it in its new site'.[154] *Cadbury* products were marketed on the basis of their purity and natural goodness, and the firm's wholesome image might have been compromised by being surrounded by new slum housing.

So George Cadbury took a close interest in the architecture and the building of the houses and the planning of his village. Standard three-bedroom houses with sitting-room, kitchen and scullery were built simply but well, many with an English cottage-style inglenook, and all with ingenious fold away baths in the kitchen or in the scullery. From the outside these houses determinedly avoided regimentation, having different elevations and being placed irregularly, 'with an eye to picturesque unity', as Gardiner wrote. It was very important to Cadbury that there should not be a repetition of the overcrowding that disfigured Birmingham's centre.

He permitted only seven houses per acre. Each was set back from a broad road and an established feel was achieved from the outset by the preservation of existing trees on the site. Every house had a sizeable garden, three times bigger than the footprint of the building. Across the Bournville site, parks, village green and other open spaces were incorporated from the outset.[155] This was a determinedly different aesthetic model from the monotonous high-density housing constructed after the Public Health Act of 1875.[156] One other element was very important: it was a central concern for Cadbury that 'all classes may live in kindly neighbourliness – the amalgamation of factory worker and brain worker in the same district is catered for as being positively desirable', said his architect.[157]

Although George Cadbury very rapidly handed over the management of the village to the Trust, he and his family continued to take the closest of interest in its establishment and growth. The gifting of hundreds of acres of land as well as of a number of community buildings was an act of great philanthropy. Yet it also provided him with an opportunity to fulfil the clear vision he had about the ways in which working-class lives could be improved and shaped. Just as he and his brother Richard sought to develop moral, temperate, industrious and thrifty workers in the Bournville factory (see chapter 2), so Cadbury from the outset sought to extend that vision to Bournville Village.

He evidently set out to create an orderly environment which aped middle-class settlements; he hoped it would develop their values too, finding in the 'rational recreations' the village offered the means to counter what he believed were the popular recreations of the lower orders, their physical violence and their drinking. Hence the importance to him of community activities, of building meeting places for religious denominations, and of establishing village schools, all out of his own pocket. He prohibited the sale of alcohol on the settlement.[158]

Gardening is perhaps the most significant area in which to observe Cadbury's desire to shape a better life for the lower orders. He was a firm believer in *mens sana in corpore sano*, the healthy mind in the healthy body. Gardening had so many benefits. The evidence of malnourished recruits for the Boer War was pertinent in his growing concern for national efficiency (the physical state of the people): at an annual gathering of Bournville tenants, he told his audience that of 10,000 Manchester men applying to enlist in 1900, only 1000 were found fit to serve.[159] Williams proffers a more transcendental reading of Cadbury's horticultural enthusiasm: 'Give each man his garden where he can come into touch with nature and thus know more of nature's God.' The garden was the site of moral, physical and spiritual restitution.[160] It was a therapy to cure the ills of a noxious industrial environment.

The Bournville gardens were planned from the outset, with lawns, fruit trees, fruit bushes (redcurrant, blackcurrant and gooseberry), and areas prepared for the productive gardening in which Cadbury believed. This was beneficial physical labour for a man, keeping him fit and out of the pub. Leisure was too easily associated with idleness, a corrupting vice.[161] The crop yield would supplement the family diet and produce enough to sell to augment weekly earnings. Alexander Harvey clearly signed up to the founder's vision: in his book about his design for the village he wrote: 'It was equally to the advantage of their (the occupants') moral lives as well as necessary to their health, that they be brought into contact with Nature. Instead of losing money in the amusements the worker usually sought in the towns, he saved it in his garden produce.'[162]

The emphasis on vegetables and fruit reflected Cadbury's own vegetarian preferences. Through lectures, training courses, shows, festivals and competitions the Cadbury style, the preferred Bournville way, was propagated. As early as 1900, the Bournville garden competition attracted over 1000 entries.[163]

This suggests many of the new village occupants bought into Cadbury's values. The villagers were moulded by the ground rules he established for his village, the standard height of hedges, the prohibition of any sheds or buildings at the front of the houses, and the earnest imprecations to weed, tidy and mow the front gardens ('Remember', ran advice in a Bournville Year Book, 'you cannot grow weeds without seeding your neighbour's garden.')[164] The aim was not just to inculcate a bourgeois value of good neighbourliness. There were larger commercial considerations. Chocolate and cocoa products were advertised as wholesome and pure, emanating from the Bournville factory in a garden. If not a village occupied entirely by Cadbury workers, Bournville did provide a green, rural environment for the business and George Cadbury exploited this remorselessly. He even tried in 1904 to persuade the inhabitants to plant yellow and blue crocuses in all the front gardens, so subliminally advertising the colours of the *Cadbury* brand.[165] Visitors were encouraged to marvel and tours were organised from the village's inception, culminating in the visit of the King and Queen in 1919. Bournville was both the host of the first Garden City conference in 1901, and an exemplar for its international delegates. The *Cadbury* product unquestionably benefited by association.

Equally one could argue that the entire strategy to rescue Birmingham working people from squalor, idleness and intemperance was devised to produce a reliable, sober workforce to the firm's ultimate benefit. More fundamentally too, no doubt, Cadbury was as conscious as was Joseph Chamberlain that violence and revolution remained distinctly possible in the fifty years up to the First World War, especially in the depressed 1880s and in the Edwardian years of feverish trade union activity. It was in the interests of the successful capitalist to do his bit to make life easier for his workers or risk the overturning of the whole enterprise.

Cadbury's response to the systemic challenge of urban deprivation and disease was to act himself, to model solutions for others. Chamberlain's was to use the powers available to city and to state to legislate for improvement. Two very different approaches; but in one regard they found common ground. Both recognised that the way land was distributed in Britain was at the root of the problem. Chamberlain articulated this, as we saw above, in his Radical Programme of 1885. He had become convinced 'that working-class housing could be improved by tapping the wealth of urban landowners, while the number of peasant farmers could be increased by carving small allotments out of the broad acres of the aristocracy', in Marsh's words.[166]

His threatening assault on landowners who had appropriated common lands – 'What ransom will property pay for the security it enjoys?' – was provocative and possibly counter-productive.[167] Yet he did at least witness the passage of Allotment Acts and a Small Holdings Act in 1887, 1890 and 1892 by a Conservative administration led by Lord Salisbury, representatives of a class Chamberlain had mocked for 'they toil not neither do they spin'. These started the process of providing agricultural labourers with a few acres for themselves. His campaign greatly influenced the next generation of Liberal land reformers, notably David Lloyd George, for their very own Land campaign from 1911 to 1914.

Perhaps it resonated with George Cadbury but more likely he arrived at his conclusions himself. He early concluded 'that the monopoly of the land was the source of bad housing conditions and he had adopted the axiom of the land reformers that land as a necessary of life should be used not to create wealth for individuals but to serve the interests of the community'.[168] A mutual interest in land reform drew him close to one of those Liberals influenced by Chamberlain's land crusade, the party leader, Sir Henry Campbell-Bannerman in the early years of the twentieth century, although their hopes for radical change were to be frustrated. He returned to his theme in 1916 when he wrote to the Chairman of the Trades Union Congress: 'The wealthy hold the land, millions of acres of which provide for a mere handful of men sport, such as hunting, shooting and racing. This land might produce ten times as much food if properly cultivated, and many acres set apart for deer forests might produce timber and provide healthy and profitable employment.'[169] Of course, Cadbury recognised that individual efforts would be puny in effecting real change; only radical government legislation could bring about the reforms he sought.

Both Joseph Chamberlain and George Cadbury devoted a considerable part of their energies to trying to improve housing and the built environment. Their impact more than a century later still shapes parts of Birmingham. Even if their lives were characterised by a steady physical distancing from the city (as they moved to Edgbaston and King's Norton) and from the focus of their environmental planning, they continued to feel an obligation to improve living conditions for others. Chamberlain's dignifying of Corporation Street and the civic centre around the Town Hall unquestionably exalted Birmingham. His work in ensuring decently paved, clean streets augmented that sense of a civilised environment. A new Council House and later a Museum and Art Gallery symbolised the aspiration to elevate and educate the citizens of Birmingham. All this was the physical expression of his philosophical commitment to municipal, and later central, government intervention to improve and reform the community. And if Chamberlain focused on the municipal heartland, Cadbury was to construct a lasting legacy in developing a spacious and decorous estate for lower middle- and working-class occupants; its cottage-style architecture, green public spaces, and generous gardens have remained to this day the exemplification of all that is best in suburban planning. This too was an architectural declaration of a deeply held faith. In George Cadbury's case, for all that his natural inclination could be controlling and inclined to moulding the behaviour of the lower orders, the most important strand in his motivation was his strong Christian conviction. Simply, it impelled him to act when confronted with the squalor of some of Birmingham's working-class housing, both as a straightforward act of Christian charity and in the hope that others would imitate him.

As we shall now see, while housing and the built environment may have been absolutely central to them, it was not the sole issue of social reform about which they concerned themselves.

SOCIAL PREOCCUPATIONS

Housing was only one facet of Joseph Chamberlain and George Cadbury's steady determination to improve the lot of the country's working classes. This chapter will consider a clutch of initiatives by which the two sought reform, including pensions and working conditions, but will firstly focus on what was for much of their adult lives the national preoccupation of many Nonconformists and many from the propertied classes, the 'Drink question'. They felt a strong societal obligation in their differing guises of employer, churchman, public servant, philanthropist and politician to make a coherent and practical response. Unsurprisingly, they answered it in their own distinctive ways.

In a speech in 1894 which spoke as much for Cadbury's views as for his own, Joseph Chamberlain averred that 'intemperance is a great blot on our civilisation and a frightful cause of misery, pauperism and crime'.[170] He was giving voice to fears that chilled the propertied classes throughout the nineteenth century. Reformers argued that drink ruined family life and eroded household finances. Public houses, they believed, enticed drinkers into drunkenness, and this led on to crime, disorder and to vice, as well as (pertinently for the businessman) to a less efficient workforce.[171] In 1881 there was one licensee to every 243 people in England and Wales; the pubs they ran overwhelmingly served working people. In 1853 it was estimated that 70% of Derby workingmen spent the evening in a pub.

Given the squalor and inhospitability of many working-class homes, and their contrast with the warmth, conviviality and social attractiveness of the public house – which even Joseph Rowntree, a long-time Quaker temperance reformer recognised for himself – it is not surprising that the pub was the great social centre of working-class life. It often metamorphosed into a workingman's club, hotel, eating place, rest place for travellers and election headquarters.[172] For many it provided a source of perfectly innocent relaxation and pleasure. The trouble was that it could at its worst also be a place which provided the quickest way to oblivion, and the consequences of that for law and order, and for the peace and prosperity of family life, concerned many middle- and upper-class observers from at least 1830 onwards. That year the Beerhouse Act was passed which, in a mistaken attempt to wean Englishmen (and women) from a dangerous addiction to gin, allowed any would-be publican to sell beer from his premises unlicensed by justices. Beer consumption increased by over 60% in the thirty years from 1845.[173]

The inebriatory consequences of the Beerhouse Act led opponents to organise themselves into a formal temperance movement. Many like Joseph Livesey, their articulate voice, signed a pledge to commit to abstinence; most were working-class men generating their own secular self-help movement, culminating in the National Temperance League in 1856. The emphasis was on moral suasion, and on a personal conversion.[174] When that moral appeal came to seem comparatively ineffectual a new, middle-class initiative emerged in 1853; based on the enactment of prohibition in the US state of Maine, the UK Alliance espoused the complete suppression of all drink traffic, all buying and selling of drink. The Alliance's teetotalism has been seen as just one aspect of a Nonconformist power play. Many radical Nonconformists attacked publicans

George Cadbury, schoolteacher, aged 20. Two years later he and his brother would inherit the family business.

The earliest known photograph of Joseph Chamberlain as a young man.

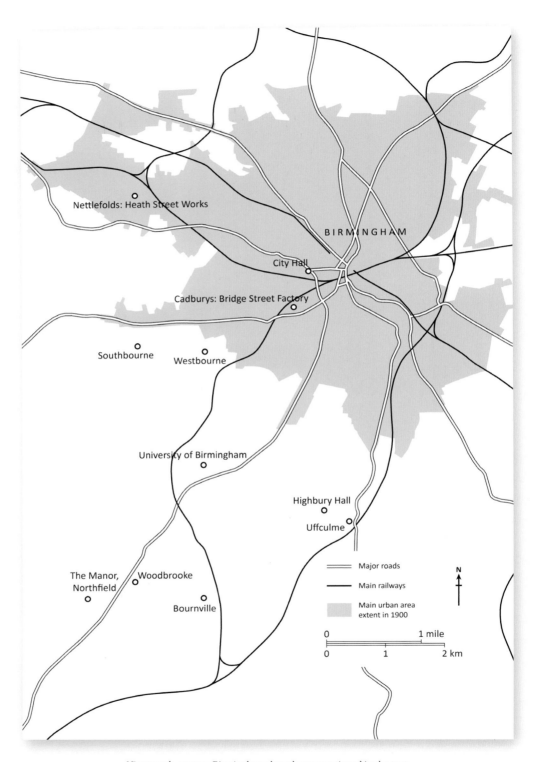

Nineteenth-century Birmingham: key places mentioned in the text.

Nettlefolds factory at Heath Street, Smethwick.

NETTLEFOLD AND CHAMBERLAIN, BIRMINGHAM,

SOLE MANUFACTURERS OF

WESTON'S   STORER'S

PATENT DIFFERENTIAL RATCHET BRACE. — PATENT OPEN TOP SUET LUBRICATOR.

SOLD BY THE UNDERMENTIONED AGENTS:—

BIRMINGHAM	Boulton, A.
LONDON	Taylor and Stevens; Andrew and Co.
LIVERPOOL	Sharp, William, 17, Brunswick Street.
MANCHESTER	Edmondsons and Co. [and Budenberg.
GLASGOW	Hunter, W., and Co.; P. and W. McLellan; Schäffer
EDINBURGH	Redpath, Brown and Co. ; Thomas Scott.
BRISTOL	Weston, J. D. and Son.
SHEFFIELD	Wilkes, Brothers and Co.
NEWCASTLE-ON-TYNE	Galloway and Co.
NOTTINGHAM	Manlove, Alliott and Co.
BELFAST	Patterson, R., and Sons.
NEWPORT (MON.)	Steel, Rake and Co.
DERBY	Handyside and Co.
SWANSEA	Steel, Rake, & Co., Oxford Buildings.
FRANCE	T. C. Hounsfield, 13, Rue Pierre Levee, Paris.
RUSSIA	Sumner, John M. & Co., Manchester.
AUSTRIA	Simon, Henry, Manchester.
ITALY, NORWAY, & SWEDEN	Baines and Tait, 86, Cannon Street, London.
GERMANY	Schäffer and Budenberg, Manchester
SOUTH GERMANY	C. Delisle, Stuttgart.

OF WHOM PRICED LISTS AND FULL DESCRIPTIONS MAY BE OBTAINED.

THESE BRACES are produced by self-acting Machinery at prices lower than the commonest hand-made Braces. They are of wrought-iron, case-hardened throughout: the parts are interchangeable, and the greatest precision is observed in the manufacture. The Ratchets are differential, and afford thereby a better hold for the pawls, while the springs are secured within the pawls, and cannot be damaged.

The Invention is applied to several new Braces for special work, and particularly to a Carpenter's Brace, G, for use with a common Swing Brace to screw and unscrew in confined places; and to an Angle Iron Brace, which will work within half an inch of the angle.

THE SUET LUBRICATOR has effected a saving of 70 per cent. in the cost of lubricating material used for Nettlefold and Chamberlain's Engines, and has now been fully tested in their works on 15 Cylinders working to 750-horse power.

Messrs. HICK, HARGREAVES & Co., of Bolton, write:—" We find the saving in *excess* of that stated in Messrs. Nettlefold and Chamberlain's Report, viz., 70 per cent., and the Cylinders to which these Lubricators have been applied are in beautiful condition. We shall adopt them for all our engines."

By this Invention the steam is lubricated before passing to the valves, while the supply of grease is uniform and constant.

A *Nettlefolds* product and price guide from 1872.

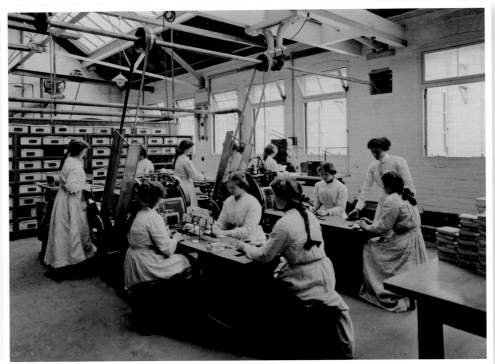

Cadburys girls packaging chocolates at the Bournville factory.

Tall and commanding, the University of Birmingham's clock tower physically expresses its founder's dominance over the city.

One of Chamberlain's many impressive Board School buildings still stands today at Oozells Street.

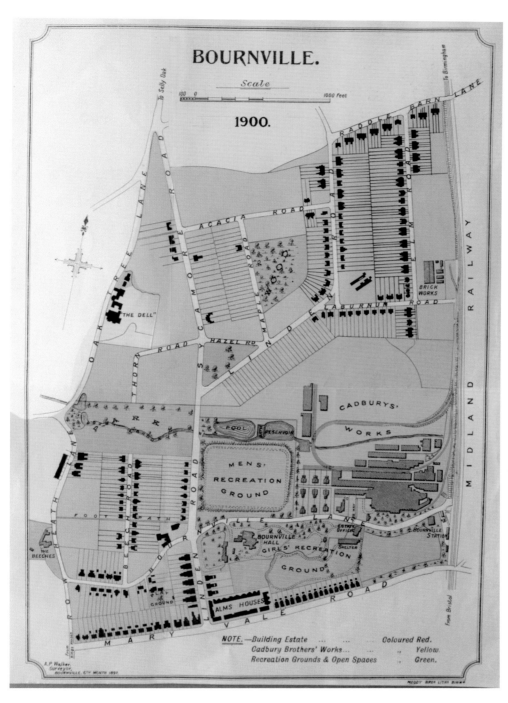

BOURNVILLE.

Scale

100 0   1000 feet

1900.

NOTE.—Building Estate ... ... Coloured Red.
Cadbury Brothers' Works... ... „ Yellow.
Recreation Grounds & Open Spaces „ Green.

Plan of Bournville showing the works and newly-established village, 1900.

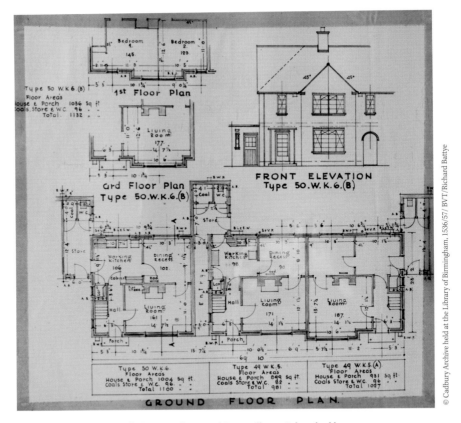

Architect's drawing of a typical Bournville semi-detached house.

Sycamore Road, Bournville, 1900. An early photo of Arts and Crafts-inspired houses.

Supplement to THE GRAPHIC, September 4, 1886

INDEX TO KEY-BLOCK

INDEX TO KEY-BLOCK

BIRDS-EYE VIEW OF   BIRMINGHAM IN 1886

Bird's-eye view of the Town Hall Fountain commemorating Chamberlain's achievements for Birmingham.

A contemporary homily on the evils of Drink. Parents continue to drink as bailiffs repossess the family furniture.

George Cadbury's masterly simple pitch - 'Absolutely Pure'.

Chamberlain surrounded by the shades of those lost fighting 'Joe's War' in South Africa, as imagined by a French cartoon.

and the drink trade as being a further manifestation of the Anglican establishment's hold on the levers of control. In this way the Alliance can be thought of as part of that radical protest movement which spawned the Anti-Corn Law League, the National Education League and the Liberation Society in the middle of the century, movements designed to overturn the status quo.[175]

The UK Alliance quickly learnt that prohibition was not universally popular. Its message made inroads in the North (for it was based in Manchester) but the South and especially London formed a 'sea of indifference'. When government did intervene, as in 1854 with the limiting of Sunday drinking hours, there were violent working-class disturbances, protesting at what men perceived to be class legislation, the interference of do-gooders, representing the propertied whose own domestic alcohol consumption (in their clubs and homes) was to be unaffected. So to achieve its goals the Alliance felt it had to advance cautiously, in stages; in truth it was disappointed by the compromises necessary in getting any legislation passed at all.

In 1872 the Liberal Home Secretary H.A. Bruce eventually carried Licensing legislation which restricted closing times in public houses, empowered local licensing authorities to refuse the renewal of licences, made public drunkenness a crime and encouraged the police to deal with infractions. Again riots – in Cheltenham, Exeter, Maidstone and Ashton – revealed working-class anger at government meddling, while publicans united to protest at threats to their property.[176] There was a strong electoral backlash; indeed, the Liberal leader, Gladstone, reflecting on his party's defeat in the General Election of 1874, believed: 'We have been borne down in a torrent of gin and beer'.[177] The riots and electoral consequences, made politicians wary of prohibition and, indeed, of even modest licensing legislation.

This helps explain why the momentum behind the UK Alliance slowed from the early 1870s; instead temperance societies, espousing personal conversion and closely allied to churches and to missions, grew in importance in these years, culminating in the Blue Ribbon movement (the unofficial name for Gospel Temperance) in the early 1880s. Then Richard Booth, an American, conducted a series of rallies across the country, in which over one million converts pledged themselves to personal abstinence (and sported the blue ribbon of the cause) in what the movement's historian, Lilian Shiman, has called a 'temperance fever'.[178] Such was the enthusiasm among Nonconformists that the Liberal Party, to which many gave political allegiance, was persuaded to incorporate local prohibition (local councils to be empowered to deny licences to all public houses) in its party programme in 1890.

This led to William Harcourt's controversial Local Veto Bill of 1894 on which, as we will see, Joseph Chamberlain had much to say. The problem for Liberals was that their association with temperance could be an electoral embarrassment; by contrast, Conservatives claimed to stand for the defence of 'the pleasures of the people and of the workingman's right to enjoy a quiet drink free from interference'.[179] Temperance by the end of the century had increasingly come to be seen by working men as a symbol of busybody interference with their drinking habits and their Sunday sporting pursuits by backward-looking Nonconformity.[180]

Unsurprisingly, a moral and societal question which provoked and divided Nonconformists and politicians prompted an active rejoinder in Cadbury and Chamberlain. A random sample of 124 UK Alliance members found that 53 were Quakers, a remarkably high proportion.[181] Just as that other Quaker chocolatier family of Rowntree was prominent in temperance circles, so too were the Cadburys, following John Cadbury, George's father, who took the pledge with Joseph Livesey in 1832. Helen Cadbury Alexander in the biography of her father, Richard Cadbury, recounts how John built a room for temperance meetings where he sought to reclaim drunkards to sobriety and decency.[182]

Filial influence ensured that George became a life-long supporter of temperance; in the 1870s when, with his brother, he was still establishing the *Cadbury* brand, he was 'associated with the extreme wing of the temperance party', becoming a supporter of the prohibitionist Alliance.[183] His sympathies, and his vigorous support for a measure of local option in liquor traffic in a meeting of Birmingham borough members, explain the passions aroused by George's candidature for the 1878 Rotton Park ward election, when 'beer could be had as freely as rainwater', as publicans unavailingly poured resources in to stop an avowed enemy of the drink trade.[184]

A few years later, in 1882, he and his brother had a Damascene conversion to Gospel Temperance, for on hearing Richard Booth they employed a full-time negotiator and organiser Edward Ward to recruit the American to speak in Birmingham. Richard Cadbury took the lead, heading the list of subscribers, underwriting the visit and inviting all Christian denominations in Birmingham to support Booth in a genuinely ecumenical mission. George was also actively involved in what was evidently a successful revivalist rally. Over 66,000 people took the pledge and donned the blue ribbon as a sign of their total abstinence. Richard would go on to initiate women's meetings to ensure domestic support for husbands embracing abstinence, and would establish the Temperance Institute in Birmingham's Corporation Street in 1889 as a headquarters for all the various local temperance groups – Band of Hope, UK Alliance, Church of England Temperance Society and Gospel Temperance.

George Cadbury was especially motivated by the urge to do something about the domestic lives of the working class. He was aware that the wretchedness of home conditions explained why men had recourse to the public house. In 1891 he – and his brother – constructed the Stirchley Institute alongside the tunnel back houses which used to accommodate *Cadbury's* resident female workforce. 'Stirchley contained a large proportion of slum dwellers,' writes Elizabeth Cadbury's biographer. 'There was no place for recreation or refreshment for these people, save the public house. They therefore decided to build a roomy institute on the main street as a social and educational centre. (It included) a coffee room, classrooms and a meeting house.'[185] Cadbury had clear views about what constituted appropriate behaviour – drinking and dancing were banned. Many of the men for whom it catered would be employees and, given the convictions of its directors, *Cadbury* took a consistent line on drink, which extended to an employee's behaviour in his leisure time, for it was vitally important to have a temperate workforce. So for example, the head of office staff at *Cadbury* wrote a letter to one employee in 1895 concerning 'his condition at Oxford station on Saturday night'. 'Such conduct ... not only brings discredit to your colleagues but is likely to reflect upon the name of the Firm. I advise you strongly to abstain from intoxicants.' When it came to establishing Bournville Village in the 1890s, George Cadbury clearly set out his preference for a temperate community. He drafted

Suggested Rules of Health for the first residents, advising them to 'avoid intoxicating liquors, tobacco, pork, aerated drinks and drugs.'[186]

It is no coincidence that for decades *Cadbury Bros.* had been propagating healthful, pure substitutes for alcohol – cocoa and chocolate. They were products from which, of course, the Cadbury brothers would draw rich commercial benefits.

In the *Trust Deed* establishing the Bournville Village Trust in 1900 a passage setting out the founder's intention to 'alleviate the evils which arise from insanitary and insufficient accommodation, and secure the advantages of outdoor village life,' concluded with instructions, limiting the extent of shops and factories and with the following injunction:

> No public house or building for the manufacture, sale or distribution of intoxicating liquor should be allowed without the unanimous consent of trustees in writing, and any subsequent profits were to be spent on alternative recreation.[187]

This suggests that his views on alcohol had much changed since his prohibitionist days in the 1870s. He was now prepared to envisage a time when the trustees might moderate his absolute position on drink. Bailey's collected oral testimonies include the reminiscences of a lady who recalled deliveries within Bournville by the Birmingham brewer Baron John Davenport, who in 1904 founded the 'Beer At Home' service. It would seem this had been regularly tolerated on the estate.[188]

George Cadbury revealed in an interview for the readers of *Sunday at Home* in 1909 just how much he had modified his position except, perhaps, on the dubious character of publicans:

> If drink is to be sold at all, I would have its sale municipalised, so that no profit accruing should go to individuals, and so that there would be no incentive for its sale, except to satisfy a reasonable demand. Therefore, under careful restrictions, it may well be acceptable to supply drink. I would rather they could procure it in Bournville for consumption at home than that they should go to some vice-ridden drink shop outside.[189]

Gardiner commented on this evolution in his retrospective of George Cadbury. He explained it thus:

> He had been brought up in the most rigid school of teetotalism and in his early life had adopted the ideal of prohibition. ... He (later) saw how largely the evils of drink were the result of social conditions (and so) his mind tended more and more to attacking the cause rather than the effect. He often used to say "Were I living in a back street with one room, where all the washing and cooking were done, and with perhaps two or three noisy children about, the temptation to visit the public house would be overwhelming." (Nor was) he wholly convinced of the value of the temperance pledge. "I believe that taking the pledge and breaking it lowers the standard of character."[190]

That understanding of the vital importance of housing and environment explains why he dedicated himself to creating a model community at Bournville. For Cadbury healthy recreation, growing vegetables, tending fruit trees and mowing the grass was the Bournville way to deflect men from the temptations of the public house; yet he seems to have come to accept by 1922 that, in the privacy of their own homes, men might indulge in the occasional glass of beer and still not be a threat to civilisation.

Joseph Chamberlain barely changed his views on the drink question from his days on Birmingham Council in the 1870s through to his last election campaign in 1906. Like George Cadbury he was led into sanitary and housing reform in response to the ubiquity of the pub culture, arguing in 1874 that: 'It seems to me ridiculous to talk of temperance to men who have every reason to leave their homes, and are driven thereby to the public house', an insight, we have seen, echoed by Cadbury at the end of his life.[191] Because many men had an unattractive domestic alternative to the public house he was strongly opposed to Sunday closing because 'that would practically affect the poor only'.[192]

Instead of prohibition, he concluded that municipal control was the solution; this is unsurprising for he was a foremost advocate of the civic gospel. Local authorities would act, where there were palpable abuses, to regulate excesses in the local drink trade. He felt that excessive competition in many towns led publicans to 'wink at abuses' and encourage cheap binge drinking and the adulteration of beer and spirits. So he became an advocate of the Gothenburg system, from Sweden, in which the town council had compulsorily acquired the public houses and bars and run them not for profit but, because subject to the will of ratepayers, in an orderly and disciplined manner as a kind of local service. He made a major speech in the House of Commons in March 1877 proposing this system of licensing reform, but met defeat.[193]

He did not give up. From the 1880 General Election through to the new century he continued to press for local control. In 1888 he persuaded the Conservative Prime Minister, Lord Salisbury, to include in his important Local Government Bill liquor licensing clauses designed to reduce the number of outlets for the sale of alcohol, while compensating licensees who thereby suffered. This drew strong – and successful – opposition from temperance supporters and the clauses were dropped. In 1892 he invited the Bishop of Chester and Richard Cadbury, among others, to his family home at Highbury to discuss the Gothenburg system again, a solution which continued to attract him even if Richard Cadbury came away unconvinced and the more determined to see a system of local prohibition enacted, like that in Maine.[194]

Chamberlain's dislike of the 'extreme men' who had seized the leadership of the temperance movement was articulated in that powerful Birmingham speech in October 1894 alluded to earlier. Prompted by Harcourt's Local Veto Bill he scorned those 'who were more anxious to prohibit drinking than to prevent drunkenness, more eager to punish the publican who after all is carrying on a legal trade'. He attacked local veto because 'it limited the local community's power to deciding just one question, whether there should be no public houses or all that exist at present'. There was no room to regulate the number of public houses. He once again called for public control of the trade, but he was clear that the Veto bill 'proposed to commit an injustice in taking away the legal property of the publican, destroying his livelihood'.[195] Chamberlain here rejected the absolutism of the prohibitionist and showed some sympathy for the publican. Now that he and his Liberal Unionists were firmly allied to the Conservatives, the party of brewers and publicans, and defenders of the rights of working classes to determine their own entertainment, that indulgence also made political sense. There is some evidence that Chamberlain's articulation of the case against this 'class legislation' had significant electoral appeal, going a long way to explaining the size of the Conservative majority in the 1895 General Election.[196]

Throughout his career he appears to have remained true to an early conviction that: 'I do not think that a moderate consumption of drink is in any way wrong on the part of the working-man.'[197] For that reason, right to the end of his life, he disliked the extremist position of prohibitionists who wanted to deny men the right to drink; in 1904 he clashed with his own brother Arthur Chamberlain, chairman of Birmingham's licensing magistrates, over his zealous, as well as illegal, policy of closing excess public houses in the city without compensation.[198] Although George Cadbury was to introduce his very own private local veto in Bournville Village, and retained his suspicions of publicans to the end, it seems fair to conclude that he too came to see that a man should have the liberty to drink in private. In that, over the years he had moved closer to Joseph Chamberlain's thinking on a deeply divisive issue.

Both men were equally involved – and significant – in the struggle to provide a financial safety net for the aged poor. Many workers were left destitute when age and ill health forced them to give up work, for there was no mechanism apart from desperate recourse to the workhouse for ensuring men and women did not starve to death.[199] Indeed Joseph Chamberlain was the first front-line politician to espouse the cause when in March 1891 he made a speech in the Aston by-election, just outside Birmingham.[200] He highlighted the aged poor's need for state help with pensions for which they were barely able to save for themselves. Even at that early stage of his thinking, it is clear that he was looking for the government to supplement the individual's efforts in saving for retirement. The state was to encourage thrift and self-help. Birmingham hosted the annual conference of National Union of Conservative Associations later that same year and here he suggested that money expended on the hated Poor Law with its inhumane apparatus of workhouses might be better directed to supporting workers' efforts to save for their old age.

The issue of Old Age Pensions was but one item in a programme of social reform by which Chamberlain was establishing his radical credentials in the Unionist alliance. For all that it had a political purpose his interest was genuine and humanitarian, and his intervention had established his pre-eminence and his expertise, which explains why he was asked by Prime Minister Salisbury to chair a committee at Westminster of other politicians and public servants on the subject. He became sufficiently friendly with the renowned campaigner on the aged poor, Charles Booth, to invite him to stay at Highbury, even if Booth was to campaign for a much greater state contribution than his host.

In early 1892 Chamberlain set out his arguments in an article in the *National Review*. He vigorously attacked the moralising view that the old and indigent were to blame for their own parlous state; he proposed a contributory system supplemented by state support with an allowance made for the worker's illness and unemployment.[201] He would continue thereafter to argue for Old Age Pensions for the 'veterans of industry'. In front of a distinguished Royal Commission established in 1893 he put flesh on the bare bones of his pension thinking: he envisaged a scheme for those who contributed a deposit before the age of 25, to continue subscriptions till 65, with government making comparable payments. On reaching 65, 5/- a week would be payable. Many including his old friend Charles Booth thought 5/- patently inadequate, balked at the inflexibility which limited the scheme to those joining before 25, and wondered how working people could ever save for the initial deposit. Conservative critics objected to the government expenditure.

This too was the rub for Chamberlain. His scheme looked ungenerous because in truth he shied away from committing to the levels of expenditure necessary to provide fully funded pensions; he never changed his position on this. He also worried that a dole would erode the working classes' sense of independence. Years earlier he had made a speech in Smethwick in which he had warned: 'We have to take care (when) attempting to remedy an evil which is greater than the one we are trying to remove; for any man who did anything in the way of checking man's thrift which would discourage this tendency to save would do a greater evil.'[202]

In thrashing around for a solution to the funding dilemma he alighted in 1895 on the idea of a corn tax; he would abandon that as politically impracticable in a country where thought of a bread tax stirred powerful folk memories of the 'Hungry Forties.'[203] Still, he returned to it when he launched his Tariff Reform crusade in 1903, only to drop it in the face of cold indifference from the working-class audiences he addressed.[204]

In 1899, when embroiled in his South African war and fully engaged on the funding of Birmingham University, he returned to the pension issue in a debate prompted by the Liberal opposition. Liberal proposals for non-contributory Old Age Pensions he dismissed as 'pensions for everybody – good and bad, thrifty and unthrifty – the waster, drunkard and idler as well as the industrious'.[205] When, in 1902 a TUC Congress meeting enthusiastically adopted a resolution favouring non-contributory pensions of 5/- a week for every citizen over 60 years of age, he condemned it outright; it did not accord with his mid-Victorian notions of self-help and in any case his expensive Boer War campaign had exhausted the Treasury's coffers.[206]

By the time H.H. Asquith carried the legislation which set up non-contributory pensions in 1908, Chamberlain was a crippled observer from the sidelines, rendered impotent by a devastating stroke in 1906. He might have reflected that his presumption that Old Age Pensions would reduce the cost of the Poor Law proved to be wildly optimistic; but he was correct that Old Age Pensions would be hugely expensive, the cost of £12.5m in 1914 far outstripping the estimated cost in 1908 of £6m to £7m. The expense had already precipitated a political convulsion in 1909 when it prompted Lloyd George's redistributory 'People's Budget'. No doubt to Chamberlain's wry amusement, it also convinced Lloyd George that the next stage in creating a safety net of health and unemployment insurance in 1911 would after all be financed on Chamberlain's contributory basis with the individual, state and employer sharing the costs.[207]

If Chamberlain was first off the mark in initiating the national debate on Old Age Pensions, George Cadbury would prove as important, in both practically implementing a scheme for his own *Cadbury* workers and in leading and financing the national campaign to persuade the Liberal Government to act on the issue in 1908. George Cadbury and his son Edward, largely motivated by simple idealism, had taken an interest in establishing a pension scheme from 1902, when one of the Directors of *Huntley and Palmers* visited Bournville to talk about their own scheme. In 1906, working with *Rowntrees*, a pension scheme for all their men between ages 16 and 50 was introduced. The Cadburys sought to inculcate middle-class virtues in their workers, and thought that 'earlier age of entry inculcates thrift before manhood'.[208] 'Thrift' coincidentally was the very quality Chamberlain also sought to develop in his working man.

The scheme was initiated with a gift of fulsome generosity – £60,000 – to cover benefits for those older workers joining the scheme when it was launched. The men made their contributions of between 2.5% and 5.5% of wages, and this was matched by the firm's subscription. A man could draw his pension when he reached 60 years of age, and would receive a pension of 1% of the worker's average wage, multiplied by the number of years for which he had contributed. Later, in 1911, a Savings Fund and Pensions Fund were established for women workers. The schemes may have been a Christian act of philanthropy, but it was good business sense in developing a loyal and hard-working labour force. George Cadbury ensured that the launch was heralded with widespread Press coverage; over 100 provincial papers carried notices about the scheme, which was the subject of interest in the London Press too. Gardiner claimed that it was 'largely the seed of a great national scheme'.[209] As we have seen, that scarcely does justice to the long-standing debate provoked by Joseph Chamberlain's promotion of the pensions issue from the early 1890s.

Yet in another sense, too, Cadbury made a telling intervention in the campaign for Old Age Pensions. In the late 1890s he became involved in a national campaign to force through pensions legislation, supporting the National Old Age Pensions League. Cadbury helped fund its conference at Browning Hall in London in December 1898, an event usually taken to be the signal for the start of that organised national movement. He was equally central to a great conference in Birmingham in March the following year, bringing together over 630 delegates from Friendly Societies, Trade Unions, Councils and School Boards in a rally addressed by Charles Booth.[210] It coincided with a debate in the House of Commons on a Liberal motion to implement a non-contributory pension scheme.

George Cadbury was prevented from speaking at his Birmingham Conference by the untimely death of his brother, Richard. Still, he did set down his views for the chairman, Councillor Stevens, writing in a letter that he and his brother had long felt that 'as a Christian nation we ought to make some effort to add to the comfort of the aged toilers of our country, of whom one third end up as paupers'. 'The workhouse was looked forward to with dread by many (working people).' He hoped ultimately to emulate New Zealand where every man or woman over 65 received a shilling a day. He repeated his notion that: 'Old Age Pensions would promote thrift.' A man assured of 7/- a week 'would be encouraged to add a trifle to it either by joining a Friendly Society or by insurance or by savings'. There was an added benefit for families: the pension 'would allow the aged people to stay in their accustomed surroundings (not transferring to a workhouse) and live possibly with their sons or daughters without being a burden to them'.[211]

From 1899 to the successful passage of Asquith's Old Age Pensions Bill in 1908, George and Edward Cadbury funded half the costs of the National Old Age Pensions League; it was George's constant refrain that giving old people pensions would not only spare them from the clutches of the workhouse, but would make them useful to their extended families. That message was regularly reinforced in the pages of the newspaper he owned, the *Daily News*. The eventual Act was less generous than he had hoped: 5/- a week for every man and woman over 70, but it was at least fully funded by the state. It was enough of a victory for the League to mark the event with a memorial tablet on the wall of Browning Hall commemorating the leading lights in the campaign; George Cadbury unveiled it in June 1910, a sign of his central role in persuading the Liberal government to enact the legislation. He showed his personal satisfaction by throwing a series of tea parties at his home, The Manor in Northfield, Birmingham for over 6,000 old age pensioners to celebrate the triumph of the movement.[212]

George Cadbury was equally committed to another national campaign, for the suppression of sweated labour, that is workers who put in very long hours of hard work for little remuneration in poor working conditions, often their own homes. As a model employer at Bournville, where he and his brother adopted the best employment practices to ensure a loyal, well remunerated, healthy and productive workforce, the abuses of sweating appalled him. His sympathies were aroused by the editor of his newspaper, the *Daily News*, who suggested, in early 1906, that the paper organise an exhibition of the sweated industries to highlight the plight of the workers. Cadbury undertook to pay half the costs.[213]

The exhibits in the *Daily News* exhibition at Queen's Hall in London moved him as much as they did many of those who attended. The exhibition handbook vividly itemises the exploitation for the figures indicate the paucity of the reward for hours of painstaking labour: a gross of button roses fetched 1s 4d, Parma violets at 7d a gross, cardboard boxes at a rate of 1s 2d for twelve hours' work; match boxes 2½d per gross, for example.[214] The system of piece work, and the predations of middlemen, made the lives of these 'home' workers utterly wretched. It was clear that these workers who were ignored by trade unions needed organising, and, despite the difficulties in establishing rates of pay for so many and varied skills, they needed a minimum wage.

The effect of the exhibition was long lasting. It spawned the National Anti-Sweating League, which Cadbury helped fund, and a conference at the Guildhall in London on the minimum wage in October 1906, chaired by Sir Charles Dilke, Chamberlain's old Radical ally. In his opening remarks Dilke talked about 'the hopelessness' of the plight of home workers, often women, who were suffering a kind of 'slavery'.[215] The Anti-Sweating League sent a deputation in early 1908 to meet the new President of the Board of Trade, Winston Churchill. Its proposals for a minimum wage in the sweated industries were adopted and passed into law in Churchill's 1909 Trade Boards Act, covering four specific industries: paper box, machine-made lace, bespoke tailoring and chain making. Again Cadbury had the immense satisfaction of having quietly worked to initiate, fund and then carry a significant reform to improve the lives of some of Britain's poorest workers.

Another campaign of the *Daily News* had been to initiate compulsory powers for local authorities to purchase land to create small holdings for workers. Cadbury was delighted with the two Small Holdings Acts of 1907 and 1908 which implemented that very policy.

If George Cadbury's methodology was to support and work through others to effect social change, Joseph Chamberlain's – as illustrated at many junctures in this book – was to be in the vanguard, articulating, politicking and persuading. Where George Cadbury worked from the outside on others to carry legislation, Chamberlain was in the thick of it, initiating and manoeuvring for himself, in the very centre of government and in the public eye. Like Cadbury, Chamberlain was much influenced, in the objects of social reform he championed, by his career as a businessman. His instincts were those of the model, enlightened employer and those objects were the correction of abuses on which he felt government should act. The aim was to compel employers to reform the conditions for their employees, if they were unwilling to do so voluntarily. His attitude, however, was not necessarily oppositional – his vision was one of cooperation and negotiation between employer and labour wherever possible.

This can be seen in his abiding interest in arbitration, from his days at *Nettlefold and Chamberlain*. He had been asked on occasion to arbitrate in disputes, and he developed a reputation as a leading practitioner in the West Midlands.[216] Throughout his political career he would return to the issue of government involvement in industrial arbitration to avert damaging strikes, rather as Bismarck had pioneered in Germany. This was an issue which appealed to George Cadbury too; in 1898 Cadbury initiated a great gathering in Birmingham Town Hall, including Labour leaders, to press for compulsory arbitration of trade disputes. He was very keen to involve Birmingham's Unionists in a cross-party campaign.[217]

When he was first President of the Board of Trade in 1880 Chamberlain embarked on a crusade to tackle the high mortality rates among seamen in the mercantile marine. He worked with Samuel Plimsoll to campaign against what they deemed the dangerous practices of ship owners in overloading and under-manning their ships. Chamberlain also believed that many ship owners allowed leaky ships to sail and then over-insured them to garner profits if they then foundered. He sought to make the ship owners responsible, effectively extending to shipping the recent Employers' Liability Act (1880), which provided a right to compensation only when the employer's negligence could be proved. He probably over-stated his case, and with his usual bluntness and cutting tongue he created such adamantine opposition, from ship owners even on his own Liberal side of the House, that Gladstone's government abandoned the Bill.[218] Still, the saga had steeled his determination to do more for workers who suffered work-related injuries.

Despite his bruising at the hands of ship owners the episode did not make him partisan on the issue of employee/employer relations. Significantly, he opposed the Liberal Government's attempt in 1893 to introduce a new Employers' Liability Bill. That Bill was effectively derailed in the Lords. The difference between his approach and that of the Liberals is apparent in the Bill's title. Liberals sided with trades unions and took aim at employers. When he was back in government and 'the question had attained such prominence that inaction would be dangerous', the bill he and Sir Matthew White Ridley (the Unionist Home Secretary) proposed was called the Workmen's Compensation Bill. He refused to play the trade union blame game, which attacked the employer for a lack of 'moral responsibility'.[219]

Instead he ensured that the employer would pay compensation in all cases whatever the cause, and he would recoup the cost of insuring himself by adding a small amount to the cost of his product. Although it did not apply to all industries, exempting agriculture, domestic service and shipping, and although he had to concede to his Conservative colleagues 'contracting out' where firms had at least as generous a scheme, it did compel mine owners to participate, a major step forward for miners and their families. Overall, the Act was notable both for easing tensions between workers and employers by treating a long-running sore, and for being a landmark of social security legislation which would be a precedent for Beveridge, as the latter himself acknowledged. Some historians have even seen the Workmen's Compensation Act as the beginning of a welfare state.[220]

In several other areas, Joseph Chamberlain demonstrated a sensitivity to labour issues, countenancing government action to intervene on the worker's behalf. For example, in that brief interlude when he was President of the Local Government Board in early 1886 (before he resigned over Home Rule), he issued a circular to the Boards of Poor Law Guardians through the country, urging them to promote public works projects for those unfortunates recently thrown out of work, as the Depression deepened. Even if it made little real difference – most especially to the long-term unemployed – the Chamberlain Circular was largely of symbolic importance, extending the state's purview into job creation, a harbinger for more far-reaching Keynesian schemes in the next century.[221]

He also continued for many years to promote the principle of the eight-hour day for miners working at the coal-face. It was both humanitarian and electoral; he knew many mining communities were in favour of such legislation. He did not succeed in enacting it.

These two chapters on the social reformative efforts made by George Cadbury and Joseph Chamberlain reveal the breadth of their interests, the sincerity of their conviction, and the remarkable energy with which they pursued their goals.

Arguably, their educational, housing and social reforms defined them. However, it is fair to say that for Chamberlain the zeal for reform dimmed as he increasingly focused on Imperial war and on tariff reform at the turn of the century. Others noticed it; his unfulfilled promises of social reform, especially of pensions, were frequently and bitterly recalled on Liberal and Labour platforms in the 1906 General Election. If Cadbury's progressive impetus slowed in the years before the First World War with incipient old age, he was still party to *Cadbury's* imaginative introduction of Works Councils in November 1918. This enabled workers to meet in consultative committees with employers to discuss pay and conditions on a very regular basis. To the end, then, he showed an active interest in the welfare of his workforce.

DIFFERENCES OVER PARTY AND POLITICS

Joseph Chamberlain rose to the top of the greasy pole, he shaped the national debate and his policies and his speeches decided general elections; by 1902 he was but one step from the highest office of all. George Cadbury on the other hand remained a private man, shunned office and honours, yet helped to articulate the Liberal social message and to generate support for political movements, like those for Old Age Pensions and Anti-Sweating. Still, if their political contributions differed in scale, a comparison between the two is fruitful and illuminating.

Both men started out supporters of the Victorian Liberal coalition. In a nineteenth century context this was entirely natural. The Liberal Party which emerged in the 1860s, led by William Gladstone, was the natural home of businessmen and industrialists who felt excluded from the aristocratic and landed classes represented by Derby and Disraeli's Conservative Party. John Vincent, wrote: 'To vote Liberal was closely tied to the growing ability of whole new classes to stand on their feet and lead independent lives.' He went on to argue that 'deep moral feeling might be involved in being Liberal'. 'For many Liberals, politics was derived from a religious centre,' and that centre was overwhelmingly Nonconformist. A particular reading of English history was common to many Liberals, an interpretation shaped by oppression and exclusion at the hands of the Anglican establishment; they remembered the fines, the distraint of goods, the barring from public office, which was the lot of Dissenters after the Restoration in the 1660s.[222] So Liberals, and especially Radicals, sought to secure reforms designed to help oppressed nationalities, religions and classes, and excluded individuals.

Successive Gladstone governments between 1868 and 1894 legislated to right some of these historic wrongs, whether in Ireland, in the armed forces, the historic universities, or the civil service. As we have seen, this also involved reform of parliament and of education, the last being for many Liberals the means to achieving a higher and better civilisation, and to eradicating intemperance and pauperism.[223] As Cadbury and Chamberlain entirely subscribed to this reformative mission, they naturally joined the Liberal Party, even if for both there came a moment when loyalty was stretched to breaking point. Chamberlain put it this way: 'I was drawn into politics by my interest in social questions, and by my desire to promote the welfare of the great majority of the population. I looked to the Liberal Party as the means for removing and remedying those grievances, as the great instrument of progress and reform.'[224]

Chamberlain was from the outset a Radical. Indeed, Birmingham was a Radical stronghold. In practice his Radicalism, when he started out in the late 1860s, was expressed by championing free education for all and the town's own particular brand of gas and water socialism. Radicals nationally operated as one wing of the great Victorian Liberal Party alliance forged by Gladstone. So through the 1870s Joseph Chamberlain represented the Liberal Party as a failed Parliamentary candidate in Sheffield in 1874 and as a successful one for Birmingham in 1876. From the first he sought both to shape the party's policies in a Radical direction (to include social reforms) and to introduce to it a whole new level of organisation and professionalism. With his understanding of the effectiveness of detailed planning, of local political knowledge, and of managing meetings and of active canvassing – accumulated through the experience of the National Education League – it seemed to Chamberlain that the Liberal Party would be improved by associating all local Liberal parties together in a National Liberal Federation.

This was launched in 1877, based in Birmingham, staffed by his trusted Birmingham allies, William Harris and Frank Schnadhorst among others, with several aims. It would unify the forces of popular Liberalism, it would help unite working- and middle-class Liberals, and it would be a powerful advocate for a raft of Radical policies, reminding the London-based leadership of the causes which were dear to the grass-roots membership. It would involve members in an ascending pyramid of democratic representation based on election and delegation, not dissimilar to the structure of the Birmingham Liberal Association, with its subsidiary ward associations, which was established in the 1860s – this was the famous Birmingham caucus system.[225] Finally, being based in Birmingham, it would be a formidable augmentation of Chamberlain's power-base. He could speak nationally with an enhanced authority, and that helped him in his meteoric rise from being a new MP in 1876 to joining the Cabinet in 1880. In the event, just under half of the country's Liberal associations affiliated (88 out of 198) and the NLF's influence became considerable in the late 1870s and 1880s. Chamberlain had, then, done much to make the Liberal party a more effective electoral force.[226]

In under a decade he had helped split that party. In 1886 he and Lord Hartington, the leader of the Whigs, the aristocratic wing of the Liberal Party, led their supporters in rebellion against Gladstone's proposed Home Rule Bill (see below). Ninety-three Liberals voted against it in June 1886 and precipitated a General Election, which was lost by Gladstone. The greater part of those rebels became Liberal Unionist MPs at that election, united almost solely by their fears for the integrity of the United Kingdom and the Empire. Although Chamberlain continued to espouse Radical policies on local government, education, land reform and pensions, bringing a Radical flavour to an increasingly close Unionist alliance with Lord Salisbury's Conservatives, he would never rejoin his erstwhile Liberal colleagues. His own creation, the NLF, sided with Gladstone against him after 1886. The Liberal Party was forced to endure twenty years of splits and of irrelevance – with the brief exception of the 1892 General Election, when it was the largest party and formed a short-lived minority government.

Chamberlain was now a Unionist, or more precisely, a Radical Unionist, being after 1892 leader of over 70 Liberal Unionists in alliance with the Conservatives in the House of Commons. Indeed, he was destined to serve as Colonial Secretary in a Conservative-dominated Unionist Cabinet for eight years from 1895, and across that time his instincts, his public pronouncements and his policies would become more and more those of a Conservative politician. Early attempts at Liberal reunion – as at the Round Table Conference in 1887 – had failed, foundering on the adamantine stubbornness of Gladstone, unwilling to forgive his disloyal, openly ambitious young ex-colleague. So Chamberlain set out on that transformatory journey from the Liberal Party to sit with the ranks of the Conservative party. By 1902 so effective had that journey been that when Lord Salisbury resigned, many Conservatives looked to the most charismatic Unionist, Chamberlain, as a potential successor. In the event, Salisbury's nephew Arthur Balfour won the crown. Critics observed that Chamberlain's Radical edge, as represented by his erstwhile passionate support for social reform, seemed blunted by the turn of the century, by which time Imperial projects had come to dominate his thinking.

That Liberal split in 1886 was as painful in Birmingham as it had been nationally. Chamberlain had secured the support of the 2000, the elected representatives of Birmingham Liberalism, at a special meeting of the local party in April 1886 called to endorse Chamberlain's opposition to the Prime Minister's proposals. Birmingham Liberals overwhelmingly sympathised with Gladstone and only Chamberlain's brilliant, persuasive, and uncharacteristically conciliatory speech – and a degree of wire-pulling by supporters like J.T. Bunce, a friend, ally and editor of the *Birmingham Daily Post* – secured the backing of the meeting for Chamberlain. The subsequent defeat of Gladstone in the Commons in June precipitated an unravelling of any semblance of Liberal unity in Birmingham. The superbly effective vote-gathering machine of the Liberal caucus in Birmingham was dismantled; Schnadhorst, its presiding genius, led a number of prominent local Liberals into Gladstone's camp.

Chamberlain's position was perilous for several years although he, his Birmingham Liberal Unionist Association and his Conservative allies (an uneasy and often fraught relationship) succeeded with difficulty and the occasional crisis in defeating Gladstonian Liberal candidates. Only after 1889, with a spectacular victory for the Liberal Unionists in the by-election caused by the death of John Bright in Birmingham Central, was Chamberlain secure. That victory demonstrated that Chamberlain's Radical Unionist policy mix of social reform and Imperialism was effective and attractive to the Birmingham working classes. It marked Birmingham's shift from Liberal allegiance to a Liberal Unionist/Chamberlainite allegiance.[227] Indeed Birmingham and the three abutting counties in the West Midlands – Worcestershire, Warwickshire and Staffordshire – became a stronghold of Chamberlain's power, his Duchy. Only George Cadbury successfully challenged Chamberlain's grip in Worcestershire North.

For George Cadbury was, despite occasional doubts as to its wisdom, a loyal believer in the true faith of Liberalism. He remained a member of the Liberal Party all his (adult) life, according to Gardiner, who concluded that 'he remained in cordial agreement with the impulse to social reform which Chamberlain brought into the Liberal movement'.[228] He had seen this social reform at first hand for himself as a member of the Birmingham Council in 1878. Even then, as we have seen, as *The Dart* put it: 'Cadbury is not a slavish follower of Chamberlain.'[229] The two would split definitively over Home Rule in 1886 when Cadbury followed Schnadhorst and others in support for Gladstone. For Cadbury the next fifteen years of Liberal politics were increasingly frustrating.

There were for him several real problems and one of them, paradoxically for Cadbury who was so loyal, stemmed from Gladstone himself, for the concentration on single-issue politics – especially Home Rule – narrowed the Liberal Party's appeal. Indeed, from around 1890 onwards the party seemed little more than a rainbow alliance of faddist enthusiasms like Home Rule, Local Veto and Church Disestablishment. A second problem was that with the flight of the wealthy aristocratic Whigs to the Unionist alliance the Liberal Party found itself under-funded.[230] Cadbury did his best in Birmingham and North Worcestershire to ensure the party in the area did not suffer financially; indeed, he received a presentation in 1895 from local Liberals as public recognition 'for the magnitude of his services to the party'.[231]

A further frustration surrounded the issue which above all others divided the party in the 1890s and early years of the new century – that of Imperialism. Liberal ministries from 1892 to 1895 were rent by arguments over British expansion into Uganda – enthusiasts like Lord Rosebery, Edward Grey and H.H. Asquith jostled with Gladstonian 'Little Englanders' such as William Harcourt and John Morley. The Boer War exacerbated the splits, with pro-Boer Radicals like David Lloyd George at odds with Liberal Imperialists keen to promote the cause of Imperial unity. A moderate majority in the middle followed the leader, Henry Campbell-Bannerman, in embarrassed neutrality. Cadbury was deeply disappointed by the signs of jingoism, of Imperial enthusiasm, he observed in the Liberal Party for his faith and temperament made him a strong advocate of peace as opposed to recourse to military expeditions.[232] This explains the growing strains in his relationship with J.W. Wilson, the MP for North Worcestershire, whose support for Chamberlain's War led to a deep rift between the MP and his financial backer which was only healed in 1902.

Finally, the consequence of party policy being an agglomeration of fads, without coherence and an overriding purpose, was a ceding of the initiative on social reform in the 1890s to Chamberlain and the Radical wing of his Unionist alliance. Cadbury greatly regretted this, for he believed that such social reform was the historic mission of the Liberal Party. On another score he was disappointed that the Liberal Party also failed to embrace representatives of the working classes, the men who would benefit from a programme of social legislation.

This explains, firstly, the strength of his commitment to those social causes like Old Age Pensions, Anti-Sweating, and Compulsory Arbitration which were addressed in chapter 4; if government, and his own party in opposition, was not acting then he was prepared to campaign and finance political action for himself. Secondly, it accounts for his growing interest in the rise of the new Labour Party; Gardiner averred 'that much of his sympathy went in that direction'.[233] Cadbury despaired of the slowness with which the evils of working-class living conditions were tackled by government and said in one speech: 'We want a hundred working men in Parliament. Then the condition of the people will become a living issue'. For him, the election of the working-class engineer, John Burns, in Battersea in 1892 was very significant and hopeful – he would be a pioneer of the principle of the direct representation of the people. He sided with trade unionists like Burns in their fight with capital in the 1890s; nowhere is this better illustrated than by Cadbury's financial contribution to the engineers' strike fund in the 1897 national strike called to resist the employers' attempts to break the trade union.

One important consequence of conflict in the engineering, boot and shoe, and railway industries was to convince a majority of trade unions that they needed direct representation in Parliament to put workers on a more equal footing with the employers. This new conviction coincided with the dawning realisation among a number of working-class politicians that local Liberal parties were actively obstructing the advancement of working men. A frustration with the Liberal Party was compounded by the fear that the ignominious collapse of Lord Rosebery's Liberal ministry of 1895 might reflect a deeper malaise, might – in fact – signal the start of a permanent decline. All these factors help explain the genesis of the Labour Representation Committee (LRC), soon to be the Labour Party, in 1900.[234]

George Cadbury was on what Gardiner called 'terms of intimacy' with a number of the new party's leading lights, most especially Ramsay Macdonald and Keir Hardie.[235] One can see what might have appealed to Cadbury in Hardie's virulent anti-war politics, his 'moralistic, principled pacifism', his almost Quaker-like severity about drinking and dancing (he was an advocate of magistrates refusing pub licences for dancing for 'if drinking and dancing took place immorality was apt to be great'.)[236] There are echoes here of the ban on dancing in the teetotal Stirchley Institute in 1901.[237] In a broader sense, Cadbury was attracted to the LRC as an organised body in favour of many of his especial enthusiasms such as peace and disarmament (though like the Liberals there were divisions on this), the taxation of land values, Old Age Pensions and municipalising liquor traffic. Cadbury demonstrated his sympathy for the fledgling party and its anti-war stance by donating generously to its election-fighting fund in 1900. Yet he remained a Liberal, and tried to ensure the funds he contributed were not used to challenge Liberal candidates.[238]

Although he remained broadly sympathetic to the Labour Party and its aims, events conspired to rekindle his enthusiasm for the Liberal Party. Members of the party were able to unite in their detestation of the 'methods of barbarism' employed by British forces in South Africa, most notably the use of concentration camps in the Rand.[239] The arguments over Imperialism within the party were stilled. In the same year that the Boer War ended (1902) and the seamier side of British victory came to light, the Unionist government gifted the Liberal Party a cause which regenerated the passionate enthusiasm of its flagging Nonconformist supporters. Balfour's Education Act slew several Liberal sacred cows, by abolishing the Board schools for which Chamberlain and his allies had fought in 1870, and by publicly funding voluntary (Church of England) schools. In parts of Britain, most markedly in Wales and the North, a Nonconformist revival was swiftly engendered and the Liberal party was – as it had always been – the beneficiary.

Only a year later another central tenet of the Liberal faith was challenged when Joseph Chamberlain electrified a Birmingham audience of Unionist faithful by committing himself to Tariff Reform.[240] Almost all Liberals could agree on the inviolable truths of Free Trade, adherence to which had brought Britain peace and prosperity. It was a cause which divided the Unionist side of the House, but which revivified the Liberals, who had been in total disarray in the 1900 General Election. These traditional Old Liberal issues explain the party's extraordinary success in the next election in 1906 when the Liberals won 400 seats (up from 186) and the Unionists slumped to 157 seats. The new Labour Party won over 30 seats.[241]

George Cadbury was delighted on several counts. The electoral arrangement of the Liberal and Labour parties (the Lib/Lab Pact) was the consummation of a long-standing ambition: 'to bring the two forces into cooperation was the main interest of his life', wrote his biographer.[242] In addition, as Peter Clarke and others have observed, there was a strong undercurrent of Progressivism, that is of social reform, in the programmes of successful Liberal and Labour candidates in the North in the January 1906 Election.[243] This was to be the harbinger of the New Liberal programme of welfare reforms carried through by David Lloyd George and Winston Churchill after 1908. Naturally, this pleased George Cadbury, a leading proponent – as we have seen – of welfare reform. Indeed, as he himself said: 'I have no interest in the Liberal Party except in so far as it promotes the welfare of the millions of my fellow countrymen who are on or below the poverty line.' Lastly, Cadbury was especially pleased at the stunning election victory because he had a great regard for the new Prime Minister, Henry Campbell-Bannerman, who he credited with reviving his own interest in Liberal politics. His respect for the Prime Minister was enhanced by the high priority he gave to land reform, a pet project of Cadbury's. There was mutual regard, too, for Campbell-Bannerman wanted to submit his friend's name to King Edward VII for appointment to the Privy Council but failed to persuade George Cadbury.[244]

Where George Cadbury prompted, influenced, and supported but remained below the political radar, Joseph Chamberlain was very different. He sought to proselytise, to convert, and to engage with the enemy firstly by his oratory. He was a charismatic, combative and energetic performer, of whom Winston Churchill would write: 'When I looked out of my regimental cradle and was thrilled by politics he was incomparably the most lively, sparkling, insurgent and compulsive figure in British affairs.'[245] He was never better than when surrounded by the adoring faithful in Birmingham. Beatrice Webb wrote that 'he attracted devotion by the mesmeric quality of his passion'.[246] He did, it is true, also understand the power of the printed word, having speeches published, financing poster and pamphlet campaigns especially in support of Tariff Reform from 1903-1906. Still, the essential nature of his politics is best seen in his speech-making, where he could bring his extraordinary force of personality to bear. From the early 1880s through to his last great effort in 1906, election campaigns were characterised by Chamberlain's national speaking tours, carrying the message of the Unauthorised Programme, then of Unionism, and latterly of the iniquities of Free Trade to the country in scores of his trademark, relentless, clear, ruthlessly logical, and often memorable, speeches.[247]

Indeed, it is true to say that, in a way that the private, reserved George Cadbury could never be, Joseph Chamberlain was a political animal to his fingertips. Decades of correspondence preserved in the Special Collections in the University of Birmingham reveal his passion for political intrigue. More than that it betrays his tireless ambition, his ruthless determination, and his employment of a range of strategies from flattery and pleas to threats and anger when he sought his way. This is well illustrated by the fight he put up to ensure his Liberal Unionist son Austen was nominated for the safe Conservative seat of East Worcestershire when a vacancy emerged in 1892; he bombarded local leaders into submission, calling in his big gun allies in the Conservative leadership to bolster his cause. The sheer energy and persistence evident in the batch of letters he wrote to break down local Tory resistance is extraordinary; he was irresistible.[248]

Joseph Chamberlain was a master of electoral politics in a way George Cadbury could never have been or ever wanted to be. His understanding of electioneering, of canvassing, of how to appeal to his voters was matched by no other frontline politician, and only Lord Salisbury himself had as acute and deep an understanding of Victorian psephology, of the political make-up of constituencies. Chamberlain transferred his commercial gifts utilised in selling *Nettlefolds* screws into selling his message and his party. He successfully shaped a personal image, the dapper, foppish statesman replete with monocle and orchid, reproduced on hundreds of thousands of the new picture postcards; the vanity involved in personalised politics repelled George Cadbury.

Where Cadbury coined a memorable marketing jingle, 'Absolutely Pure', to sell *Cadbury* chocolate, Chamberlain had the successful advertiser's ear for a political catchphrase like 'Union is Strength', 'Work for the Unemployed' and 'We Are Seven' (to celebrate the seven Unionist MPs of Birmingham). He also had an eye for visual referents like his cultivation of the orchid buttonhole, recruiting the Union Jack (and John Bull) to his cause for use in Unionist meetings and posters from 1886 onwards.

Chamberlain's love of every aspect of adversarial politics from speech-making, debate in the House, electioneering, and private intriguing, extended to an altogether darker side. No contemporary understood better than Joseph Chamberlain the value of political violence to intimidate an opponent. Even if direct proof of his involvement is difficult to come by, a number of incidents in Birmingham over a twenty-year period have Chamberlain's prints all over them. For example, a Conservative rally in Aston in Birmingham in 1884 (when Chamberlain was still a loyal Liberal), was the subject of violent disruption by rowdies who swarmed over the park walls, invaded the house and stormed the platform where Lord Randolph Churchill presided. It is inconceivable that the man who knew Birmingham Liberal politics inside out was unaware of the Liberal circular, widely disseminated: 'Churchill leaves the Exchange Rooms at 10.30pm; meet him and greet him'. These riots were the subject of a long and personal attack on Chamberlain by his Conservative opponents in the House of Commons in October 1884 who accused him of 'inciting the riots himself'.[249]

From that time on the suspicion that Chamberlain directed a willing mob to do his business clung to him. He made Birmingham a physical as well as a metaphorical fortress, as David Lloyd George discovered in December 1901 when he came to speak at the Town Hall. His intrepid and persistent investigation of the Chamberlain family's business interests in South Africa had already alienated many Birmingham Unionists, protective of their hero's reputation. So this visit was seen as a provocation. Again, Chamberlain cannot have been unaware of what would then transpire. Sandwich-board men paraded the streets calling on the people to 'Defend King, Government and Chamberlain against Brum Boers'. False tickets were printed for the Town Hall meeting, and a mob was summoned to invade the Town Hall, nearly lynching Lloyd George who made an unheroic exit disguised as a policeman. Chamberlain made no public denunciation of violence involving the loss of life.[250] The point is that for Chamberlain passionate engagement with political controversy was his whole life, and issues were so strongly felt, so personal to him that he was prepared to countenance physical violence in pursuing them.

George Cadbury was almost the polar opposite temperamentally. Whilst he felt strongly on certain issues, he remained steadfastly uninterested in the wiles of politicking and absolutely opposed to the sort of violence discreetly supported by Joseph Chamberlain. With the occasional exception when he made speeches at Bournville to employees or residents, it would seem that Gardiner was correct in his judgement that 'his disposition throughout life was to avoid publicity', a consequence of his being 'curiously self-depreciatory as to his own merits, and conscious of his intellectual limitations'. If speech-making was not for him, he was much happier influencing opinion through newspapers. In 1891 he bought a group of four weekly papers in Birmingham with the aim of 'raising the civic and moral standards of public life'. As such the papers did not engage with big issues of national politics. In 1900 that all changed as a result of the revulsion he felt towards Joseph Chamberlain's South African War (see chapter 7). He was profoundly dejected by the attitude of the London Press. Once the *Daily Chronicle* and the *Daily News*, the two Liberal penny newspapers in the capital had come out in support of Chamberlain's War, there was no anti-war organ to counter the influence of *The Times*, the *Daily Telegraph*, the *Morning Post* and the *Daily Mail*.[251]

It was that up-and-coming Welsh Radical David Lloyd George who persuaded George Cadbury to become involved in a scheme to take over the *Daily News* in late 1900. John Grigg, Lloyd George's biographer, amusingly describes how Lloyd George read aloud his draft letter to Cadbury to a friend, Harold Spender, over port, cigars and coffee at a London restaurant. Grigg mused on what picture of the letter-writer the teetotal George Cadbury might have conjured in his mind's eye – more likely, of a puritan, Nonconformist idealist, and most unlikely of the reality of a cigar-smoking bon-viveur and man of the world.

Cadbury came to have a high opinion of Lloyd George, for his courage in holding the anti-war line, and for his bravery in entering the lion's den when he came to Birmingham to make that anti-Chamberlain speech in December 1901. He believed Lloyd George to be the most constructive of the Liberals in social reform and welfare. That letter did the trick, persuading him that it was his duty to help capture the *Daily News* and eliciting this response from George Cadbury, when he excused himself from a meeting on the subject in London: 'At this time of the year I am overwhelmed with work. All you want is the money and that I have promised… The venture is unlikely to pay unless common sense and business capacity are combined.'[252] In truth, even his business capacity would not make the *Daily News* a financial success in these years.

The impact which resulted from securing the paper was immediate. Even allowing for his partisanship as editor of the *Daily News*, most historians agree with Gardiner that 'the spirit of Liberalism revived under its energetic and audacious leadership'. The anti-war party had its mouthpiece, but at considerable financial cost; the paper suffered disastrously on the advertising side. Some of the backers who joined Cadbury in the syndicate created by Lloyd George to finance the paper withdrew. Their departure, and the prospect of the *Daily News* falling into other hands and reverting to its original pro-War attitudes, bore Cadbury along to a personal crossroads. As he wrote to C.P. Scott, the Liberal editor of the anti-war *Manchester Guardian*: 'We could sell the paper to those who are supporting the war, but this seems to me a terrible responsibility as the *Daily News* ought to be a power for peace in the South of England as the *Manchester Guardian* is in the North.'[253] It was a responsibility and a duty which he decided to undertake, and so he became sole proprietor in early 1902.

Sales of the paper rose from 30,000 to 80,000 and this reflected not simply an increased sympathy for the *Daily News* anti-war stance. The paper became the vehicle for the 'new spirit of social reform' evident once the war was over. Its editorials and campaigns championed the politics of C.P. Masterman, Lloyd George, Winston Churchill and others, men who were aroused by revelations of poverty, malnutrition and general deprivation, highlighted by recently published inquiries such as those of Rowntree and Booth.

The *Daily News* also led the charge against Joseph Chamberlain's Tariff Reform both on the grounds that Free Trade was hallowed and also because it argued that Chamberlain's campaign was designed to 'divert the public mind' from the need for government to act on the condition of the people – which, for Chamberlain, was precisely what he felt he was addressing by his concentration on tariffs as a solution to working-class unemployment.[254] The *Daily News* advocated a number of other causes, especially in the years before the 1906 Election – opposition to Chinese slavery (the employment of Chinese coolie labour in the South African mines), to Balfour's Licensing Bill and to his Education Act. It campaigned for Old Age Pensions, the development of small holdings, and the suppression of sweating (see chapter 4). Cadbury, says Gardiner, 'rejoiced in the influence the *Daily News* gave him of bringing the facts of the poor home to the national conscience'. The newspaper vigorously supported the Penrhyn quarrymen in their action against their anti-union employer Lord Penrhyn, raising £2,500 in 1902 in an appeal in the *Daily News* to pay for the damages and costs incurred by W.J. Parry, one of his opponents; later it highlighted a national scandal with its Exhibition of Sweated Industries in May 1906.

In 1910, now well over 70 years old, George Cadbury drew up memoranda to step away from active involvement and transfer the ownership of the *Daily News* to his son, Edward and other trustees. In a covering letter he set out the philosophy which had underlain his tenure of the newspaper. 'I had a profound conviction that money spent on charities was of infinitely less value than money spent in trying to arouse my fellow countrymen to the necessity for measures to ameliorate the condition of the poor, forsaken and downtrodden masses which can be done most effectively by a great newspaper.' He went on to caution his son: 'If you champion the cause of the poor who cannot do anything to recompense you, you must expect savage attacks from those whose interests may be affected. I have been bitterly attacked in society papers, also on the other hand by anarchists who desire a violent revolution, and who know that progressive legislation will make this impossible.'[255]

Cadbury had placed the *Daily News* firmly in the vanguard of the progressive crusade to persuade government to act to improve the lot of the country's poorest inhabitants. He could point to a number of victories. His newspaper had championed the Liberal Party in the years up to its spectacular landslide triumph in 1906; it had called for control of sweated industries, for the implementation of non-contributory old age pensions, for compulsory land purchase by local authorities to create small holdings for workers, and all these projects came to fruition in the Liberal Campbell-Bannerman and Asquith ministries after 1906. He could feel vindicated in his support of Lloyd George and the New Liberals who had used the levers of power to enact a series of important social reforms which would lay foundations for a later Welfare State. Of course, it was not simply or singly George Cadbury and his *Daily News* which achieved this substantial legacy of reform, but he and his paper were significant players in a wider progressive movement for change in these years.

It could be argued that in this he had a greater impact in the early twentieth century than had Joseph Chamberlain. The latter, despite all his great speeches and for all his early creativity, became mired in matters of colonial policy and of war, and at the end of his career pursued the chimera of Tariff Reform, with disastrous consequences for his party and absolute failure for the cause of overturning Free Trade. Yet as a political figure, even a hundred years after his death, the name of Joseph Chamberlain still retains an aura, both as the greatest British statesman not to have become Prime Minister and as Birmingham's favourite son, the architect of its municipal revolution and the man who made the city nationally significant.

THREE DIVIDING LINES

E ven though Chamberlain and Cadbury had so much in common with their mutual reforming interests, they were to be irrevocably divided on political matters by the time Joseph Chamberlain retired in 1906. Part of the explanation lies in those temperamental differences explored in the previous chapter. However, there were also deep divisions of principle and this chapter is concerned with three bitterly contested areas which underlined the gulf between them, just as it estranged other Liberal Party members from each other. The ramifications of the debates over Irish Home Rule were to continue up to the outbreak of the First World War and beyond. The South African War entrenched party political positions and split the Liberal Party comprehensively. Chamberlain's surprise espousal of Tariff Reform (Protection) in 1903 profoundly divided his own Unionist party and very effectively succeeded in uniting the Liberals for whom Free Trade was an absolute article of faith. In each controversy our two Birmingham titans found themselves on opposite sides of the political debate.

Ireland had been a running sore for all Westminster governments throughout the nineteenth century. Irish grievances were many. On the land tenants were subject to rack-renting (extortionate rents) and eviction at the hands of often absentee landlords. The Established Anglican Church in Ireland ministered to barely 10% of the population while over 80% of Irishmen were Roman Catholics who had to pay taxes both for Protestant clergy and for the upkeep of largely empty Protestant churches. Catholic MPs until 1829 were barred from sitting at Westminster. Protestant Trinity College in Dublin had a monopoly over university education in Ireland. Most intolerable of all was Pitt's Act of Union, passed in the shadow of possible French invasion in 1801; it dissolved the Irish Parliament, initiating direct rule from Westminster. Until the mid-1880s the policy of successive governments had been to assuage Irish outrage by tackling a range of other – social, educational and religious – issues in hopes that the underlying demand for the return of an Irish parliament (Home Rule) would disappear.[256]

William Gladstone had initiated more in the way of constructive reform than any other nineteenth-century English politician. When first Prime Minister he had enacted the disestablishment of the Irish Church and a series of Land Acts in the 1870s and early 1880s to deal with eviction and unaffordable rents. Yet, to his dismay, he had had to institute measures of coercion (suspension of *habeas corpus*, the imposition of curfew) to tackle endemic rural violence. Equally, that dismay was compounded by the realisation that all this effort had diminished not a jot the indomitable demand of men like Charles Stewart Parnell (leader of the Irish National Party) for Home Rule for Ireland. Parnell stood at the head of a formidable movement. The General Election of December 1885 had seen 85 MPs returned for the Irish National Party and they held the balance in the new House of Commons in which the Liberals under Gladstone formed the largest party. So, a mixture of political realism ('Ireland has spoken', said Gladstone) and a growing conviction in the rightness of the cause, propelled Gladstone towards a fateful conclusion – that his new Ministry's mission was to pacify Ireland by restoring a Parliament to Dublin.

It was fateful because Home Rule was deeply unpopular with sections of his own party; his stubborn refusal either to be open about his plans or then to modify his Home Rule Bill in early summer 1886 to win over critics consigned him to defeat in the Commons, and sentenced his party to an irreparable severance. Joseph Chamberlain led the attack on Gladstone within Liberal ranks, earning the sobriquets 'Judas', and 'the man who killed Home Rule', as a result. His stand wrecked his prospects in the Liberal Party forever, and indeed for three or four years his very future in politics was imperilled. Why did he hazard everything over this issue?

With Chamberlain there was usually a personal dimension to his political actions. He felt slighted that his own proposal in Cabinet to meet Parnell's insistent demands had been turned down by Gladstone; he had suggested a Central Board for Ireland, a glorified municipal council with local responsibilities rather akin to those of Birmingham.[257] That rejection sharpened a growing frustration with a Prime Minister who would insist on soldiering on – he was 76 years old in 1886 – rather than handing over to a younger more vigorous man. For Chamberlain was deeply ambitious. Frustration turned to anger and dislike as a result of the way he was treated by Gladstone in early 1886; the Prime Minister determined to humiliate him, offended by Chamberlain's pretensions and continuing insistence on propagating his own unofficial Radical programme. So he offered him the meanest Cabinet position and then proceeded to widen the gulf with a series of calculated rebuffs. Others, even on Gladstone's side, observed this regretfully.

Lord Kimberley, although a Gladstone ally in the Cabinet, recorded in his journal that 'our Chief's management of his relations with Chamberlain was inexplicable to me and certainly unfortunate'.[258] Chamberlain's behaviour over the Home Rule Bill should then be understood as at least partly an exercise in revenge, a settling of a score. In addition, Chamberlain greatly resented the way that Home Rule drew the party's and the country's attention away from the raft of social reforms on which he campaigned with his Radical Programme (chapters 2 to 4) and for which he had originally joined the Liberal Party.

Nevertheless, his arguments against the bill itself were strongly felt, brilliantly articulated and persuasive enough to win over a sufficient number of Radicals and Whigs to defeat Gladstone. Those arguments were to form the core of the Unionist case right up to the Government of Ireland Act in 1920. In speech after speech Chamberlain repeated a fundamental belief. 'Is there any man among you,' he asked an audience of Birmingham Liberals, 'who believes any settlement of the Irish question will be permanent that does not yield to the full demands of Mr Parnell?'[259] After all, as he reminded his audience, this was the man who had told supporters: 'None of us will be satisfied until we have destroyed the last link which keeps Ireland bound to England.' Later Chamberlain would elaborate in the House: 'There is no finality in this Bill and until you come to separation you cannot stop or satisfy the (Irish) Honourable gentlemen opposite.'[260] That would undermine the cohesion of the hitherto United Kingdom. It would seriously endanger the Mother Country in a time of war. It would indeed threaten any plans for closer ties with the colonies, instead providing a precedent for the Empire's dissolution. Here is the outline of that Imperialism for which he would become a leading apologist at the end of the century.

He developed a battery of further arguments. An essential feature of Gladstone's Bill was that Irish representation at Westminster would cease. The Irish would have no part to play in the foreign and colonial policy made at Westminster, would surrender all control over the army and navy, and would be permitted to manage barely one quarter of Ireland's tax revenue and be denied any control over customs and excise.[261] This he said, in the Birmingham speech already cited, 'is contrary to all the principles of our representative government'. It gave fresh impetus to the old rallying cry of 'No taxation without representation'.

He had worries about the threat that was implicit in even this reduced Irish Parliament. After all, as Whigs like Lord Hartington and old Radicals such as John Bright pointed out, Ireland was being handed over to a criminal element, which had gloried in intimidation, boycottings and arson in the recent Land War. They greatly resented the idea that crime had paid off. Chamberlain saw the danger to Ulster Protestants of a vengeful Catholic majority, bent on supremacy. Ulster, he said in a speech in Belfast, 'is connected by ties of race and religion and sympathy with the greater nation'. 'I fear your submitting to the rule of an authority officered by the men who invented the Plan of Campaign and the No Rent manifesto.'[262] As much as Lord Randolph Churchill, Chamberlain played the Orange card, arousing Ulster to the dangers of majority Catholic rule under Home Rule. The success of the campaign to awaken Ulster's feelings for the rest of the United Kingdom culminated in Ulster's mass defiance, aimed at another Liberal government, in 1912/13.

Many of these ideas he articulated early on in the Home Rule struggle in April 1886 when he spoke to Liberal constituents in Birmingham. As we have seen in the previous chapter, that day he won the support of the 2000 for his stance in resisting Gladstone's Home Rule Bill, even if thereafter significant numbers of local Liberals defected to the Leader's camp. George Cadbury was one who was never convinced by Chamberlain's arguments. The issue of Home Rule led to a parting of the ways. Cadbury's reasons were several. He was to the end a loyal supporter of Gladstone's, with whose mission causes to bring about justice to the oppressed he sympathised. As a Quaker he cleaved for all his life to the ideal of peace in international relations, a principle which equally motivated Gladstone even if he could not always live up to it in practice. Another article of faith for Gladstone was that nations had a right to self-government. He had got into a lot of hot water for his injudicious remarks during the American Civil War in which he had shown support for the secessionist ambitions of the Southern States, which he recognised as 'having made a nation'.[263]

Equally, in 1883 and 1884 Gladstone sympathised with the objectives of the India National Conference, the forerunner of the Congress Party, which aspired to Indian self-government.[264] He extended this logic to Ireland in the Home Rule debate: 'The true key was this; that it was not properly borne in mind that as England is inhabited by Englishmen, and Scotland by Scotchmen, so Ireland is inhabited by Irishmen.'[265] Just so, Cadbury followed his party leader in seeing Irish Home Rule as being fundamentally about a nation justifiably calling for self-government, about Ireland being for the Irish.[266] He never followed the logic of this to embrace Chamberlain's notion of Ulster for the Ulstermen.

This reading of the Irish Question would determine Cadbury's political allegiance thereafter. While Chamberlain was cast out of the Liberal Party, in exile forming the Birmingham Liberal Unionist Association and the National Radical Union, Cadbury, with loyalists like Schnadhorst, stayed true to Gladstone. However, as we have seen (chapter 5), he became frustrated that Gladstone's mission causes deflected Liberal attention in the 1890s from the campaigns for social reform most dear to his heart. It was ironic, then, that Chamberlain, increasingly close to his Conservative Unionist allies, should in that decade be so active in precisely this area of social reform – in education, compensation, arbitration and in pensions. Cadbury would watch this from the other side of the party divide.

The onset of the Boer War then widened the gulf between them, summoning from George Cadbury an unprecedented depth of hostility towards his Birmingham rival. For both men the South African War from 1899–1902 would be the central action of their political lives. For example, many have followed Lord Salisbury when he dubbed it 'Joe's War'. In truth the causes of the war were far more complex and enduring than could be attributed to the agency of one man. Throughout the nineteenth century the British had extended their hold over Southern Africa and the Boers had trekked ever further north from the Cape, to Orange Free State and Transvaal to evade them. Britain pursued them and sought to annex the Transvaal in 1881, though being defeated at Majuba Hill; subsequently they were forced to recognise Transvaal's essential independence. Still, in successive conventions Britain was confirmed in its control of the Boer state's foreign policy. Until the end of the century this claim to ultimate British suzerainty (sovereignty) was resented and resisted by the President of the Transvaal, Paul Kruger, just as actively and passionately as it was promoted by the Colonial Secretary, Joseph Chamberlain. The stakes were raised by the discovery of gold in Witwatersrand, in the Transvaal, exploited overwhelmingly by British and German mining engineers. These Uitlanders (foreign immigrants) were treated poorly by the Boer administration: they were effectively disenfranchised.

Chamberlain's reputation had been sullied early in his period of office in 1895 by association with an abortive and farcical raid into Transvaal territory by Leander Starr Jameson, whose intention mirrored that of his rich and powerful employer, Cecil Rhodes. The idea was to provoke an uprising of the Uitlanders in the Transvaal to overthrow the Boers, grab control of the mines and usher in British rule. Chamberlain, the Colonial Secretary, vociferously denied that he ever knew of the plans (see chapter 7). Whether true or not, the effect on Kruger and the Boer leadership was to confirm their mistrust of perfidious Albion and make them more intransigent. Some have seen the outbreak of the South African War in 1899 as an attempt on Chamberlain's part 'to recoup earlier losses', that is the failed Jameson Raid, but this is to assume that he set out with the express intention of fomenting war, and the evidence just does not bear this out.

Other historians, like Eric Hobsbawm, have judged that 'the motive for the Boer War was gold', but there is no documentary proof that Chamberlain, or indeed Salisbury, conceived South African problems in terms of gold, tempting though it would have been to ensure British control of this precious metal.[267] Far from pushing for hostilities relentlessly in the months before war in 1899, he appears to have thought his usual confrontational style of negotiation would ensure Britain had her way peaceably. Only by late August, and the realisation that Kruger was not to be bullied into concession, did Chamberlain contemplate war. In truth, he and his Cabinet colleagues still operated in 'a pervasive political culture inimical to force', which explains how ill-prepared the British military was for war and how unsuccessful it was in the early months of conflict.[268]

Chamberlain was the government's articulate advocate, who set out the twin war aims in a speech in the House of Commons on the eve of war: 'We are bound to show that we are willing and able to protect British subjects everywhere, wherever they are made to suffer from oppression and injustice and, in the interests of South Africa and of the British Empire, Britain must remain the paramount power in South Africa...for since 1881 they (the Boers) have by imperceptible steps been trying to oust the Queen from suzerainty.'[269] That he was the spokesman does not mean that he was the sole responsible party for the conflict. The British High Commissioner for South Africa, Alfred Milner, was adamantine and inflexible when negotiating with Kruger. The latter, in his determination to win complete unfettered independence for the Boers, was equally immovable. Lord Salisbury, the Prime Minister, appears more hard-line than Chamberlain in that summer of 1899.[270] Perhaps in any case so deep-seated were enmities between Boer and British that there was an element of inevitability about the resumption of the hostilities of 1881.

Still, once the war was underway, in a number of ways it did indeed become Joe's War. Supporters and opponents identified the war with the Colonial Secretary personally; he was a deeply divisive figure and he attracted 'a terrible amount of hatred', as he himself ruefully confessed.[271] Across the course of the war his analysis of war aims evolved, and he became the apologist for a more metaphysical Imperial mission. The war was part of 'a greater scheme by which we hope to make our Empire something more than a geographical expression. We hope to make it a living entity in which each part shall contribute to the success and security of the whole.'[272] On another occasion he spoke of the Empire of 400 millions as 'one family', bound together by mutual sentiment, common ideals and noble aspirations, bringing 'freedom and justice and civilisation and peace to its dependent races'.[274]

In a remarkable way, during the course of the war he established a unique reputation: when the mood was black after military reverses, much of the country exempted him from criticism. When things went well he was fêted in scenes of jingoistic delirium. So, if it was not simply 'Joe's War', the 1900 General Election in which he alone of the Unionist leaders quartered the country speaking about the war (in which British fortunes had taken a turn for the better) was 'Joe's Election', with his Unionist party securing a majority of over 120.[274]

Chamberlain was the centre of attention in another regard, too; for Lloyd George ensured that his personal probity was the focus of intense scrutiny. Chamberlain had provoked him, accusing him and other Radicals of treasonable dealings with the Boer leaders after a cache of their letters was seized by the British military at recently captured Bloemfontein. In retaliation Lloyd George set about investigating the extent to which the Chamberlain family benefited from war contracts, starting with *Kynoch's*. Joseph's brother Arthur Chamberlain ran the firm, one of the three biggest cordite manufacturers in Britain; Lloyd George alleged that 'it had been practically made by the War Office' and that it had received preferential treatment simply because of 'the unconscious influence of a powerful personality'.[275] He went on to point out that

Hoskins (in which Joseph's sons Neville and Austen were prominent shareholders) supplied the Navy, and that Austen was Civil Lord of the Admiralty. Herbert Chamberlain was deputy chairman of *Birmingham Small Arms*, whose munitions supplied British forces in South Africa. As Peter Marsh points out, here was 'a family federation of companies manufacturing metal supplies and munitions for the armed forces to fight a war brought on by the senior member of the family, the Colonial Secretary'. It did not look good, however valiantly Chamberlain denied any impropriety; how could he effectively distance himself when, for example, the major shareholders of *Hoskins* all lived under his roof?[276]

Lloyd George, as we have seen, played a significant part in drawing George Cadbury into funding and then owning a major national Liberal newspaper, the *Daily News*. George Cadbury succumbed to his blandishments because Lloyd George was an outspoken critic of the Boer War and Lloyd George's arguments resonated with him. Lloyd George challenged Chamberlain's vision of maximum Imperial integration and consolidation by arguing for its polar opposite, local autonomy and Home Rule all round. This exactly replicated Cadbury's 'simple, fundamental belief in the principle of self-government'.[277] Cadbury objected to Chamberlain's war on other grounds too. He abhorred the way that the tone of politics during the war had become debased, that those who opposed the war were instantly labelled pro-Boer and their motives questioned. He greatly disliked the jingoistic tide which bore Chamberlain and Unionists aloft at times of great popular excitement, as with the celebrations of the Relief of Mafeking. For him the aim was for his newspaper to be 'a power for peace in the South of England', a brave stand given the largely overwhelming majority for the war.

Although he refrained from involvement in Lloyd George's assaults on the Chamberlain family, he did believe that the war was 'carried on on behalf of speculators at Johannesburg, and that they are responsible for it'.[278] He meant 'the machinations of the mine owners', amongst whom might be counted Cecil Rhodes, who came so close in 1895 to effecting an uprising in Transvaal to his material advantage. Cadbury sits in a long line of left-leaning critics of the war, from J.A. Hobson to Eric Hobsbawm who saw capitalist greed as the motor of the government's Imperial policy.

Even if matters in South Africa, military and civil, were the business of men on the spot, the generals like Buller, Kitchener and Roberts and the British High Commissioner himself, Chamberlain was bound to be in the firing line when things unravelled at the war's end. Cadbury's *Daily News* led the attack on 'methods of barbarism', the military's use of concentration camps to break the spirit of Boer families. This was an issue in which Chamberlain was caught out, being ignorant of the details; he was privately very critical when he discovered the truth. Still it was embarrassing to be part of a regime which employed such methods.

Another decision made in South Africa by Milner rebounded on Chamberlain and Unionist politicians; this was the policy of importing Chinese labour to the mine fields to supplement local labour. Trade Unionists objected because here were employment opportunities of which British workers might have availed themselves. Cadbury and many other Liberals were outraged at least as much by the conditions in which Chinese coolies were housed and employed. Again his *Daily News* was at the forefront of the campaign and it was evidently effective. Chinese Slavery continued to be a live issue right up to the 1906 election when Liberal poster campaigns employed images of Chamberlain in Chinese costume and when pigtailed and manacled Chinamen were familiar on the streets and at Liberal election meetings! Chamberlain himself knew that Chinese labour 'had completed the disillusionment of the country with the Boer War', a humiliating reversal from the heady days of the Khaki Election victory in 1900 when Imperialism was a vote-winner.[279]

By now, as Gardiner wrote, George Cadbury 'had a deepening distrust of Chamberlain's political purposes, and an intense dislike of the ruthless suppression of anything like free opinion'. 'The rupture (over the Boer War) was never healed.'[280] Cadbury's hatred of acquisitive Imperialism is even reflected in changes made in the packaging and promotion of *Cadbury* products. In the 1890s *Cadbury Bros.* were 'typical of many firms which relied upon representations of royalty, colonial travellers and explorers to promote their products. This all changed at the beginning of the Boer conflict.' Advertising instead now centred on the home, on the domestic housewife, emphasising how women, 'Absolutely Pure', were destined to counter the unhealthy passions of jingoism.[281] Cadbury's disapproval of the war extended from packaging to his 'refusal to tender for orders of chocolate and cocoa for the British army', a stand only later abandoned when the Queen commanded him to supply her (chocolate) Christmas present to the troops. Even after this, the chocolate bar for the troops was unbranded, so preserving *Cadbury's* distance from a war that George roundly condemned.[282]

The conclusion of the war in 1902 certainly allowed Liberals to begin the process of reunification after a period of painful internecine hostilities. To Cadbury's pleasure, amity was restored with the pro-war J. W. Wilson, the MP for North Worcestershire, who George Cadbury had helped financially. Many of the legacies of the war were damaging for the Unionist government. There was the cost and the loss of life. The methods used to win the war, concentration camps and scorched earth, damaged Britain's reputation. Optimism about Imperial expansion took a considerable knock. Yet, these unwelcome developments did not affect Joseph Chamberlain's maturing vision for Britain and its Empire. It contributed to his apostasy in 1903 when he came out as a Protectionist; that completed his alienation from George Cadbury.

For most of the nineteenth century the overwhelming majority of Britons accepted Free Trade 'as a good, like virtue, holiness and righteousness to be loved, admired and honoured', in the words of the *Economist*.[283] Free Trade, its many apologists argued, promoted trust and toleration at home and harmony not greed, competition or exploitation, overseas. It was associated with purity in politics and with having the interests of the consumer at heart. To tax food would be to drive those on the margins out of civilisation and into barbarism and social anarchy.[284] Joseph Chamberlain was at first an enthusiastic Liberal and fully bought in to this orthodoxy. When Birmingham's Chamber of Commerce invited him to be President in 1887 he fastidiously rejected the offer: 'The Chamber has recently adopted a resolution in favour of Fair Trade and, as I am opposed to Protection in any shape or form, I could not with propriety accept.'[285]

A little over a decade later he was changing, and profoundly. His conversion was prompted by a number of factors. It was a fundamental truth that he was first and foremost a Birmingham businessman and was not immune to signs of increased backing for action to protect local manufacturing industry. He detected this enthusiasm throughout the town's business community. When a Royal Commission on Depression of Trade and Industry in 1885 asked the Birmingham Chamber of Commerce for its views on the requisite measures to improve ailing trade, it called for 'the imposition of an import duty on foreign manufactured goods'. This body, which represented most of the leading Birmingham manufacturers, in subsequent years continued to hammer away at the same theme: other countries like France, Germany and USA imposed high tariffs on British exports injuring local industry, with metal working being especially vulnerable. It added to the list of grievances the evidence that foreign countries were dumping cheap goods in Britain to undercut domestic products, and that those same countries were benefiting from cheap labour, and from longer working hours than were possible in Britain.

This idea of levelling the playing field is the essence of 'Fair Trade', a movement which gathered strength from the early 1880s in the Conservative Party, where Protection had probably never died away, even after Peel's Repeal of the Corn Laws ushered in a long era of tariff reduction. It was particularly well supported in the West Midlands. All seven Conservative candidates in the 1885 General Election were Fair Traders, and though they lost, they performed creditably in what was at that time a Liberal citadel. Chamberlain observing this commented: 'Fair Trade, you have no idea what a hold it has on the artisans.'[286] Its attraction to a class of potential supporters he needed to woo had not eluded him. As persuasive would have been his growing pessimism about the future of the national and local economy.

We can see this in speeches he made once he felt emancipated from the obligation to defend Free Trade. For example, at Bingley Hall in Birmingham in November 1903 he spelt out the damaging impact of foreign tariffs on local trade. The litany of woe included the facts that: imports were growing faster than Birmingham exports in jewellery, brass manufacturers faced up to 60% tariffs abroad, pearl button employees had shrunk from 6,000 to 1,000 because of America's McKinley tariffs and the cycle industry's exports had fallen by half a million pounds over ten years thanks to foreign tariffs. This all fed into a broader narrative, that of relative national decline in the face of unscrupulous foreign competition. He worried that Britain was becoming less a country of manufacturing than of consumption, finance and service industries.[287]

So, Joseph Chamberlain was an interested party in the fortunes of Birmingham's business. His own entrepreneurial outlook was reflected in the way that he looked at the Empire for which, as Colonial Secretary from 1895, he had a special responsibility. He viewed it as a great estate which demanded development. It was Imperial concerns that helped convince him of the need to break with Free Trade and introduce tariffs. He was unquestionably moved by the response of the far-flung Empire to requests for help in the Boer War, for 60,000 colonial troops augmented British forces. At the same time he could see the benefits from closer ties, for an Imperial bloc of millions more customers in a *Zollverein*, a free trade area, would be a formidable competitor to the rising powers of Germany and the USA.

Canada showed him the practical steps to achieving that greater union; in 1897 it raised the prospect of unilateral Canadian preference on British imports. The logical response was for Britain to give Canada a reciprocal preference in British markets for her corn. That inevitably involved a tax on grain from other countries.[288] Chamberlain by 1902 had been converted to this idea of Imperial preference, and thought he had seen a way to achieving it and giving that corresponding gesture to the colonies that they said they needed, before committing to greater integration. The Chancellor of the Exchequer, Hicks Beach, that year had imposed a one shilling per quarter tax on corn to plug the financial hole created by Boer War expenditure. Cabinet agreement to use this as the basis for Imperial preference was then, to his dismay, overturned and the tax abolished while Chamberlain was out of the country touring defeated South Africa.

This was the proximate cause for Chamberlain's open and defiant commitment to Tariff Reform in his speech in Birmingham on 15 May 1903. He was equally motivated, no doubt, by a desire to distract attention from the politically damaging story of Balfour's Education Act, which had split Chamberlain's own Liberal Unionist party. Another part of him wanted to give the flagging Unionist party a goal, a mission, to rejuvenate it in the aftermath to a controversial war. Whatever, the result was that: 'No speech in British history has ever caused such a sensation or led to such momentous consequences', as Julian Amery, Chamberlain's biographer, claimed.

Chamberlain probably underestimated the depth of the passion he would stir in opposition to his plans. The Unionist alliance fractured. His own Liberal Unionist party split, with the Duke of Devonshire its leader in the Lords abandoning it. The Conservative party would enter the 1906 Election with some members openly campaigning against other members of the party; indeed, Chamberlain himself aggressively attacked leading Free Trade Unionists like Lord Hugh Cecil.[289] By contrast, Liberals who had been at sixes and sevens over the Boer War and – in a wider sense – over Imperialism in general, now buried their differences in reaction to a dangerous challenge to the established order. For Free Trade was thought, along with Christianity and democracy, to be one of the key elements in Britain's unique liberal civilisation, which it gifted to the rest of the world. Revived Liberal unity, and the defence of Free Trade, brought a spectacular victory. When the *Manchester Guardian* reflected on the 1906 Election results beyond Chamberlain's Duchy it concluded:

> A candidate only had to be a Free Trader to get in, whether he was known or unknown, semi-Unionist or thorough Home Ruler, Protestant or Roman Catholic, entertaining or dull. He only had to be a Protectionist to lose all chance of getting in, though he spoke with the tongues of men and angels.[290]

If he underestimated the virulence of the reaction, neither did Chamberlain at first quite know what the income yielded by these tariffs would be for. He commenced by arguing that the taxes would fund social reform like Old Age Pensions. In the face of working-class indifference to that he suggested using tariffs to subsidise for them the cost of foodstuffs, raised by his very own food taxes, which he conceded were an inevitable corollary of Imperial preference. ('There the murder is out', he admitted in a speech in 1903.) Food taxes were a gift to the opposition, which revived memories of the 'Hungry Forties', for the 1840s were a time of political violence and real deprivation.

Steadily, across the course of the period from 1903 to 1906, he became more and more a full-blooded Protectionist, wanting to prevent British factories from being undercut by German, American and French rivals. By 1906 he was campaigning on electoral platforms under banners which promised 'Work for the Unemployed' as he realised that conventional Free Trade solutions had failed to stem the rising tide of unemployment in Edwardian Britain. Only by stopping cheap foreign goods coming into the country could British firms and men's jobs be secured.[291]

Not all industrialists in Birmingham felt as threatened as Chamberlain and his Tariff Reform League (based in the city) evidently did. George Cadbury, a manufacturing magnate, was vehemently opposed to the imposition of tariffs. No doubt his son Edward was reflecting his father's attitude just as much as his own when he reported to the *Cadbury* Board in 1901 that while on a tour of the white Dominions he had granted £50 to the funds of the Free Trade party in Australia and had met the leader of the Free Trade party to show support.[292] Yet Free Trade was unquestionably making things difficult for *Cadbury* as sales of Swiss milk chocolate doubled in Britain in 1902, with evidence presented to the Board that the Swiss firm of *Lindt and Sprüngli Ltd.* 'were proposing to wake things up a bit in the UK', taking on larger and better premises and appointing a new representative in the UK.

Cadbury might have been expected to flirt with the Tariff Reform nostrums fashionable among many of Birmingham's businessmen, but if for no other reason, commercial reality forced it to reject protection. The firm recognised that even if its home market was under pressure from European businesses, protective barriers would threaten the loss of important export markets in retaliation. Indeed, one Swiss manufacturer spelt out what action it would take if the principal export market for Swiss chocolate (45% of total Swiss chocolate exports by 1903) were threatened by tariffs. 'Should Mr Chamberlain's proposals ever be accepted by the British public, the principal continental chocolate factories would manufacture part of their output in the U.K.'[293] In Paris, a leading Swiss chocolate firm had already built a factory to be able to compete successfully with French industry.[294] The lesson was that *Cadbury* needed to compete effectively without tariff protection, and indeed Chamberlain's Tariff Reform campaign coincided with its determined effort to master the making of milk chocolate, which culminated with the successful launch of *Cadbury Dairy Milk* in 1905 (see chapter 1). From now on *Cadbury* could compete effectually with the Swiss.

George Cadbury did not need commercial considerations to confirm him in his adherence to the Free Trade faith. He reveals his thinking in a letter withdrawing his financial support for the *Clarion* vans, which circulated round English and Scottish villages with copies of the *Clarion* socialist paper edited by Robert Blatchford. Cadbury wrote that he was very disappointed 'that the '*Clarion*' goes in for Protection. It appeals to us as other large manufacturers in England and would probably mean an increase in our profits of 25% to 50%. Protection appeals to every selfish interest, especially among the wealthy manufacturers, and I am perfectly sure it would mean terrible suffering for the poor. I am sorry to withdraw my offer for the van. No doubt there are plenty of wealthy landowners, liquor dealers and protectionist manufacturers who will take my place.'[295]

Here he articulates a strong contemporary argument against Tariff Reform, that it was designed for the benefit of the rich businessmen, not for the consumer, who would pay more for their food. Cadbury's dislike of self-seeking plutocrats, among whom he counts his old enemies, the publicans and liquor traffickers, is manifest. It is a Manichean world-view, of Free Trade good pitched against Protectionist evil. Free Trade with its connotations of peace and trust sat well with his strong religious convictions.

On this issue he was indeed on the side of the angels; and also, as it happened, of the future. Chamberlain had blundered in embracing Tariff Reform. It cost the Unionists the next three elections. George Cadbury's Liberal Party was re-enthused and reinvigorated for a decade or so by his decision. True, it was briefly enacted in the 1930s Depression when Joseph Chamberlain's son Neville was Chancellor of the Exchequer, but since the Second World War the prevailing *zeitgeist* in British politics has been international and tariffs have been the panacea for those campaigning for a socialist siege economy.

Three defining political moments centred on England's view of itself in a wider world and determined men's alignments. On each issue, of self-government for Ireland, of aggressive expansion of the British Empire through a South African war, and of the abandonment of Free Trade, Joseph Chamberlain and George Cadbury found themselves on opposite sides of a deep divide. Such were the passions their allegiances inspired that by the time Joseph Chamberlain was abruptly removed from the fray in 1906 they were irreconcilable political enemies.

SCANDAL

J oseph Chamberlain was no stranger to controversy; he was combative, took risks and sought publicity for his views. Inevitably, across a political career spanning over thirty years there were scrapes and embarrassments. Still, the seriousness of the charges against him with regard to the Jameson Raid in 1895 was in a class of its own and threatened him with political oblivion. With George Cadbury it was different. He shunned the cut and thrust, and was an innocent unused to a world where honest motives could be called into question. Yet even so he was to find himself deeply implicated in a scandal, party to a libel action in 1909 involving alleged complicity in importing slave-grown cocoa, which rebounded uncomfortably on him and on *Cadbury Bros*. It is an additional curiosity that there appears to have been something of a role reversal: unworldly George Cadbury, arguably guilty of dereliction of responsibility on a most serious moral question, while Chamberlain, a man who had long experience of intrigue, may despite all the innuendo have been innocent of the worst charges brought against him.

At issue for George Cadbury was the sourcing of raw cocoa for the major British chocolate firms. By 1900 56% of *Cadbury's* cocoa supplies came from the Portuguese islands of São Tomé and Príncipe in the Gulf of Guinea off the west coast of Africa.[296] The Board minutes of *Cadbury* record that it was not until 1901 that the first intimations of slave labour on the islands reached George Cadbury and his fellow directors. A report from São Tomé 'seems to confirm other independent reports that slavery either total or partial exists on these cocoa estates'. It comprised an inventory of an estate for sale on the island which included 200 black labourers valued at £3555, detailing the means by which these workers were secured through contracts with African chiefs in Angola's interior.[297] Association with such practices for the Cadbury family, prominent Quakers and long-time agitators on the issue, who had spent a fortune on Anti-Slavery campaigns such as Fox-Bourne's Aborigines Association and the Congo Reform Association, was extremely compromising.

Despite this there is no evidence in the Board minutes of any subsequent urgent action. Instead an entry from April 1903, two years later, records: 'We believe at the moment no useful purpose will be served by publishing the particulars of past abuses as the Portuguese government and its Colonial Secretary are establishing the new labour regulations'. This refers to a recent Portuguese royal decree (in 1903) governing the conditions under which *servicais* (labourers) were imported from Angola, and the treatment they were then to receive from the planters. The Cadburys, then, were at first content to wait and see how the decree affected the cocoa islands, even though it was clear that as far as the Portuguese were concerned the issue was simply a matter of the conditions in which labourers worked. British critics were much more concerned about the loss of personal freedom, and so about the issue of whether workers were enslaved.[298] Later in the year, the Board concluded that they needed to find out the facts for themselves, and William Cadbury, George's nephew, was authorised to go to Lisbon to interview government officials there.

His visit coincided with a British Foreign Office report by the British consul in Angola, A. Nightingale, which did not raise any concern about slavery on the islands, although he did mention the high mortality (20%, largely through sleeping sickness) and the constant demand for replacements. He typified the Foreign Office cautiousness about not offending an old and valued ally (Portugal). That diplomatic fastidiousness only served to help reinforce the Cadburys' pedestrian response. British officials were even more wary because they were conscious of their need of Portuguese labourers in the gold fields of recently conquered Transvaal.

The following year (1904) George Cadbury and his Board agreed to delay any decision to act on reports of slavery, on the grounds that 'the authorities maintained that the conditions of labour would be vastly improved and labourers would be returned home from the colony after their term of service (five years)'.[299] Yet with independent evidence that repatriation of workers from the islands to Angola was 'a perfect farce', they concluded they needed their own trusted information from Angola and the islands. So (with the involvement and approval of the Frys) the Board engaged a fellow Quaker, Joseph Burtt, to go to Portugal, learn the language, then travel on to investigate conditions in West Africa.[300]

That process took nearly two years; five years had elapsed since the first indications of slave labour on the islands. Meanwhile a pioneering American journalist, H.W. Nevinson, who had covered the siege of Ladysmith, then the 1905 Russian Revolution, became determined to expose the African slave trade. In articles in *Harper's Monthly Magazine* in 1906 entitled 'The New Slave Trade' he described his 250-mile trek by ox-wagon on the slave route through the interior of Angola, down to the slave port of Benguela, where 4000 slaves a year were transported to the cocoa islands.[301] He chronicled the human remains and discarded manacles, which littered the track, and the inhumane treatment of men and women marched by armed escort to the boats in Benguela harbour. 'Thus it is that England and America can get their chocolate and cocoa cheap,' he witheringly concluded.

Nevinson was to be *Cadbury's* 'nemesis', for he was a knowledgeable, persistent and voluble critic.[302] He was irritatingly persistent in his calls for action, most particularly, for a boycott of Portuguese slave cocoa. William Cadbury, at first prevaricated for he still 'trusted the Portuguese overseers and accepted incremental progress'.[303] By 1907 Nevinson's frustration was growing and he was writing that *Cadbury* was indirectly employing one third of the slaves on the Portuguese cocoa islands; he also found the Foreign Office to be adept at equivocating.[304] George and William Cadbury experienced that official procrastination for themselves in December 1906. While they were still awaiting Burtt's report they arranged to see the Foreign Secretary, Sir Edward Grey, to discuss the cocoa islands. The Board Minutes record: 'Sir Edward Grey asked us to refrain from calling public attention to the subject until he had the report of our commissioner and had had the opportunity to speak to the Portuguese Minister on the subject.'[305] And so a potentially damaging state of affairs first revealed in 1901 remained unresolved in 1906; and now was to continue into 1907.

By 1907 William Cadbury had himself become eager to get going; his correspondence with Burtt reiterates the urgency of having the report 'at the earliest convenient time'. In early 1907 he at last received it, and it made harrowing reading, detailing the death rates (44:1000 on São

Tomé, 110:1000 on Príncipe), and the reasons for this: the tsetse fly, the 'mental distress and hopelessness of young men when separated from their family', the relentless hours of work and the corporal punishment.[306] Burtt and his assistant went on to describe conditions in Angola, providing anecdotal evidence of *serviçais* bought in the slave port of Benguela, of slaves shot by their handlers, and of high mortality on the slave route in the interior. They concluded by highlighting the contrast between the theory, the system of labour laid down by the Portuguese government, and the reality of slavery as it existed in practice.

With the overwhelming evidence of their own specially commissioned report it might be thought that the Cadburys would act immediately. However, they kept the report under wraps to allow discreet pressure applied through diplomatic channels to take effect. As became apparent in the libel trial – to some incredulity in observers – George and William believed it had been agreed at that meeting that they had to wait until Sir Edward Grey contacted them before they could safely publish. He never did. In a speech to the Liverpool Chamber of Commerce in March 1907, William Cadbury gave another reason for caution: he was reluctant to boycott Portuguese cocoa because the company would lose its ability to effect change.[307]

Just a month later George Cadbury was writing to his own editor of the *Daily News*, H.N. Brailsford, who was impatient for a boycott. He said that 'had we taken the course in question we would have been in a far worse position in doing anything on behalf of the natives of Angola', and that after correspondence about a boycott with other firms we found 'we could not'.[308] George Cadbury was also concerned to avoid offending Portugal, for to do so 'would make it impossible for missionaries in Portuguese West Africa to stay at their stations'.[309]

When *The Daily Graphic* carried an article in October 1907 alleging that Cadbury 'make their chocolate and cocoa powder from slave-grown cocoa – they do not appear to care a pin', William Cadbury heatedly replied that 'the Foreign Office expressly requested us NOT to be drawn into newspaper agitation', and called the article libellous. *The Daily Graphic* apologised, saying that 'the three chocolate firms have suffered a grave injustice through their inability to reveal the steps they have taken in the matter'.[310] But the incident undoubtedly affected William Cadbury whose correspondence in 1908 betrays an irritation both with the Foreign Office, which had not yet published Burtt's report, and with the Portuguese (planters and Government) for the methods of recruiting labour in Angola remained unchanged.[311] By the end of 1908, he was quite determined to 'discontinue the present purchase of São Tomé and Príncipe cocoa'.[312]

The Board of Directors resolved in January 1909 'to clear at once all cocoa on order and to have used it up as soon possible' because 'we are quite satisfied that the conditions of labour have not been reformed'.[313] After much havering and delay, the boycott for which observers like Nevinson had agitated was at last a reality. It seems that perhaps the Cadburys privately regretted the length of time it had taken: Gardiner was alleged by Nevinson to have told him that the directors 'agreed how stupidly they had mismanaged the whole thing'.[314] However, it was too late to quiet critical murmurs in the Press.

In September 1908, while William Cadbury was once again on São Tomé, and was locating new supplies of non-slave-grown cocoa on the Gold Coast, the *Standard* published an editorial about which George Cadbury felt so strongly that he sued on behalf of the firm; this time there was to be no retraction. Influenced by Nevinson in its criticisms of the Cadburys, the most offensive of its charges were:

> The white hands of the Bournville chocolate makers are helped by other unseen hands some thousand miles away, black and brown hands, toiling in plantations or hauling loads through swamp and forest. In the plenitude of his solicitude for his fellow creatures Mr Cadbury might have been expected to take some interest in the owners of those same grimed hands. His conscience seemed to be more concerned with Chinese labourers.... And the worst of this slavery and slave driving and slave dealing is brought about by the necessity of providing a sufficient number of hands to grow and pick cocoa on the islands which feed the mills and presses of Bournville.[315]

George and William Cadbury recognised the serious danger to their reputations. They were determined to justify their actions and clear the company of all allegations of hypocrisy. For the *Standard* had pointed out that a company which prided itself on its treatment of Bournville workers, and a managing director (George Cadbury) whose newspaper the *Daily News* led the campaign against Chinese labour in Transvaal, now tolerated slavery in West Africa when it suited it, for commercial purposes.

The libel trial opened on 29 November 1909 in Birmingham, at George Cadbury's request, at the new Victoria Law Courts. It pitted against each other two future Attorney-Generals, Sir Rufus Isaacs for the plaintiffs and Sir Edward Carson for the defence. It played out against the background of the bitter struggle in Parliament over Lloyd George's People's Budget, in which the Conservative-dominated Lords rejected the Liberal government's Finance Bill. Many observers of the trial saw in it reflections of national politics, for here was a Unionist newspaper, the *Standard*, attacking the behaviour of a prominent Liberal, the owner of the *Daily News*. Even the two counsel were partisan, Isaacs Liberal and Carson Unionist. Furthermore, a number of contemporaries wondered if a Birmingham jury could remain immune from the strong influence of Unionism and Chamberlainism in the city, which might be prejudicial to a prominent Liberal's prospects.[316]

Isaacs argued from the trial's opening that the *Standard* should have known about the Cadburys' unswerving dedication to ending slave practices, and that the firm was following the advice of the Foreign Office in not acting precipitately. He showed how the Cadburys had paid for investigations into cocoa growing practices and how William had travelled and researched extensively himself. He was not helped, as he hoped he would be, by the appearance of Grey, who developed a bad case of diplomatic amnesia. Grey was unable to recall details of his meeting with George and William Cadbury in October 1906, or to confirm that he had advised the firm to continue purchasing cocoa while pressure was brought on Portugal.

When his turn came Carson set out to show that the Cadburys had acted slowly on the evidence they had gathered on slave labour, and deliberately discouraged its dissemination to protect the business. In cross-examining William Cadbury, he poured scorn on his version of the meeting he and George had had with Sir Edward Grey, in particular the idea that the Foreign Secretary would remember to ask the Cadburys to stop purchasing cocoa from the islands at 'the appropriate moment'. He said:

'You never took pains to put it down on paper for him? And you expected him to retain the matter in his mind, and drop you a card when he wanted you to give up buying?

'Yes', Cadbury replied.

Carson then focused on the delay in acting on the evidence of slavery.

'Knowing that slavery was atrocious, you took the main portion of your supply of cocoa for the profit of your business from the islands, conducted under this system?'

Cadbury replied: 'Yes, for a number of years.'

Carson: 'You did not look upon this as immoral.'

'Not under the circumstances', Cadbury replied.

Carson: 'As far as I can see in the year 1905 there was nothing done?'

'Probably not.'

Carson: 'Nor anything in 1906 when you saw Sir Edward Grey.'

'No, probably not.'

Carson went on to substantiate the *Standard's* charge of hypocrisy by showing how Quaker families, engaged in acts of philanthropy in England, wished to continue purchasing cocoa; so, in 1904 *Rowntree* warned *Cadbury* 'that a boycott would involve serious pecuniary loss'. He finished his cross-examination of William Cadbury with a devastating final sally:

'Have you formed any estimate of the number of slaves who lost their lives in preparing your cocoa during those eight years?'

'No – No' was the anguished reply.

Observers thought Carson's performance quietly devastating.

He moved on to question the seventy-year-old head of the firm, George Cadbury, altogether less aggressively but it must still have been a considerable ordeal to face one of the most combative and intellectually agile advocates of the age. At the outset George was forced to admit that while 'sentiment' ruled that the firm should stop purchasing Portuguese cocoa, 'common sense' dictated that it continue to do so to influence the Portuguese government to act. George Cadbury complacently added: 'I believe I <u>can</u> say that nearly the whole of the profits since that time have gone to a benevolent fund.' Nevinson, attending the court that day, later wrote: 'I well remember the painful sense of derision with which I and others heard the worthy old man make that irrelevant excuse.'

Carson went on to score a palpable hit when he showed that George Cadbury as principal owner of the *Daily News* 'obviously restricted what (his paper) carried about Portuguese West Africa'. Cadbury was forced to concede that although the paper conducted a determined campaign against Chinese slavery in South Africa, it ran no articles on São Tomé or Príncipe. He admitted that his editor, Brailsford, had threatened to resign if the newspaper remained silent on São Tomé and Príncipe slavery. George's reasoning seemed lame: 'I thought it injudicious because my nephew was risking his life at the time in the islands.'

Carson's summing up at the end of the trial focused on two points. By the high ideals of journalism, the *Standard* was required to reveal the heinous nature of the slavery that had been tolerated by *Cadbury* in order that it continue its profit-making. Secondly, Carson contended *Cadbury* was not an ordinary company. It presented itself as a humanitarian firm: 'They put themselves forward as champions of proper conditions of labour, and they put themselves on a very high pinnacle of public morality.' For eight years, he charged, the firm had supported human exploitation by buying £1.3million worth of cocoa beans, and had continued because it feared that to switch suppliers would be to suffer loss of profits.[317]

The verdict when it came was an extraordinary one. The jury found for *Cadburys* but awarded a derisory farthing's damages.[318] Carson believed that 'the jury were disgusted with the plaintiffs for dealing so long in slave cocoa'. Most of the Birmingham papers, on the other hand, agreed with the *Birmingham Daily Post* when it averred that 'Messrs. Cadbury have always been known as honourable men and so they will continue to be known.'

The waters soon though closed over the trial, for two general elections, the death of a king, and struggles over the powers of the House of Lords formed distractions enough the next year. Yet some damage was done to *Cadbury*; the Cadbury papers contain a file of abusive letters sent – often anonymously – to the firm in an Edwardian form of trolling. Criticism centred on such themes as 'Bournville's slavery', and 'after all your slimy hypocritical cant about Chinese slavery' and 'it took you seven years to make up your consciences'.[319] It must have been especially galling that rivals also made hay, with *Van Houten* complacently advertising that: 'We wish to state that never during eighty-odd years of its existence has any slave-grown cocoa been used in its preparation.'

For George, now in his dotage, the whole episode must have been both painful and draining. More wounding would have been attacks on his integrity, especially on the honesty of his philanthropic endeavours. It is no coincidence that the end of the trial should have been followed so swiftly by his divesting himself of the *Daily News*, for the trial had uncomfortably drawn the *Cadbury* business into wider politics, and his ownership of the paper had been a gift to the defence.

It is a striking coincidence that the scandal engulfing Joseph Chamberlain, like George Cadbury's, came out of Africa. Before exploring the dark recesses of the Jameson Raid which threatened Chamberlain's political survival it is important to set out a simple narrative of what happened.

As we saw in the last chapter, South Africa was host to the competing ambitions of Boer, British Imperial government and Cecil Rhodes's British South Africa Company ('the Company'). The success and wealth of the Boers' Transvaal state was a constant provocation to the British, yet Chamberlain and Rhodes did not see entirely eye-to-eye on how to act accordingly. When Chamberlain assumed office as Colonial Secretary in 1895 he inherited the previous (Liberal) government's policy of encouraging Rhodes's expansion into the area north of the Transvaal – Zambesia, renamed Southern Rhodesia – and into Matabeleland. He also inherited Lord Rosebery's promise that Southern Bechuanaland (now Botswana), to the west of the Transvaal, should be handed over to Cape Colony, British Southern Africa, and that the Northern part of Bechuanaland, the British Protectorate, should pass into Company hands. As soon as Chamberlain was installed in office Rhodes dispatched his associate, Rutherford Harris, to press him to hand over the land, on the grounds that the Bechuanaland Protectorate territory was needed to accommodate a railway from the Cape into Zambesia, the first stage in realising his Cape to Cairo vision. That railway would circumvent and surround the hostile Boer Transvaal republic, threatening it with eventual absorption into British Cape Colony.

Chamberlain was wary of the Company's pretensions and did not immediately concede. He had his own vision of a united South Africa with British South Africa, native protectorates, the Company and Boer Transvaal lands all gathered under British Imperial rule.[320] His reluctance to fall in with Rhodes's plans was fortified by the concurrent arrival in Britain of three Bechuana chiefs – Sebele, Khama and Bathoen – who petitioned Chamberlain on his first day in office that 'they still wish to remain under the government of the Great Queen…. for (they) had heard much of the injustice and oppression which the Chartered Company inflict on the tribes who live in the North (the Matabele) and fear very much lest they should be killed and eaten by the Company'.[321] The three chiefs, dressed in top hats, dark suits, collar and tie, sporting accompanying umbrellas and with a natural grace and courtesy, charmed audiences the length and breadth of Britain.

Perhaps their greatest triumph was in Birmingham where they attended Carr's Lane chapel, visited the *Cadbury* factory at Bournville and then lunched with Richard Cadbury at Uffculme, before travelling on to visit Chamberlain's Highbury home. Both Cadbury brothers approved of the chiefs' fierce disavowal of liquor; the chiefs had written on this point to Chamberlain, before coming to Birmingham, fearing that 'the Company will take our land, sell it to others, and will fill our country with liquor shops like Bulawayo'.[322] In a speech at the Birmingham Town Hall to members of the Missionary, Temperance and Peace societies with Richard Cadbury in the chair, on 27 September 1895, Sebele asked: 'Can it be that we shall be given away in ignorance, the government not knowing the things that they do, because we are not like a man's oxen?'[323]

In November 1895 Chamberlain met the chiefs and Harris, the Company representative, to pronounce on the issue. 'It is necessary the railway be made', he said, 'and we will take the land we want for the railway and no more.' 'The chiefs shall rule their people themselves as heretofore … and each of the chiefs shall have a country within which they shall rule under the protection of the Queen.' In view of later suggestions that Chamberlain and Rhodes were intimate allies, this decision in the chiefs' favour clearly suggests a less amicable relationship. Rhodes was furious when he heard, cabling Harris: 'It is humiliating to be utterly beaten by these niggers.'[324]

Chamberlain's reason for ceding this strip of eastern Bechuanaland between 6 and 10 miles wide (known as the Pitsani Strip) was not only for the railway, but to make the Company responsible for the security of the border region abutting Transvaal. He allowed it to recruit a police force from Imperial officers. He was not unaware that they might be needed, for across the autumn of 1895 rumours circulated of an uprising of the Uitlanders, the embattled foreign settlers in Johannesburg. In fact, he said as much in the Commons in February 1896: 'Practically, I may say that everybody knew about the probabilities of agitation.' 'The (Uitlanders') revolt was an open secret.'[325] Sir Hercules Robinson, the High Commissioner in Cape Town, wrote to him in December 1895 about what he planned to do should 'a revolution' occur in the Transvaal, proposing to issue 'a Proclamation directing both parties to desist and submit to my arbitration', with the aim of transforming by non-violent means a republic into a British colony and of forestalling a Boer appeal to Germany to intervene.[326] Days before Christmas Edward Fairfield, head of the South Africa Department in the Colonial Office, wrote to Chamberlain saying that his source in Rhodes's Company 'advises that Johannesburg will begin to move in about ten days'.[327]

The next he knew, Chamberlain was being informed, just after Christmas, that the zeal for an Uitlander revolt was cooling– 'the gas is out of the balloon'. The news prompted Chamberlain to speculate to Prime Minister Salisbury that 'the Transvaal business is going to fizzle out'.[328] Almost as he wrote this an ominous new development occurred; Fairfield reported to Chamberlain that Rhodes's London solicitor had told him of Rhodes's mounting frustration. 'He thought Rhodes might be driven into frenzy, and unreason, and order Jameson to go in from Gaberones (on the Bechuanaland border) with the Company's police and manipulate a revolution.'[329]

Within hours that eventuality had come to pass and Chamberlain acted instantly. On hearing of the raid of 400 armed horsemen into Transvaal, and recognising that 'If this succeeds it will ruin me', he left his dinner party, boarded the midnight train to London and telegraphed Kruger to repudiate the raid, days before it was clear whether it would prevail. He ordered High Commissioner Robinson to recall Jameson. He then briefed the Press. Subsequently, within a matter of hours Jameson's men were outnumbered, shot down, surrounded and arrested; in sum it comprised a complete fiasco.

Chamberlain's whirlwind of action helped to lessen suspicion of British involvement, and for the next weeks and months his stock rose. His reputation for energy and competence was augmented by his becoming the personification of British resolution when, at the start of the New Year, Kaiser Wilhelm II sent a telegram congratulating Kruger, which was intended to embarrass Britain but only succeeded in rousing its patriotic fervour.

That was not the end of the saga. Jameson had to be dealt with and tried on conspiracy charges in Britain; found guilty, he was jailed in July 1896. Meanwhile, feelings about Rhodes had turned, too; telegrams had been seized from one of Jameson's officers at the end of the raid, which suggested Rhodes's complicity in trying to stir up – manufacture even – the Uitlander revolt in Johannesburg. A Parliamentary inquiry was then initiated to examine uncomfortable questions of complicity; pertinently for Chamberlain, 'to what extent had the Colonial Office been involved in planning an attack on another sovereign power?' Rhodes himself wanted the inquiry buried, and tried – through Bourchier Hawksley, his solicitor – to blackmail Chamberlain into abandoning it. He threatened to reveal the contents of telegrams from Company employees in London to Cape Town, which allegedly deeply implicated Chamberlain in Jameson's plans. Chamberlain faced down the threat. Rhodes later became unwilling either to appear at the Inquiry in 1897, or to allow the telegrams to be released to the Inquiry members, both because they implicated him too, and because Chamberlain had told him that if the telegrams were released the Company's charter would be revoked.[330] Chamberlain's coolness and resilience under intense pressure from a practised bully, Rhodes, is remarkable.

The Select Committee investigating the Jameson incident concluded Rhodes was largely responsible for the plot and judged that – in the absence of proof emerging from the telegrams withheld by Rhodes – 'Mr Chamberlain had no foreknowledge of the Raid, nor of the preparations for the Raid.' 'Your Committee fully accept the statements of the Secretary of State (and of Under-Secretary, Lord Selborne) and entirely exonerate the officials of having been in any sense cognisant of the plans'.[331] It appeared that with one bound Chamberlain was free. From then on he was enabled to put the business to one side and carry on to an apogee of public approbation in the years spanning the Boer War.

Still, even at the time, there were many unconvinced by the Inquiry's official line, mordantly dubbed by John Morley, 'Lying in state'. Although barely months after the raid some observers in South Africa were accusing the British government of complicity, for decades after, most historians were content to accept the version propagated by Chamberlain and Selborne. Only careful re-examination of documents published by Chamberlain's biographer, J.L. Garvin, in 1932, led some critically to scrutinise Garvin's bullish conclusion that 'Chamberlain had not a shadow of complicity in the Raid'.[332] That scrupulous re-examination suddenly made the case against Chamberlain seem embarrassingly persuasive.

Rhodes's Company telegrams raised awkward questions: firstly, did Chamberlain know that the strip of Bechuanaland he had ceded would be used as a jumping-off point for an invasion? After all, one telegram from Harris to Rhodes in early August 1895 says: 'We decided therefore to inform the Sec. of State guardedly (of the) reason we wish to have base at Gaberones (on the Pitsani strip).'[333] Chamberlain must have suspected something nefarious; he metaphorically clapped his hands to his ears so that he could not hear. As he recalled later: 'One of the deputies began to talk of the state of affairs in Johannesburg and of the probability of disturbance. I at once stopped him and said "I do not want to hear about that."'[334] Rhodes's associates thought they understood the game – the story must be officially deniable. So on 21 August a telegram to Rhodes ran: 'You are aware C. states Dr J.'s plan must not be mentioned to him.' Again, later, Harris informed Rhodes: 'Chamberlain will do anything to assist, provided he officially does not know of your plan.'[335]

Another telegram in November informed Rhodes that Harris had seen Edward Fairfield in the Colonial Office saying '... he had spoken open to Fairfield and told him Rhodes required an armed force on Transvaal (borders) in event of disturbance in Jo'burg so it could be used in connection with uprising'.[336] The implication was that Fairfield would have communicated this to his Secretary of State, Chamberlain. Together these telegrams make Chamberlain look dangerously complicit, 'avoiding all connection with the plot, because he favoured it', in the words of H. Winkler, the first revisionist historian to subject the telegrams Garvin quoted to searching analysis in 1949. It certainly does seem incredible that a politician as decisive, controlling and intellectually curious as Joseph Chamberlain remained as ignorant as he claimed of the developing plot through the five months between his appointment as Colonial Secretary and the commencement of the raid.[337]

A second controversial area was the extent to which Chamberlain was involved in determining the timing of action in and around Johannesburg. Chamberlain appears to have urged that action on. So, Harris on 7 November 1895 telegraphed Rhodes to say: 'Sec. of Colonies says you must allow decent interval and delay fireworks for fortnight,' presumably to avoid unseemly haste as Chamberlain had just two days earlier met the chiefs and settled the Bechuanaland strip on the Company. In December 1895, with rumours multiplying that Uitlanders might rise up against their Boer masters, Chamberlain telegraphed Robinson in Cape

Town: 'I take for granted no movement will take place unless success is certain – a fiasco would be disastrous.'[338] Indeed it would.

In the run-up to Christmas 1895 there was an added urgency, for a dispute with Venezuela threatened to draw in the USA too, and Chamberlain was anxious to clear the decks of South African difficulties as soon as possible. He wrote to Fairfield: 'I again repeat the worst time for trouble anywhere would be six months hence. I cannot say that any time would be a good one but can the difficulty be indefinitely postponed?' The next day he reiterated the message to the Permanent Secretary at the Colonial Office, Sir Robert Meade, saying: 'The longer it is delayed, the more chance there is of foreign intervention. It seems to me it should come at once or be postponed for a year at least. Can we ensure this?'[339] Collectively these comprise an implicit message to Rhodes to 'hurry up', a message endorsed by the Colonial Editor of *The Times*, Flora Shaw, an unofficial intermediary between the Colonial Office and Rhodes's Company. She relayed to Rhodes an indiscreet private chat Chamberlain and she had had that December: 'Joe (is) sound in case of interference with foreign powers but have special reason to believe (he) wishes you do it immediately.'

The insistent question is: 'What sort of action ('fireworks') did Chamberlain think he was hurrying up?' Those involved in the plot were sure he approved and took it for granted he was implicated both in the timing of the Uitlander uprising and in Jameson's Raid.[340] Rhodes's lawyer Bourchier Hawksley later wrote to Fairfield in orotund prose: 'It cannot truthfully be denied that certain statements were in fact made to Mr Chamberlain and that certain persons in South Africa were informed that those statements were so made with the result that responsibilities were undertaken in the belief that they were done with the approval of the Imperial authorities.'[341] Chamberlain simply argued he had not heard and had been misunderstood; so he conveniently distanced himself from the Raid when it came.

Yet his behaviour in these months after the raid appears that of a man with much to hide. He tampered with witnesses, as with Flora Shaw, rehearsing with her the story she would be telling the Select Committee about what Chamberlain knew of the raid. Because the High Commissioner would inevitably have had to communicate what he knew to his Colonial Secretary master in London, Chamberlain and his minions persuaded minor officials in the High Commission in South Africa to say that they had kept from Sir Hercules Robinson the intelligence they had gathered about the raid in South Africa. G. Bower and F. Newton sacrificed their careers and carried the can at the Inquiry, for someone had to take the blame. Poor Edward Fairfield at the Colonial Office, so central to communications with Rhodes and his associates, was denigrated by Chamberlain at the Inquiry both for not keeping him informed, and because he was deaf and 'hadn't heard'. [342]

Perhaps the most extraordinary thing was that Chamberlain got himself appointed to the committee engaged in the parliamentary inquiry into the raid. As Travis Crosby caustically observes in a recent biography of Chamberlain, he did so '... not to facilitate (it) but to subvert it. By delay, obfuscation and transparent witness tampering he attempted to defuse the various components of the Transvaal fiasco.'[343] A reading of the Select Committee Report illustrates just how much he dominated proceedings, interrupting witnesses, ensuring his side of the argument was heard, and even leading and coaching witnesses.[344] With such a dominant character on the committee it is not entirely surprising that it found in favour of its most overbearing member.

Ethel Drus, in an influential article, wrote that the charge against Joseph Chamberlain was that '... he was fully informed of the Jameson raid to invade the Transvaal and overthrow its government'.[345] But the truth seems less bald. Firstly, the telegrams need careful handling; they comprise versions of meetings and conversations, and interpretations of Chamberlain's responses recorded by Rhodes's associates for a demanding and impatient master (Rhodes). It is possible Chamberlain really did not understand the guarded allusions of Harris and Grey. One telegram sent to Rhodes in October 1895 about the urgent need for the strip of Bechuanaland territory to facilitate a Raid runs: 'We dare not mention (to JC) the reason'. As Chamberlain noted on the copy of this telegram he had obtained: 'This proves that nearly three months later (i.e. after that August meeting when Harris had hinted of Rhodes's real intentions) the sender was aware I had not been put in possession of the facts.'[346]

It is important to separate the putative Uitlander uprising from the Jameson Raid. Chamberlain's urgings to get on with 'the movement' and hurry up are surely proof enough that he thought Rhodes and his associates were in a position to hasten the rebellion. But as for the raid, his panicked response on hearing the news and his instant demand that Robinson recall Jameson even before the fate of the raid was known, show that he thought Jameson an impetuous maverick who had gone far too far in precipitating the invasion of another country. On this reading his nobbling of witnesses and tampering with evidence was simply the recognition of how incriminating his discussions and his communications would seem after the raid. He was trying – too hard – to tidy up the evidence to ensure the Inquiry was left in no doubt about his fundamental innocence. Flora Shaw told Garvin years later that 'in the conspiracy to make an explosion he played no part'.[347] Earl Grey had also conceded to Chamberlain: 'I most certainly can confirm you when you say you did not know and could not know of any plans or intention of Mr Rhodes, for I did not know myself.'[348]

The last months of 1895 in the Colonial Office were characterised by mysterious allusions, by diplomatic games of smoke and mirrors; it is very possible Chamberlain did not know fully what was being plotted. He admitted to Flora Shaw as much: 'I can hardly say what I knew and what I did not. I did not want to know much. Of course I knew of the precautions, the preparations if you like, in view of the expected trouble in Johannesburg, but I never would have imagined that Jameson would take the bit between his teeth.'[349]

Even if he was not guilty of involvement in the plot, it was not his finest hour. Although at the Inquiry's end Chamberlain had lavishly praised Rhodes, as a 'man of honour' who had made a mistake, he still lived in fear of what yet might emerge from South Africa. Where George Cadbury's slave cocoa tarnished his reputation in some circles, Joseph Chamberlain's embroilment in the Jameson Raid threatened him at one time not merely with temporary embarrassment but with total ruin. In a curious way they were more like each other than one might at first suppose; both men contrived not to know too much of a truth of which they could have asked a great deal more. By remaining incurious they hoped to avoid having to take responsibility.

PRIVATE PASSIONS

This chapter is about the interior lives of two sharply contrasting individuals and the different ways that these manifested themselves in public life. In many ways there was much common ground between the two men. They were both highly significant and influential members of the Birmingham upper-middle-class elite at the end of the nineteenth century. As such they were subject to the same influences of taste, social behaviour and culture, and so they shared similar interests, most particularly with regard to domestic life on the outskirts of Birmingham. Yet, they were two profoundly different people – the serious and religious juxtaposed with the society darling; the man struggling with the guilt and weight of expectation of the very wealthy, as opposed to the man who took real pleasure in the enjoyment of wealth; and the man conscious of an inherited religious and social hinterland, set against the man emancipated from Nonconformist strictures on education, social interaction and behaviour.

For the central point about George Cadbury was that his religion was not a hobby, was not compartmentalised as just one of his interests. It percolated his whole life and evangelism was at its core. This can be seen in his dedicated work with the Adult School and Class XIV where for over fifty years – in his own words – he helped pupils to 'put off the old man and (become) the new man'.[350] Decades later when he spoke as President at the Free Church Council in 1898 he exhorted its members to: 'Go out into the highways and hedges and compel them to come in', directing his focus especially on the country's youth whom he believed to be abandoned and neglected.[351] He fought a long battle to ensure that the Free Church Council remained focused on spiritual matters not on political campaigning, on Gospel propagation to stop the drift away from religion he discerned at the end of the century.

This evangelism was, as for many Nonconformists, but 'the obverse of a spiritual coin on whose reverse was social work, for winning a man's soul meant changing a man – from a drunkard and a spendthrift – and in consequence, changing the social environment, for him and his family'. Cadbury was motivated to act altruistically because his faith taught him 'the importance of mutual aid, of bearing and sharing mankind's burdens'.[352] It explains George Cadbury's zeal in a multitude of causes ranging from school-building, workers' housing, further education, crippled and sick children, sweated workers, and the dispossessed.

Joseph Chamberlain, as we have seen, first became involved in public life when convinced of the inadequacies of public education and the horrors of an unsanitary urban environment; thereafter he placed social reform at the forefront of his political prospectus. But his motivation was very different from George Cadbury's. Brought up a Unitarian, and in a particularly rationalist branch of the creed, he was to abandon what little faith he had after personal tragedy.[353] The death of his second wife, Florence, in 1875 in Peter Marsh's words '... tore him loose from his Unitarian religious convictions', for Chamberlain wrote to his then close friend, John Morley: 'I refuse to try and buy comfort by forcing myself into insincere conviction.'[354]

Later, Beatrice Webb recorded a revealing conversation about declining faith in which she said to him: 'It seemed to me that part of the Englishman's nature which has found gratification in religion is now drifting into political life.' He answered: 'I quite agree with you and I rejoice in it. I have always had a grudge against religion as absorbing the passion in man's nature.'[355] The result of his rejecting the religion with which he grew up can be seen in protean ways: in his irritation with hard-line Nonconformist agitation against Balfour's Education Act, in his support for the foundation of non-sectarian Edgbaston High School for girls and for Anglican Rugby School which educated his sons, in the ease and comfort he showed in high Anglican society and in his unabashed enjoyment of his wealth once ensconced in Highbury.

While it is true that the brand of Unitarianism he adhered to as a young man was characterised by rationalism, reflected in an interest in social analysis and in finding practical solutions to society's problems, the fact is that the mature Chamberlain developed his own secular religion in which social conditions, like bad housing, inadequate sanitation and polluted water were the source of sin (not an absence of the Gospel) and legislation – the power of the state – was the means by which people were improved.[356]

Cadbury, on the other hand, never abandoned the Quakerism into which he was born. He was in his last years the country's leading Quaker. His faith coloured all his social and familial relationships, determining his own and his children's marriages, the education of his sons (at Leighton Park, the new Quaker school), the guests he invited to Woodbrooke and The Manor, and his circle of friends. His central role in a regional network of Quaker contacts not only reinforced a certain unintentional exclusivity but it helped consolidate the national business connections of a small minority sect.[357] Still, he had a horror of an ossified, stringently orthodox faith which failed to move with the times, and his claim to national eminence in Quaker ranks rests on his success in transforming English Quakerism into an altogether more dynamic and outward-looking creed, less concerned with matters of dress and old formalities of speech ('thee' and 'thou') and more responsive to the profound social problems of the time. He brought about changes in the form of service augmenting the traditional Quaker silence with hymn, scripture reading, and sermon, and by so doing he injected a new vitality to the faith's formularies.

His biographer quotes George Cadbury speaking in 1897 at an annual meeting of the Friends and saying that: 'We have dwelt too much on looking inward instead of lifting up our eyes.'[358] And that sense of regret and a missed opportunity explains the burst of creative energy harnessed in the foundation of the five Selly Oak Colleges at the start of the twentieth century, the first of which was Woodbrooke, which he established with the express purpose of 'combining a spirit of reverent and frank enquiry, with a practical devotion to social service'. Woodbrooke, on Birmingham's doorstep, would provide a forum and a base for developing a 'multitude of experiments in social amelioration, which could be studied (in the city) on a large scale'. This was the first of a number of practical steps to focusing religion and the religious on effective and workable solutions to society's many problems and to professionalising the church's response. So, West Hill was established to train Sunday school teachers so that they could adequately educate their young charges; and Kingsmead was founded properly to equip missionaries with the religious, anthropological and geographical knowledge effectively to take the Gospel message abroad.[359]

The point about West Hill and Kingsmead is that they were non-denominational, reflecting George Cadbury's impatience with the doctrinaire squabbles of the different Christian denominations. Instead, he developed excellent relations with the Anglican bishop of Birmingham, Dr Gore, and with Cardinal Newman. He gave land on the Bournville estate for the foundation of an Anglican church; he also contributed generously to the Salvation Army, greatly approving its practical response to poverty. His ecumenicism was given impetus by the results of a religious census he had sponsored in Birmingham in November 1892.[360] It found that only 42.4% of the population in total attended church, and over half of churches and chapels had congregations barely approaching 50% of capacity; many people in working-class inner Birmingham never attended church at all.

What concerned George Cadbury was the unproductive competition between Nonconformist churches. Division deflected churchmen from applying Christianity to the very real problems of the poor and the oppressed, the ill-housed and the neglected. He wanted 'cordial cooperation for social ends'. The eventual result of his project to promote church unity was the National Free Church Council in 1895, of which he was first president – and a significant financial backer. Its aim was to promote a new parish-style structure, with individual Nonconformist churches responsible for spreading the Word and tackling the dearth of spirituality in a defined area, with particular regard to winning young people to the church. It had shocked Cadbury that 9 out of 10 children who had attended Sunday schools thereafter belonged to no church at all. Different denominations were to work together on this mission.

George Cadbury's faith was expressed in his daily life. His belief in the efficacy of prayer was translated from his own personal devotions to morning prayers in his household and to his work people with the morning assemblies at Bournville. His religion determined his attitude to drink, to dancing and to hunting. It coloured his attitude to society – he maintained a cool distance from London society, from grand dinners and from Court and conventions like 'coming out' for his daughters. More importantly, his beliefs determined his attitudes to wealth and to charitable giving. He and his brother Richard each left over £1m and over and above that it is calculated that George Cadbury had already given away over £500,000 to a variety of good causes, a sum matched only by Josiah Mason in this period in Birmingham.[361] For this was the age of low taxation, of great disparities in wealth, and the era of the philanthropist.

He would have absolutely concurred with Gladstone who argued that the possession of wealth carried an obligation to give lavishly to the poor and unfortunate.[362] For he was indeed lavish; in all modesty he told Dr Gore, in a letter in 1906, that: 'I have for many years given practically the whole of my income for charitable purposes.'[363] Those charitable purposes encompassed working men's institutes (Stirchley and Selly Oak), the gift of land for the Bournville Trust, the building of schools and meeting houses on the Bournville estate, the money he gave to Birmingham Children's Hospital and the Birmingham Cripples' Union, the land he donated for children's recreation areas in Birmingham, Woodbrooke and the other Selly Oak Colleges, financing the London Missionary Society's project in Papua New Guinea, funding the Anti-Sweating League, the Birmingham religious census, the Band of Hope and the Free Church Council, benefactions to the Salvation Army, help for Leighton Park and – for he saw it as a charity which helped the working man – a sum for the foundation of the Labour Party. And that is but a partial list.

He even joined with his political adversary Joseph Chamberlain, at the height of their differences over the Boer War, when together they helped raise money in 1902 to rescue the Birmingham Rowton House scheme, an organisation to provide shelter, a bed and the basics of life for the city's down-and-outs.[364] Yet this was a rarity. Chamberlain did not give a large percentage of his wealth in philanthropy. Firstly, his wealth was a small fraction (perhaps one tenth) of Cadbury's; he left about £125,000 on his death. In any case he had a very different attitude to private philanthropy. He wrote near the start of his national career in politics that 'more can be done by Act of Parliament than by all the private charity and individual beneficence of the upper and middle classes', and he remained consistent in that view to the end.[365] His biographer acidly observed that after his third marriage, 'though he gave little to charity, he lavished jewels on Mary'.[366] Unlike George Cadbury, Joseph Chamberlain did not have a faith which determined the way he responded to pressing social issues. Thoroughly rational, and entirely convinced of the efficacy of politics, he looked to legislative action to solve the country's problems not to the whim and the generosity of the wealthy individual.

A further expression of Cadbury's generosity can be seen in the extent of his entertaining in the grounds of firstly Woodbrooke, where children of the Birmingham poor were entertained to tea in their hundreds, then after 1894 in the extensive estate of The Manor, Northfield. He annually hosted some 25,000 guests at the barn he built for the purpose; but it was as much the fresh air, the grounds, the baths and the games he organised that attracted visitors unused to the space and freedom he offered. Joseph Chamberlain opened the gardens of Highbury to a different class of people, and in a much less philanthropic vein. His guests included local and London political contacts as well as family and friends, and from Easter through the summer his house parties offered croquet and tennis and the famous hothouses and gardens as diversions. Mary Chamberlain's At Homes, social occasions of over 500 guests designed to repay the legion of 'calling' cards she received, were dwarfed by garden parties like that of the West Birmingham Liberal Unionist Association which rewarded 5-6000 loyal political allies, by his very final garden party for his constituents in 1914 when 4000 people came, and by the Moseley and King's Heath Horse Show and the Moseley Flower Show, which in a quasi-feudal sense reinforced the Chamberlains' local eminence.[367]

If in the nature and purpose of their guest-lists they differed, with regard to the rationale and the character of their new houses and estates, Cadbury and Chamberlain had much in common. Reference has been made elsewhere in this book to our two subjects' various property transactions and eventual purchase of Highbury and The Manor. The editor of *The Villa Gardener* magazine in 1870, long before their respective moves to these estates, identified a national social truth: that of 'our well-to-do population's movement outwards from the turmoil and din of a busy city or town life to the free air of the country and the pretty villa'.[368] The attraction of a suburban location for both was that they could continue to engage in business and social activities in the city while at the same time adopting a lifestyle which aped that of the rural gentry. Both of them uprooted themselves to gain space and larger estates. For the philosophical George Cadbury, it was all of a piece for it reflected the same faith in the spiritual benefits of reconnection with the natural world which underpinned his vision of a

Garden City at Bournville (see chapter 3). Both families followed a similar pattern of repeatedly moving to preserve that rural idyll, escaping a city which remorselessly pushed outwards. So Richard Cadbury moved from Moseley Hall to Uffculme, George Cadbury from Woodbrooke a mile further out to The Manor in Northfield, and Joseph Chamberlain, from Southbourne further out into the country at King's Heath, where he built Highbury. George's sons fled Birmingham entirely for the Lickey Hills.[369]

In 1895 the Chamberlains were agitated by the news of the erection of a row of small houses on the Grange Estate, on the far side of the railway line marking the southern boundary of the Highbury estate in King's Heath; they would overlook Highbury and interrupt their unbroken views of rural Worcestershire.[370] It prompted a flurry of tree planting to mask the unsavoury sight.[371] Even George's saintly brother Richard strove to maintain a rural privacy at Uffculme, building a wall along the road, which ensured that his favourite vista across the valley to the Lickey Hills and Rednal was preserved for personal enjoyment, unsullied by the public.[372] There seems to have been a fastidious desire in them all to avoid daily, visible reminders of the unseemly objects of their philanthropy.

George Cadbury and Joseph Chamberlain both built houses exemplifying a fashionable late nineteenth-century revulsion against Victorian Gothic. Where Highbury was built from scratch, The Manor was a 1750 farm homestead remodelled to Cadbury's taste, heavily influenced by the Arts and Crafts movement with mock-Tudor timber framing, tiled elevations, and, inside, lavish use of oak panelling in the Jacobean style. Its vernacular was that of Bournville Village. The total costs of house, and estate of nearly 100 acres with its long tree-lined avenue and parkland and large pond were, at around £16,000, under half what Joseph Chamberlain was to expend on Highbury (£35,000).[373] Birmingham's favourite civic architects William Martin and J.H. Chamberlain (no relation) were employed to build for the latter's namesake a grand house in the same Venetian Gothic style adopted in the city's new public buildings, where 'it was the brand of the Civic Gospel'.[374]

A Venetian style was a conscious reminder that Birmingham's civic values echoed those of the great marine republic. No expense was spared, inside or out, even if the décor did not appeal to all. Beatrice Webb wrote in February 1886 that '... inside there is very much taste and all very bad. At first you admire the bright softness of the colour and the general luxurious comfort of the rooms and furniture but after four and twenty hours the whole palls on you and you long for a bare floor and a plain deal table.'[375] This beside, Highbury was primarily 'built to enhance the impression that a man of immense political importance was to be found inside it'.[376] Indeed, in calling it 'Highbury' to recall his London roots he was consciously suggesting that 'his seat should command attention from the perspective of London as well as Birmingham'.[377] Thereafter, it was very much the expression of an industrialist who had made his money innovating; so, Chamberlain employed the latest technologies for heating the house (and the all-important conservatory and near-by hothouses, which in themselves were a marvel of new glass and metal developments) and it seems was the first person in Birmingham to introduce electricity to his home in 1888.[378] As we will see, this openness to new ideas would be reflected in his introduction of new plant species, of new structures for the garden, and (with Austen) of innovations in animal husbandry on the estate. In the same way George Cadbury, whose successful business had been built on scientific management, was equally alert to its application to his model farm.

Unlike The Manor, Highbury was designed specifically with entertainment in mind. Mary Chamberlain (his third wife) early in her marriage excitedly wrote to her mother, back in America: '... this is a charming house for a ball, for the Hall is just the place for it and so large that a great many people can be disposed of. What with the Drawing Room, Boudoir, Breakfast Room, Conservatory and Fernery and Dining Room there are plenty of places' (for entertaining over 200 guests). She also said that the invasion of conservatory plants in the house added to a sense of theatre: '... the long corridor with its festoons of creepers and flowering vines is extremely pretty and when lighted at night is mysteriously effective.'[379] This then was the backdrop for extensive socialising, hosting local worthies such as Robert Dale and Henry Crosskey (important ministers in Birmingham), aristocrats, and political allies like the Duke of Devonshire, John Bright and Sir Charles Dilke.

Joseph Chamberlain revelled in the social perquisites which accompanied his rise from civic mayor to national statesman. He and Mary enjoyed visits to the Queen at Windsor, dinners with the Prince and Princess of Wales, balls and dinner parties in London, weekends in aristocratic country houses, and they reciprocated as hosts back in Birmingham. A profile in 1885 entitled 'Society in London' before he married Mary, dubbed him 'the chief lion and ornament', a man comfortable 'at some of the most eligible houses in the capital', where he charmingly excelled in the gossip, political chat and mild flirtations which were meat and drink at such occasions.[380] When he hosted his gentlemen's dinners, or larger entertainments, there were few signs of a Nonconformist aversion to drink or to tobacco. Indeed, wine and whisky flowed, and guests and family smoked both in company and alone (Joseph often repairing to his study for a cigar, or occasionally a cigarette, barely with a break, and Austen and Neville smoking heavily in a room an observer called 'a shrine to My Lady Nicotine').[381]

Although it is true that George Cadbury relented in his abhorrence of tobacco, building a smoking room at Winds Point (his Malvern retreat), The Manor was still teetotal. In a more fundamental sense he differed from his Highbury rival; although extremely wealthy, he did not live as a plutocrat, and he did not utilise his money in the pursuit of high social position, or engage in frenetic social competition. Membership of the Society of Friends dictated he and his brother pursued a simpler lifestyle and eschewed many of the attractions of the Birmingham and London social scene. His first wife, Mary Tylor, shy and retiring, had done nothing to encourage George Cadbury out into society, and for a number of years after his second marriage, to Elizabeth, he remained averse to dining out in society, just occasionally accepting invitations to large-scale entertainments, the rare At Home and Royal Garden Party. At The Manor they did entertain Bournville visitors, the occasional political ally like Lord Runciman, they hosted large Quaker gatherings like that of over fifty Friends in 1903 which planned the Quaker College, and they returned hospitality dispensed on Elizabeth's social calls with summer garden parties from 1905 onwards.[382] Tea tents visibly established the difference from Highbury's tolerance of drink. For the prevailing style of Cadbury

Birmingham celebrates Chamberlain's many achievements over 30 years representing the town as an MP.

A cartoon mocks Chamberlain's autocratic approach to politics, the 'Birmingham Method'.

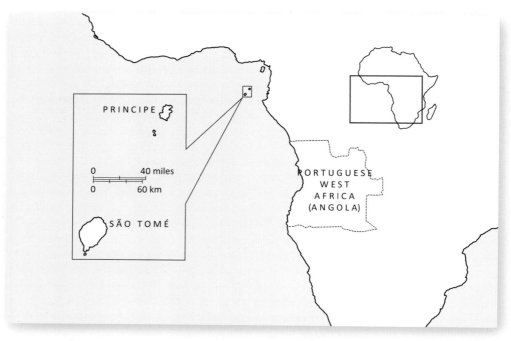

Location of Portuguese cocoa islands São Tomé and Príncipe.

LINED UP ON THE PIER AT SAN THOMÉ

Lined up on the pier at São Tomé. Illustration from *A Modern Slavery*, Nevison's 1906 book about cocoa growing.

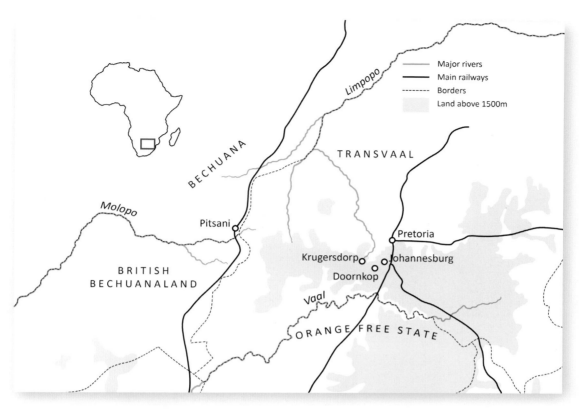

The Pitsani strip, a key strategic area on the Bechuanaland/Transvaal border, ceded by the British Government to the British South Africa Company in 1895 for the building of a railway. One month later, Jameson launched his raid towards Johannesburg from there.

Jameson leads his 400 mounted troops into the Transvaal on his ill-fated raid.

Highbury, the estate Joseph Chamberlain built for himself south-west of Birmingham.

Joseph Chamberlain in the study at Highbury, his centre of operations.

Woodbrooke, the Selly Oak estate George Cadbury first rented then purchased.
View of the south side from the garden, 1885.

George Cadbury, the keen gardener.

Cadburys host King George V and Queen Mary at Bournville in 1919.

Tens of thousands celebrate Chamberlain's 70th birthday in July 1906.

Joseph Chamberlain and his third wife, Mary Endicott.

The Chamberlain family: Neville (standing left), Austen (centre), Beatrice (seated left) join Mary and Joseph, on the right.

George and Elizabeth Cadbury.

George and Elizabeth Cadbury and their growing family: George Junior is standing left, Edward to the right.

entertainment was that of Quaker hospitality for family, Friends and philanthropic causes. Only in 1919 did George Cadbury overcome his Quaker reservation about dancing, and The Manor then hosted forty of his younger son Laurence's friends to music and dancing.

Beyond the important matter of entertaining, the two houses were bases from which both men pursued their disparate interests. For Chamberlain politics, letter writing and researching policy absorbed him; he read widely. So, mornings at Highbury were often spent in his study, and that study served as his political base.[383] The Kenricks (especially Archibald, his father-in-law), had done much to shape his wider tastes, supporting his jousts in the Edgbaston Debating Society, introducing him to the Triennial Music Festival which, though himself unmusical, he continued to patronise and support decades later, and as we shall see below, developing in him a life-long passion for gardening.[384] They also collected Pre-Raphaelite paintings and perhaps it is not too fanciful to suggest that Highbury's colour and hectic detailing was influenced by tastes Chamberlain formed when in the Kenrick circle. His interest in art can be seen in the encouragement he gave to his friend Jesse Collings' foundation of Birmingham's new Art Gallery in 1885. His concerns extended to the dramatic arts too for he and Mary were enthusiastic patrons of the Birmingham Theatre.

Although he had a large estate with scope to ride and walk – and as a young man he climbed the Matterhorn in 1858 – he developed an aversion to strenuous physical exercise. His children rode horses stabled at Highbury, Austen played tennis and became president of the local Wake Green Tennis Club, but Chamberlain's exercise was more modest, generally consisting of steady walks around the hothouses and the gardens abutting the house. In this and in so much else he differed radically from George Cadbury.

The latter took a conventionally Quaker attitude to culture in his lack of interest in the arts. Although his brother installed an organ at Uffculme, music only gradually entered George's home through the efforts of his wife Elizabeth, who employed an orchestra and brass band for a garden party for the first time in 1905. Nor was he a reader, Gardiner recording that '... his intimacy with the Bible was extraordinary. It was the one work of Literature that really appealed to him. Imaginative work, whether poetry or fiction, was outside his intellectual interest.'[385] So, he did not spend mornings reading in the study. He was much more likely to be taking physical exercise. We saw in chapter 1 how as young directors at Bridge Street and at Bournville, Richard and George relished games of football and cricket with employees, and how central to creating the ideal of a sober, healthy and productive workforce were the Bournville works athletics clubs and facilities.

George never lost that enthusiasm, and The Manor estate had a seven-hole golf course, tennis courts, informal cricket and hockey pitches in one of the paddocks, a lake for boating and fishing and stables to enable the Cadburys to ride. Where Chamberlain's physical activity shrunk to strolling around his hothouses and flowerbeds, Cadbury in his 70s invariably walked to the top of Herefordshire Beacon from his second home in the Malvern Hills, a demanding early morning climb. He communicated that relish for physical activity to his children, encouraging them to be proficient in riding, tennis, golf, swimming, rowing and even – though he himself had no taste for it – shooting, and surprisingly he put up little opposition to

Laurence's big game hunting in Alaska.[386] But on this much he and Chamberlain were as one; neither liked field sports, Chamberlain putting up steady – if ultimately unsuccessful – resistance to daughter Ida's desire to ride to hounds, which she eventually did at Bromsberrow.

In reality George Cadbury and Joseph Chamberlain shared more than a mutual distaste for the Hunt. For both ran sizeable estates, developed model farms, and had a passion for their gardens. At The Manor we are told by Gardiner that George Cadbury, for all that he had a farm bailiff, took his farming activities very seriously:

> Both at Woodbrooke and The Manor he carried on experimental farming. The home farm developed into a considerable enterprise, and George Cadbury took hardly less interest in demonstrating the effect of good conditions on the health and productiveness of cattle than he did in the influence of environment on workpeople. His cattle sheds and pigsties were models of sanitation and common sense, applied to farming. (It was) not a hobby but it too was an object lesson.[387]

The object lesson was more in how, like his employees at Bournville, decently housed livestock would produce a higher yield, rather than it was in the adoption of new technologies. Until the First World War he did not introduce any mechanical innovations, only in 1915 buying haymaking and milking machines. But the important thing to note is how seriously he applied a methodical, business-like attitude to his dairy, pig and poultry farming, 'even if it never amounted to fully commercialised agricultural production'.[388] He clearly found it difficult to leave behind at the factory gates the business methods he had refined in establishing and developing *Cadbury's* chocolate and cocoa production when he went home, and the farm was a fulfilling and challenging diversion.

At Highbury a similar seriousness of purpose is evident in the creation of its model farm. First the land had to be found and in a nice irony the 42 acres, which Joseph Chamberlain added to the estate, were leased from a Cadbury, Richard in 1894. His Uffculme estate abutted Highbury. With over 70 acres, 18 of which comprised house and gardens, there was now the opportunity and space for Joseph Chamberlain to indulge in some serious farming. Whilst he himself was interested and encouraging, his role was as financier – in 1894 he allocated an annual budget of £500 for the farm. It was to be his elder son Austen's responsibility. From 1888 Austen had set out to make a serious study of agriculture to such good effect that when his farm was visited by Professor Long of Cirencester in 1894, the Professor wrote in *The Times*: 'Mr Chamberlain is not only informed agriculturally but working upon thoroughly sound and advanced lines'. Austen, he judged, unlike many hobby farmers, had followed methods dictated by 'scientific observation and research of the past few years'.[389]

It was apparent to the family that not only was 'Austen infatuated with his pigs', but that 'he cannot exist long without the farm'. Joseph's correspondence shows his own engagement in the farm, including references to the birth of Highbury's (39) lambs in 1895 while Austen's letters detail the purchase of cows, the improvement of the herd, butter production and milk yields, the slaughter of sheep and geese. By and large the farm was supplying the needs of the household, and the demand was voracious, given the extent of the Chamberlains' entertaining. Still, meat (beef, pork, lambs, geese) and hay surplus to Highbury household needs was sold at the market. Austen wrote to brother Neville, marooned on his sisal plantation overseas, to tell him at Christmas in 1891 that a monster pig had been sold at a Gooch Street butcher's shop and it had been labelled 'bred and fed by the Rt. Hon. J. Chamberlain', drawing a sizeable crowd.[390]

As it was for George Cadbury, Austen's enterprise was 'a leisure occupation based upon business and scientific principles'. Austen's solicitousness about the accommodation for his Jersey herd (his sister Beatrice called it the cows' 'new palace') and his careful monitoring of the feed to ensure maximum nutritional value and yield, all echo *Cadbury's* methods. But his purchase of the best milk separation machinery, butter-making plant and chick incubation technology in the early 1890s show a quicker apprehension than George Cadbury of the value of investing in innovatory machinery. However, in sum it all comprised a thoroughgoing professionalism which went beyond mere hobby farming.

Interestingly, just as we have seen that George Cadbury had hoped his farm would be seen as an 'object lesson' so, using the identical phrase, Professor Long concluded his 1894 article with the hope that Austen Chamberlain's suburban hobby farm would provide an 'object lesson' for ordinary smallholders.[391] Sad to relate, Austen's burgeoning political career from 1895, then his father's stroke, and his own marriage, brought about a fading of interest in the farm; Ida and her sisters could not sustain the energy levels or the involvement after 1906, and the model farm lost its exemplary reputation. The Manor, on the other hand, did not suffer from the loss of its energising force and its model farm continued for over twenty years to absorb its owner.

In reality, Highbury's great attraction for Joseph Chamberlain was not the model farm. It and the estate as a whole made a statement in a modest way about the arrival of a successful industrialist in the ranks of the landowning classes. That aside, what really absorbed him was floriculture and garden design. Harriet Kenrick, his first wife, had fostered his interest; in 1861 she wrote to his mother: 'Joe is developing a fine taste for gardening and I believe he will shortly take it entirely out of my hands. As it is he waters with a vigour that promises well for the future and pruning is second nature to him.'[392] It seems entirely unsurprising that vigorous excision would suit the radical politician. A burgeoning gardening literature in the second half of the nineteenth century sought to articulate the attraction and the value of gardening, and the hardworking statesman would have recognised the truth of the *New Penny Handbook's* assertion that '... the mind insensibly relaxes its nervous tension by contact with the peaceful and regular operation of nature; habits of observation and reflection are induced and fostered'.[393]

In a number of ways Chamberlain's gardening at Highbury reflects the character of the man. When he had a new political cause he absorbed himself in its detail and made himself thoroughly expert. So he became an authority on his passions too, the visiting Lady Dorothy Neville commenting that 'the host's knowledge of botany renders a walk there (at Highbury) instructive as well as pleasant for there is not much of orchids that is unknown to him'.[394] He went into orchids in a serious way; Highbury boasted 25 hothouses, of which 14 were dedicated to the cultivation of a collection which was renowned in its day, so much so that he appointed the two head gardeners, who led his team of 18, from Kew Gardens.

New varieties, and prize-winning examples were grown; for instance, silver medals from the Royal Horticultural Society in 1897 and 1898 were awarded for his orchids, while he generally shared the orchid prizes at the Birmingham Botanical Gardens exhibition. Yet they came at a cost, the *Moseley and King's Heath Journal* reporting in 1894 that Chamberlain placed a single order for orchids to the value of £1800. For they were very much a rich man's hobby, a visiting journalist at Highbury in 1899 being appalled that 'three fleshy fingers were valued at £10'.[395] Chamberlain clearly treasured them for their beauty, and was fulfilled by the challenge of propagating a difficult species. He daily sported their flamboyant showiness in his buttonhole; the orchid became his signature, as the cigar was to be for Winston Churchill. A twice-weekly supply of flowers was sped from Highbury to 4 Prince's Gate, his London home when he was in town. He quite evidently relished the flashiness of conspicuous consumption, the flaunting of wealth, which their cultivation represented.

There was more to Highbury than orchids. The gardens and hothouses displayed varieties of bamboo, tropical ferns and magnolias from the East and the eclectic mix reflected the owner's own imperial vision. P.D. Ballard in her article 'Rus in Urbe' on Joseph Chamberlain's gardens concludes that 'the development of the Highbury grounds indicates the more dynamic qualities of a garden where new ideas culled from a variety of sources could be introduced'.[396] So for example Highbury's evolution saw the creation of a Dutch garden of 1901 with tulips, and daffodils planted in broad naturalised sweeps. It was inspired by a visit to the Continent, as one suspects was the later Italian garden dubbed 'The Pleasaunce', with its dwarf cypresses and its Sienese cast-iron gates.

When he followed fashion, and built a rockery, he was praised by a contemporary critic for avoiding the pitfalls to which so many succumbed, that is of 'making very much rockery and very little garden'.[397] Once again one sees reflected in his horticulture his characteristic desire to do things properly. However, it was not that Highbury was simply about flowers; Chamberlain valued his kitchen gardens, which provided asparagus, peas, salad, celery, melons and cucumbers for the table, and his hothouse vines. Some of the produce was sophisticated and exotic compared to George Cadbury's vegetable and fruit cultivation. Beyond the succession of gardens to which he added in the years before his stroke, the Elizabethan garden and the last, the tea garden, the grounds were used both for farming and for parkland, conspiring to conjure that image of a wealthy gentleman's country estate which he craved. At their peak the gardens he laid out were magnificent, 'arguably the most elaborate of the many gardens created by Birmingham industrialists and professional men in the late nineteenth century and, due to Chamberlain's high political profile, widely written about'.[398]

George Cadbury's interest in gardening started much earlier than had Chamberlain's, whose horticultural education only really commenced with his first marriage. For George was a small boy when 'working in (his own) gardens, helping with gathering fruit, top and tailing gooseberries and shell peas, (competing with his brothers) seeing who could fill a basin first', records Helen Cadbury Alexander in her biography of Richard, her father.[399] Gardiner augments this Edenic portrait, writing that:

(His) happiest memories were of summer evenings when he sat at his mother's knee at the window looking out over the garden while she read aloud. Thus he was never satisfied with any housing scheme unless it provided the worker with a vegetable patch, but with a bit of ground that could be made into a thing of beauty adjoining the cottage. He was not insensible to the practical value of a garden, but it was its use in cultivating the mind and feeling of the child that appealed to him most.[400]

These early influences shaped his later attitude to gardening. He highly valued spade horticulture, writing that 'one acre of garden ground will produce twelve times as much food as one acre under pasture'. So The Manor, like Highbury, had productive vegetable gardens. He cultivated flowers, even if he never rivalled Chamberlain, for he had one small orchid house; he certainly did not challenge Chamberlain's eminence in the big flower shows. It may be that the flower beds at The Manor were Elizabeth's responsibility for, in line with a number of contemporaneous female writers, at Bournville he certainly saw the flower garden as a woman's domain. Although it wasn't his central concern and he did not reach the professional standards of his Highbury rival, he evidently loved the flowers grown in the gardens, wearing the undemonstrative cornflower in his buttonhole to symbolise his belief that 'the love of flowers leads to the love of all natural and wholesome things'.[401] By the same token he invariably distributed flowers from his gardens to men from his Adult Class and to visiting children. Still, the abiding impression is that for George Cadbury it was the productive capacity of The Manor estate which really interested him.

Highbury and The Manor were shaped and animated by the forceful spirits that created them. For decades they provided congenial and stylish semi-rural settings for the political, philanthropic and agricultural activities of their owners. Although Elizabeth Cadbury would continue her husband's work at The Manor into the early 1950s, the Chamberlains by contrast could not afford to maintain a costly estate on Joseph's death in 1914, a combination of loss of income, disappointing investments and Mary's inability to economise sealing its fate.[402] The breaking up of the hothouses and the sale of the house soon after is a sadly anti-climactic note on which to finish. At least the house survives, managed by the Highbury Trust. The Manor suffered more, being demolished in 2015 after an arson attack the previous year, a thoroughly bathetic ending for a significant piece of Birmingham history.[403]

CHAPTER NINE

FAMILY AND DYNASTY

Both our subjects had large families, for that was the pattern for the prosperous in Victorian England, often as insurance in an age of higher mortality. Joseph Chamberlain was married three times and had six children from his first two marriages. George Cadbury fathered eleven children with his two wives. They both suffered the grief of losing young wives in childbirth, events which hardened and temporarily desensitised Chamberlain. Both men, strong characters, had a profound effect on their children, most especially on the careers of their sons who dutifully – and with great success – followed the paths their fathers had determined for them. It is not possible to write about the lives of all seventeen children; so, the wartime exploits of Laurence Cadbury and Beatrice Chamberlain, and the considerable professional and voluntary work of other siblings, cannot be given their due here. Instead, the focus will be on the significant work of the older Cadbury sons and Chamberlain's two political heirs; and on the two surviving wives of long-standing, Mary Chamberlain and Elizabeth Cadbury.

The success of both these marriages can be attributed to the fortunate fact that each absolutely fulfilled the contrasting functions their markedly different husbands sought from a wife. Not unnaturally Mary Chamberlain and Elizabeth Cadbury were very different in temperament and in outlook. Joseph Chamberlain by the mid-1880s had firm views on the role of a wife. Florence Kenrick, his second wife, had been a political partner and had helped develop in him advanced views on the role of women.[404] Yet, a decade later he had changed and Beatrice Webb wrote in frustration: '... the simple way he assumes, almost asserts that you stand on a level far beneath him and that all that concerns you is trivial.... And if I married him I should become a cynic as regards my own mental life. I should either destroy my intellectual individuality or I should become a mere observer.'[405]

In America, and in Mary Endicott, Joseph Chamberlain found a beautiful young woman (just 23 years old) who would play the appointed part for him. For in the letters he wrote her, when courting her across the Atlantic, he had clearly regressed in his attitude to the role of women. 'The details of policy and modes of action are for men to settle, (if) the principles which underlie our work are sometimes clearer to the pure in heart than to the well-worn conscience of the politician and man of the world.' This was the sentiment of a typical nineteenth-century anti-suffragist for whom women were the morally pure sex, 'the Angels of the house', best suited to the domestic sphere where they would remain unsullied by the world's harsh realities.[406] Indeed Chamberlain wrote to Mary of his loathing 'for the odious crew of (suffragist) strong minded women all of them more or less unsexed'.[407] It seems Mary and the rest of the household agreed with him. Austen would later write of 'how my soul revolts' against the suffragette movement 'and all it means in politics and social life'.[408] Unsurprisingly, Mary promised to obey Joseph when taking her wedding vows, and for Chamberlain this was entirely natural, for the man's relationship to the woman was as 'her guide and counsellor'.[409]

Mary proceeded to be the wife he hoped she would be. She was supportive politically. 'She was always with him, but never spoke on her own. She made no speeches, asked for no votes.'

She listened when he talked. She followed the debates in the Commons, observed a friend, Diana Whitehall Laing.[410] As Mary Chamberlain explained herself: 'A woman can use her good influence behind the scenes in her home (rather) than in jostling about in the world of men.'[411] In truth, in the politically traumatic and hectic months before his stroke in 1906, she became more active, as her husband's political secretary, even briefing his close allies on the outlook for Tariff Reform. Furthermore, she did what a lady of her class would do in the way of voluntary work, being for a time a vice-president of the Colonial Nursing Association. Yet, for most of the previous twenty years she had had a different role, that of beautiful society hostess at Highbury. She had undergone an excellent apprenticeship for this in the Endicott home, for her family was steeped in American patrician politics and in the accompanying entertaining.

In contrast to Elizabeth Cadbury her interests were not charitable and socially reformative; instead, the letters back to her mother have a good deal about wedding gifts, jewels, clothes and entertaining.[412] Yet, in another way the early years of both young brides were similar, being spent winning the affection of their step-children, for whom they rapidly became surrogate mothers, bringing warmth and vitality into the home. Mary had no children of her own. She became a close friend to Beatrice and Austen Chamberlain, with whom she was comparable in age; she and Austen were allied in helping Joseph Chamberlain accommodate to the social life of his new Conservative allies, for both were conventional in inclination.

Mary relished the stays in the country piles of new aristocratic colleagues as Chamberlain rose to Cabinet rank and to the leadership of the Liberal Unionist party.[413] Entertaining in Highbury – garden, dinner parties and balls – excused her expensive tastes and Joseph's indulgence of her; yet between 1890 and 1895 (the year that Joseph and Austen started to earn ministerial salaries) and again after 1903, those tastes contributed to the family's financial worries. Indeed, by 1910, with her husband crippled by a stroke, she was conceding to a concerned Neville that '... our expenses have increased... Unfortunately, the general scale on which we live – the power of entertaining family and friends – Highbury and last but not least Cannes (have created) the great trouble which has come upon us.' She had no idea how to economise and indeed she carried on spending.[414] She was irreplaceable from 1906, protecting her severely impaired husband from intrusion, nursing and encouraging him, and also keeping him informed about, and close to, the centre of political affairs in the fraught years up to the First World War. She was a devoted companion in trying times, for Joseph Chamberlain was now but a pale shadow of that earlier dashing and irresistible self who had swept her away in 1888/9.

George Cadbury's Quaker faith conditioned him to the idea of women assuming an active role in the world. In Elizabeth Taylor he found much more than a surrogate mother for his children on Mary Tylor's early death. Unlike Mary Chamberlain she was from the start her husband's equal, and a partner sharing his every project and interest. It was an ideal match. Brought up a Quaker in London, the young Elizabeth had (like George Cadbury) run a bible class, and started a boys' club. She had, again like her future husband, become interested in working-class housing, in her case in Ratcliffe, Burnhill and Shoreditch in London's East End, and planned to live among the poor in the slum streets before marriage intervened. As a result, her husband drew on her experience and intuition in the laying out of Bournville Village; her biographer wrote that 'she was a moving force in all his plans'.[415] In some ways she was broader in her talents than George; she was fluent in French and German, for she was educated in Saxe-Meiningen, and she was a good musician and an enthusiast for the theatre, both areas treated with the greatest suspicion by the Society of Friends. When she first met George he persuaded her to speak at a Temperance meeting, a cause with which she sympathised.

Marrying like Mary Endicott in 1889, then moving to Woodbrooke and overcoming the suspicion of her new step-children (later having five children of her own in as many years) did not diminish her determination to do valuable educational and social work. In a subsequent address she said she taught her children not to 'disregard inequalities of opportunity, position and wealth'; she made her home a place where 'the just regard of the industrial workers for decent conditions, for adequate wages, for respectable homes and the amenities of life' were not ignored.[416]

Her motivation to reform differed from Joseph Chamberlain's for she wrote: 'In my own belief, nothing less than a religious motive can supply the needed spirit of social service.'[417] Spiritual fellowship with God 'was the spur for her philanthropic work'. More than that she approached participation in housing, education and health work from a maternal perspective.[418] Like her husband her first 'social service' was in education. She created a Women's Adult School for the wives of George's Class XIV working men. She was the moving force in the foundation of a school at Northfield and at the Bournville schools where she fought the Local Education Committee for proper staffing. Later she would become President of the Parents National Education Union and would serve on the body of school managers responsible for schools in South West Birmingham after the First World War.

Elizabeth Cadbury had a much greater faith than either Joseph or Mary Chamberlain in the potentiality of women. As might be expected from one who as a girl attended Miss Buss's pioneering girls school, North London Collegiate, she believed in developing women's intellectual side, and supported suffragists who advocated the right of women to vote.[419] George Cadbury sympathised with her on this, sharing her bitter disappointment at the failure of the Government's Conciliation Bill in 1912 framed to allow women to vote. Indeed, he survived long enough to see her living out the message of emancipation and enfranchisement to become a councillor (an Independent) for King's Norton in the 1919 election. In 1923 she stood as a Liberal candidate on the Free Trade ticket in the General Election called by Baldwin to endorse Protection. She lost gamely in Unionist-dominated Birmingham.

She blazed a trail for women in politics. She was also 'instrumental in encouraging female participation in housing and planning reform'. Her efforts in publicising Bournville proved an inspiration to other women in the Garden City movement.[420] She also achieved much for women in other practical ways. She was the first Warwickshire President of the Young Women's Christian Association (YWCA), and for many years President of the Birmingham Union of Girls Clubs and Treasurer of the Union of Women Workers. She regularly attended, and addressed, the International Council of Women.

She also used to good effect her growing understanding both of the domestic circumstances in which many families lived, and of the ill-health which blighted many working-class lives.

Suffragists had argued that women could bring to politics a sympathy for, and interest in, family issues, and Elizabeth Cadbury proved the point. She took a leading part in Birmingham in shaping and directing the service established in 1908 to monitor and care for the physical condition of children. From 1911 she served on a sub-committee of the new Greater Birmingham City Education Committee, chairing the hygiene committee to such effect that she drove through a plan for clinics to be set up in the city's hospitals and dental hospital to administer general health, dental and eye tests and to perform throat and adenoid operations. Both Cadburys were concerned for children who were then – in the unfortunate contemporary terminology – labelled 'cripples'. They founded Woodlands for crippled children in 1909; after George's death in 1922 Elizabeth would manage its subsumption into the new Royal Cripples Hospital.

Woodlands exemplified the extent to which the Cadburys worked together. This partnership was also very evident at Bournville. Elizabeth was involved from its inception, herself declaring that the housing conditions of the working classes were 'a disgrace to England, their dreary, unhealthy, crowded quarters a menace to the health and morals of a large proportion of the population'.[421] Her involvement ranged from the maternal visitation of tenants in their homes to chairing the Bournville Village Trust for decades after George's death, when she paid particular attention to housing for single women, promoting schemes for flats and maisonettes. Some historians have seen those Bournville visits as 'a thinly disguised attempt to revive forms of pre-industrial deference', seeing her as one of a breed of middle-class women philanthropists bent on imposing their values and their social ascendancy.[422] The truth appears more likely to be that if she started with that air of condescension common to many of her class in the 1890s, the reality of experiencing urban deprivation led her to seek social justice and abandon any ideas of 'making the poor like their betters'.[423]

Her partnership with her husband is also illustrated by her support for George Cadbury's Free Church Council; like him she was out of sympathy with inter-denominational infighting. Yet in other ways she was different from her husband. As has been shown, she was more consistently politically active and involved than he; his most durable campaigning work was effected through journalism. They both believed passionately in the cause of International Peace. She acted on the conviction, in 1914 becoming chairwoman of the Peace and International Relations Committee of the National Council of Women; she went on to be treasurer and vice-president of the National Peace Council. She attended the Versailles Peace Conference with other leading women to plead that they be admitted as delegates. Between the wars she was a frequent attendee at the League of Nations assembly in Geneva. In 1936 she spoke at the World Congress of the International Council of Women in India. Increasingly lame and nearly blind, in her eighties she also travelled to, and addressed, Ecumenical Conferences on the Continent between the wars.

Unlike her husband she was not so devout a Quaker that she would turn down an honour, in her case of being made a Dame of the British Empire in 1934. A rejection of the unworldliness of strictly orthodox Quakerism extended to her love for and patronage of music (she became President of the Birmingham Symphony Orchestra) and of theatre for she helped sponsor the Birmingham Repertory Company.

She could not have been a greater contrast to Mary Chamberlain. Mary remarried in 1916 and lived quietly for many years after Joseph Chamberlain's death as wife of Canon Carnegie of St Margaret's Westminster. Elizabeth Cadbury, both in George's lifetime and for another thirty years until her death in 1951 (when aged 93), was an important and assiduous figure in her own right, creating a significant legacy in terms of health, education, and housing. She rapidly established a reputation as an effective and constructive chair of the numerous committees on which she sat. She was, indeed, an extraordinary and pioneering woman of whom George Bernard Shaw, a demanding judge, said: 'If there is life after this she is one of the very few people I would like to meet there.'[424]

If Chamberlain determined Mary's role, how much more closely did he map out the careers of his two sons. Austen, the elder was Harriet's son from Chamberlain's first marriage, while Neville's mother was Florence, Chamberlain's second wife. Austen was destined for high office; education at Rugby, Trinity College, Cambridge, and then on the Continent developed both his intellect and his ability to mix with the country's leading families. His father's powerful personality impacted on Austen for much of his life; to some observers he seemed 'father-haunted'.[425] Filial piety came close to crippling him, for he bore the weight of his father's expectations for decades. He was a manufactured statesman from the first. He dutifully followed his father into the Commons, firstly sitting for East Worcestershire from 1892, then obediently succeeding him in Birmingham West. His father's importance to the Unionist alliance with Salisbury explains Austen's rapid advance to ministerial rank as Civil Lord of the Admiralty, and then his surprising appointment as Chancellor, when he was a sort of hostage in the developing struggle over tariffs between Balfour and Joseph Chamberlain.

For long he lived under his father's roof at Highbury and it was only when moving into 11 Downing Street in 1904 that he cut that umbilical cord. It prompted him to write to his father: 'It is at once a great encouragement and a great responsibility to be heir to so fine a tradition of private honour and public duty and I will do my best not to be unworthy of the name.'[426] He continued to be aware of his father's long shadow, writing in 1911 to Mary Chamberlain: 'I think more and more of what I owe to father. He has made me in every sense of the word.'[427] He remained willing to exploit his link to his famous father. His 1922 election posters bore two portraits of the two side by side, surmounting a slogan: 'You voted for Joe. Vote for Austen.' They did.[428] Even in his seventies, and out of office, he consciously chose to sit in the seat in the Commons his father had occupied.

Austen joined his father's Liberal Unionist party and adopted his policies as if he could dare to do otherwise, though his feelings for Tariff Reform were lukewarm in comparison. Throughout his life (and forty-five years in the House) he aped him physically, sporting the trademark hair parting, monocle and orchid, and the wing collar, the stiff cuffs, and frock coat becoming 'like a beached whale of Edwardian formality in the 1920s and 1930s'.[429] He shared too with his father the dubious distinction of being defined by his ultimate failure to win the Prime Ministership.

Yet in many ways he was a very different political animal. He may have been, as Roy Jenkins has written, 'immensely his father's superior in both decency and loyalty', but he had nothing of his drive and dynamism. Indeed, he conceded that he had a dislike of exertion and tended to indolence. Being naturally cautious and conservative, he found the strain of the violent battle over Tariff Reform almost too much. Then, and later, at times of great stress he was afflicted by sciatica or exhaustion, having a far less robust constitution than Joseph Chamberlain. So traumatic was the Unionist infighting provoked by his father between 1903 and 1906, in which storm Austen found himself a central player, that one recent biographer has concluded that these years changed his personality from 'open and amiable' to the 'aloof, prickly and reserved statesman of later years'.[430] Compared to Joseph '... there was little of that exultant joy and the visceral thrill of political combat which had characterised his father's struggles'.[431] Perhaps it is not surprising that he was a natural coalitionist in the war and that his happiest time in politics, and his greatest (if relatively fleeting) success should be when he was Foreign Secretary. Patient diplomacy, negotiation and compromise, as at the Peace of Locarno in 1925, suited his essentially non-confrontational personality.

Consciousness of his father's reputation as 'Pushful Joe' and for occasionally dubious behaviour made Austen hyper-conscious of behaving with integrity and without vulgar ambition. Leo Amery who knew both Chamberlains wrote: 'Austen had an exaggerated fear of being regarded as pushful or other than scrupulously correct in his dealings.'[432] That scrupulousness was evident, for example, when he resigned as Secretary of State for India in July 1917, taking responsibility (even though it was slight) for the disastrous outcome of the Mesopotamian campaign at Kut in the middle of the First World War. It was the honourable course, and not one which commended itself to Joseph Chamberlain at the time of the Jameson scandal.

When Balfour had tendered his resignation as Unionist leader in 1911 it looked as if the leadership would pass to a Chamberlain. Yet such was his punctiliousness that Austen absented himself from the Commons and the London clubs to avoid seeming to try too hard to influence the MPs' choice. In 1921 his steadiness, reliability and reputation as a safe pair of hands in Balfour's, Asquith's and, much later, Lloyd George's cabinets saw him at last succeed to the leadership of the party. This time, however, a combination of misplaced loyalty to a political dead duck, Lloyd George, and his own arrogance, insensitivity and failure to listen to his backbenchers, saw Austen ousted. His tenure of just over a year had been historically brief and in being driven out he lost the last chance of assuming the mantle of the Prime Ministership. These serial mishaps explain why he is remembered as a perennial 'number two' and why an epigram of uncertain provenance has gained such common currency: Austen, it is said, 'always played the game and he always lost it'.

In truth, Austen Chamberlain was a considerable figure in his own right. Forty-five unbroken years in the House; Chancellor of the Exchequer and Foreign Secretary; honoured as a Knight of the Garter (for a commoner, unprecedented) and with the Nobel Peace Prize, for his efforts in bringing Germany, France and Belgium together at Locarno; leader of the Conservative Party – it is a formidable achievement. Although many of these glittering prizes were won after Joe's death the evidence is that something of the truth about Austen had been revealed to Joe in the 1911 leadership contest. Austen, he said, was content to administer for 'he had been born in a red box, brought up in one and would die in one'.[433] He had stepped aside to allow Bonar Law to seize the crown. It dawned on Joe that Austen fatally lacked the necessary ruthlessness, strength and resolution but that quietly his unsung second son Neville was revealing just the requisite drive and toughness to make it to the very top.

Neville's early years had been inauspicious, with little evidence that he would be the Chamberlain to top the greasy pole by becoming Prime Minister. An undistinguished career at Rugby decided his father to direct his second son into business, sending him to Mason College in Birmingham to study a curriculum designed to equip students for work in Midlands industry. Subsequently he sent him to Andros in the Bahamas, where Joseph invested heavily in a sisal plantation. Neville was its manager. All his best efforts failed to make the project a success. Rugby, Andros, the death of his mother, and life at Highbury dominated by a grieving and undemonstrative father, conspired to mould Neville's chilly, defensive, very private persona, in David Cannadine's words 'just like his umbrella, stiff and rolled up tight'.[434] He was well aware of his father's disappointment after Andros, a scheme that had severely dented family fortunes. Yet within a few years Neville was giving cause for some family pride, for both as a director of *Elliott's* (a metal-working company) and then as owner in reviving and expanding *Hoskins*, manufacturer of ship's berths, he started to show a real talent for business.

In this, and in his enlightened attitude to his workforce, establishing himself as a model employer, he was emulating his father. In fact, for all that Austen was the favoured son, the chosen one, it was Neville whose career most closely paralleled that of their father. Setting aside an early dislike for politics he, like Joe, learnt the craft of public speaking at the Birmingham and Edgbaston Debating Society, developing a style of oratory which echoed his father's, being clear, precise, closely reasoned and ruthlessly combative.[435] His experience in business convinced him before other Chamberlains of the urgent need to impose tariffs; his father's campaign found a willing advocate in Neville and he made his first forays into politics chairing the Tariff Reform Committee, deputising for his father in Birmingham from 1903. Like his father, but unlike his brother Austen, he enjoyed, and found he had a gift for, political organisation. Joseph got him involved in running the Birmingham Liberal Unionist organisation; at the end of the war he effected a harmonious amalgamation of Liberal and Conservative Unionists in Birmingham and right on into the 1930s it was Neville Chamberlain who raised funds for, and energised the campaigning of, the Unionists in the city, maintaining the Chamberlainite control of the Duchy.[436]

Brother Austen lived in London or Sussex; Neville based himself at Westbourne, his Edgbaston house, as his father had done at Highbury. Neville proved a worthy successor to his father in municipal politics. He became a councillor in 1911, specialising from the start in Town Planning, at the relatively advanced age of 42; he had resisted the call until *Hoskins* was quite clearly a business and financial success. Like his father he had a strong desire to do social good, seeing collective action as the most effective means to transforming the life chances of the poor in Birmingham. Indeed, when in 1913 as chairman of a special committee investigating housing conditions he wrote 'a large proportion of the poor in Birmingham are living under conditions of housing detrimental both to their health and morals', he was perhaps unconsciously echoing the words his father used in speaking to the Sanitation Conference in 1875 (see Chapter 3).[437]

In 1915, in the middle of the war, he became Mayor of Birmingham. His term of office was marked by familiar Chamberlain characteristics; he injected the same sort of restless energy which older citizens would remember from the mid-1870s, planning for the new Greater Birmingham born in 1911. He identified problems and found solutions across a range of issues from stockpiling coal for the poor, providing antenatal care for young mothers and cultivating 24,000 acres of green space in the city to provide much-needed food. That interest in the wellbeing of ordinary citizens was carried on into his rapid advance through ministerial ranks, even if an outwardly stern, unbending image effectively masked a deep concern. It showed itself when he sought to maximise house-building in his short term as Minister of Housing in 1922. As Minister of Health from 1924 in Baldwin's government he announced root-and-branch reforms of pensions, housing, health, rating, Poor Law and local government in a programme whose radicalism brought to mind Joseph Chamberlain's Unauthorised Programme. It was a solid and enduring achievement, and more complete and rapid than his father's radical prospectus. Just like his father, he provided the progressive energy for an entire administration.

Of course, in the end he surpassed his father. After a term from 1932 to 1937 as Chancellor of the Exchequer, when his cautious stewardship restored the country's finances after the political and economic crash of 1931, he succeeded Baldwin as Prime Minister. The qualities which up to then had seemed virtues – clarity, certainty, energy, decisiveness – now became character flaws in his very personal pursuit of Appeasement with Adolf Hitler, and explain the humiliating failure of all his plans for enduring peace and growing prosperity after Munich in 1938.

All through his career he remained conscious of his demanding and overbearing father. He confessed as much in 1932, writing: 'Like Hamlet I have been haunted by Father's Ghost.'[438] He was aware of that ghost when donning the mayoral chain of office in 1915, admitting to Mary: 'At the moment of putting on my armour I feel far short of what Father's son should be.' It was clearly prompting him in 1923 when he unavailingly asked Baldwin for the post of Colonial Secretary in his new government, declaring like his father in 1903: 'Our future belongs in the Empire.' In campaigning for Tariff Reform in the 1923 election, when Baldwin gambled on his father's policy as the cure for Britain's inter-war economic ills, he deliberately called to mind Joe's strategy with the message 'Keep British work for British workers'. The ghost reappeared when he became Minister of Health, for he wrote to his sister Ida: 'If I have four or five years of office, I may leave behind as great a reputation as Minister of Health as Father did as Colonial Secretary.'[439]

Above all it was carrying his father's tariff and imperial preference policies to fruition in February 1932 that most keenly reminded him of the Chamberlain legacy. He even alluded to it emotionally on the floor of the House of Commons, saying:

> My father would have found consolation for the bitterness of his disappointment if he could have foreseen that these proposals, the direct and legitimate descendants of his conception, would be laid before the house in the presence of one (Austen), and by the lips of the other of the two immediate successors to his name and blood.[440]

Months later, when leading a British delegation to the British Empire Economic Conference at Ottawa, he remarked to some of its members: 'It was a great addition to his satisfaction (in obtaining a measure of Imperial Preference) that there are still so many of the family left to rejoice in the fulfilment of Father's policy.' Brother Austen, who had nevertheless treated Neville all his life with barely disguised condescension, for once wrote with some degree of admiration to him: 'Father's great work will be completed by his children.'[441] Father's Ghost even reappeared when Neville assumed the highest office. While he negotiated with De Valera, the Irish President, in 1938 he mused to his sister that '… it would be another strange chapter in our family history if it fell to me to settle the Irish Question after the long and repeated efforts made by Father and Austen'.[442]

In so many ways Neville was like his much-admired father. He was an enthusiastic and knowledgeable cultivator of orchids. He had his robust physical and mental constitution. He even talked like him, Beatrice Webb recording that when making that most dramatic of broadcasts – to announce the outbreak of war on 3 September 1939 – his voice 'sounded strikingly like his father's'.[443] Neville also inherited the capacity to make enemies. Joseph was a good 'hater' and could be bitter, cruel and ruthless to his opponents, Home Rulers like Morley or Free Traders like Lord Hugh Cecil; where Austen avoided upsetting people, Neville showed deep disdain for those – especially some critical Labour MPs in the 1920s – who crossed him. Yet in one regard they were very different. Although Neville Chamberlain worked unceasingly to improve the security and conditions of working-class men and women, he always appeared stern and humourless, a corvine undertaker. He lacked the warmth, loyalty and charisma that characterised his father's relationship with a significant part of the electorate.

George Cadbury determined the pattern of his sons' careers every bit as precisely as did Joseph Chamberlain. Like their father they started as businessmen and once established diversified into making significant contributions to a number of educational, political and social causes. They both followed their father as devout Quakers and as committed Liberals. Edward and George junior went into the firm as young men, materially advancing *Cadbury's* development and modernisation.

Of the two sons George was marginally the more prominent in public life. After Leighton Park, the new Quaker school, and a year at University College London, George junior was summoned to help run the firm; in his early twenties he and brother Edward found themselves Directors in the wake of their uncle Richard's death in 1899. George's scientific interests led him to specialise at first in manufacturing processes; when only nineteen in 1897 he was sent to learn from *Stollwerck's* factory in Pressburg to see how continental firms produced better, smoother chocolate. Subsequently, he practised what he learnt, developing appliances to enrobe different centres with chocolate covering, and later pioneering mass production methods for the making of milk chocolate. He can take credit, then, for *Cadbury's* most iconic products, *Dairy Milk* and *Milk Tray*. Of equal value was his work to create a smooth, pure cocoa, which resulted in 1906 in the launch of *Bournville Cocoa*.[444] Realising the importance of controlling the quality and quantity of vital raw materials for chocolate manufacture, he was responsible for the building of the milk condensing plant at Knighton, linked by river and canal straight into the Bournville factory. He lived on site to supervise Knighton's construction; later he would extend his brief there to monitor the quality of milk from suppliers' dairies.

His interests at *Cadbury* were not confined to product development. On a personnel matter which trespassed on Edward's specialism, George junior travelled to America in 1901 to visit enlightened businesses which had developed employee suggestion schemes; his enthusiastic advocacy of this on his return led to *Cadbury's* own scheme which had the twin virtues of firstly providing a fund of good, practical ideas for improving productivity and also of demonstrating a positive, collaborative attitude to the workforce. It helped to establish a much less confrontational relationship between management and labour than prevailed in many firms.[445] In that vein in 1917 he chaired the committee of management and employee representatives developing Works Councils at Bournville which effectively dealt with a range of local workshop issues, be they disciplinary, about industrial accidents or the sick benefit scheme.

His concern with personnel extended to the prospects of young adult workers. So, he founded the Works Education Department in 1911, starting up evening classes, and later half-day classes in the firm's time, compulsory for young employees under eighteen. Those classes reflected his strong conviction that the firm should foster the intellectual and spiritual development of the young. He wrote that 'as employers we only have the right to use the labour of young people if we make sufficient provision for their development'. His ideas influenced the 1918 Education Act and the creation of County Colleges in the Butler Act of 1944.

He also founded *Cadbury's* new transport department after the First World War, pioneering the development of railhead warehouses to stockpile *Cadbury* products prior to wider, more efficient distribution; from London in 1924, thence to Manchester, by 1930 he had created fifteen depots in all.[446]

Although George junior is of interest as a successful businessman, with his brother establishing his firm in the leading ranks of British food and drink manufacturers, his importance – as for his father – lies in his wider career. He may not have been a leading minister as were the contemporaneous Chamberlain sons, but within Birmingham and the West Midlands his contribution was considerable, and illustrates the preoccupations of enlightened men and women in his generation. As we have seen education had become a particular enthusiasm. He learnt its value when following his father as an Adult School teacher at the Severn Street Schools, ministering (for thirty years) to illiterate and innumerate adults. He even bicycled to the class each Sunday, taking flowers, just as his father had done. He learnt, too, from George senior the value of continuing education, supporting Woodbrooke College, his father's Quaker College.

But he branched off in a different direction to found two adult residential colleges of his own, influenced by the Danish High School movement. Firstly, he opened Fircroft in Selly Oak for adult workers to broaden their minds by studying the liberal arts, and to learn more from 'the art of (simply) living together', as he put it. He funded it and became its President. Then he established Avoncroft (first at Offenham, then Stoke Prior near Bromsgrove) intended for agricultural workers, both to broaden their minds but also to give them a sound introduction to plant breeding, improved cultivation and animal husbandry.[447] In his intention to do something to renew rural life, equip young farmers to run smallholdings, and stop the inexorable population drift to the cities, he was closer to Joseph Chamberlain's views than he might have realised. Both institutions still exist, though Avoncroft now hosts historic rural buildings as a museum.

A preoccupation with the built environment was natural for the son of Bournville Village's originator; indeed, George junior had helped host Ebenezer Howard's visit to Bournville in 1897 and had learnt something of the Garden City movement.[448] The establishment of Greater Birmingham in 1911 when the city doubled in size coincided with the election of Neville Chamberlain (Unionist) and George junior to the Council. George was a councillor for sixteen years and an alderman in 1921, far exceeding his father in length of office and in enthusiasm for municipal service.

Both new councillors from either side of the political divide were passionately interested in town planning, Neville rapidly becoming Chairman of the new Town Planning Committee. George junior articulated his ideas in an influential book, *Town Planning* (1915) which became a standard text. Its main thrust was to advocate central control of planning, so that a responsible body would set down transport links, green spaces and the limitation of houses so as (in his own words) 'to prevent some of the evils incidental to crowding, (to) checkmate land sweating (which is the desire to get the maximum return from land irrespective of the comfort and health of its inhabitants)'.[449] Such ideas carry an intriguing echo of Neville Chamberlain's election address to the electors of All Saints ward in 1911 when he spelt out the need to control the growth of undeveloped districts, provide for open spaces and parks and prevent a repetition of the current overcrowding.[450]

In several other ways George junior gave proof of his commitment to protecting and improving Birmingham's environment. For fifty years he took a leading part in the Bournville Village Trust, succeeding his stepmother as Chairman. More originally, he gave proof of his passionate belief in preserving Green Belt land around big cities by purchasing land on the Lickey Hills with his brother Edward, then by buying Beacon Hill and the Rosehill Estate, all south west of Birmingham. In each case, and in that of the 414 acres of the Chadwick Manor Estate stretching from Beacon Hill to Waseley Hill, the land was given away in perpetuity, either to the City Council and its Common Good Trust or to the National Trust, to ensure the preservation of green unspoilt countryside for future enjoyment. That gift has been as important as any other Cadbury – or indeed Chamberlain – legacy down to the present day.

In a number of George junior's initiatives, Edward his elder brother was a most supportive partner. So, we find him contributing to the funds to sustain Fircroft and – as we have seen – he was a generous donor of Green Belt land in the Lickey Hills. Like his brother, Edward supported his father's ambitious scheme of Quaker education at Woodbrooke, building the Rendel Harris Library there. Later he would be prominent in the management of the Selly Oak Colleges, being the architect of the unification of the separate institutions into one large scheme.

Clearly, he too was profoundly influenced by his father. Edward founded a class for youths at Bristol Street, a branch of the Severn Street Adult Schools movement. He was a director of the Garden City Association and an organiser of the conference and that visit to Bournville at which Ebenezer Howard gave impetus to the whole notion of the Garden City. He joined his father as a prominent member of the National Old Age Pensions League, his name engraved along with George senior on the memorial tablet in Browning Hall to commemorate the passing of Asquith's Act in 1908. He was equally prominent in the *Daily News* campaign to outlaw sweated labour in 1906/7. Along with his younger brother Henry he helped his father rescue and then revivify the *Daily News*. George wrote in 1910: 'I have had during the last six years the help of Edward without which I would have given up the struggle as apparently hopeless.'[451] That year, in the aftermath to the gruelling inquisition of the São Tomé libel trial, George handed over the newspaper to a group of trustees to manage, with Edward as the chairman.

The campaigning for pensions, and even more, the preoccupation with the *Daily News*, did not affect his leadership of *Cadbury*. He started out in the firm developing export markets, visiting Australia and later South America. At the same time his responsibility as one of the four directors was for the women's departments in the works, a brief he held for twenty years from 1899. Still, the area that piqued his interest was that of personnel and productivity. He wrote several studies touching on this area: *Women, Work and Wages, Sweating* and in 1912 his most important book, *Experiments in Industrial Organisation*, which he described as 'an attempt to show how the organisation of the works (*Cadbury*) aims at minimising some of the disadvantages and drawbacks of factory life'.[452] It was conscious PR, for the Cadburys were ever aware of the need to foster a positive image of the firm. More than that, however, it proselytised a powerful message for businessmen that by scientific management productivity could be maximised.

Workers, he argued, should be scientifically selected, there should be (a relatively new idea for British factories) time and motion studies, time registering machines should be introduced, slow workers and ill-discipline should be rooted out, tools and equipment should be standardised, and – his particular enthusiasm – piece work should be introduced to replace set wage rates. In many ways his book did much to introduce Britain to the scientific management theories popularised in American business circles by Frederick Taylor. Edward Cadbury recognised that the results could be dehumanising, could lead to greater monotony and nervous strain as employers sought for increases in productivity, and so he put great emphasis at Bournville on welfare schemes, on sport, on community and on pensions as a way of winning support from employees and keeping trade unions at bay.[453]

The Cadbury sons were as much a product of their background – especially of their strong-minded and deeply conscientious father – as were Neville and Austen Chamberlain. It is of course very difficult to compare them, as difficult as comparing apples and pears, for how can we evaluate the relative merits of international statesmen as opposed to successful business leaders and philanthropists? Occasionally we can see points of shared experience, notably with Neville and George junior, both well-reputed Birmingham businessmen committed to town planning and better housing, sitting on the same Council from 1911 to 1918, but thereafter their paths diverged as Westminster drew Neville away to join his metropolitan brother. What we can say with confidence is that all four of them flourished and achieved in their own ways, and that quite evidently the interests and preoccupations of their fathers determined their careers and the direction they took to the end of their lives.

Timeline of Events

1836	Joseph Chamberlain born in Camberwell, London.
1839	George Cadbury born in Edgbaston, Birmingham.
1854	JC moves to Birmingham to join *Nettlefold and Chamberlain*.
1859	GC starts teaching at the Severn Street School.
1861	GC and brother Richard inherit family cocoa business on Bridge Street, Birmingham.
1863	GC starts his own Adult School class, Class XIV, which he runs for over 50 years.
1867	Second Reform Act passed; need now to educate newly enfranchised voters. JC joins George Dixon's new Birmingham Education Society.
1869	JC co-founder of the National Education League. JC elected a town councillor in Birmingham.
1870	Forster's Education Act.
1873	JC becomes Chairman of the Birmingham School Board. JC elected Mayor of Birmingham.
1874	GC and Richard Cadbury move *Cadbury Bros.* factory to Bournville outside the centre of Birmingham. JC retires from business and sells up. JC pushes through the municipalisation of Birmingham's gas supplies. In December Birmingham Council agrees to purchase waterworks.
1875	JC pilots the Birmingham Improvement Scheme through Council.
1876	JC becomes one of Birmingham's three MPs.
1877	JC and allies found the National Liberal Federation in Birmingham. JC in the Commons advocates the Gothenburg scheme for municipalisation of the drink trade.
1878	GC elected a Birmingham councillor; resigns after a year.
1880	JC included in Gladstone's 2nd Ministry Cabinet as President of the Board of Trade. JC moves into Highbury.
1882	GC and Richard Cadbury organise Gospel Temperance rally in Birmingham.
1884	Aston Manor riots as Liberal activists wreck a Conservative rally to welcome Lord Randolph Churchill to Birmingham. JC implicated in the plans for violence.
1885	JC launches a national Radical campaign for his Unauthorised Programme of education, land and tax reform in Birmingham.
1886	JC briefly President of the Local Government Board – issues Chamberlain Circular to Poor Law Guardians advocating public works for temporarily unemployed.

JC leads the fight against Gladstone's Home Rule Bill – and splits the national and the Birmingham Liberal party.

Lord Salisbury wins the General Election.

JC founds his own party – the National Radical Union.

1888   JC's influence on his new Unionist Conservative allies seen in passing of Local Government Act, a long-standing goal of his.

GC marries Elizabeth Taylor.

1889   Victory in Birmingham Central by-election for Chamberlain's Liberal Unionist candidate, Jacob Bright, proves Chamberlain's and Liberal Unionism's electoral potency.

JC marries Mary Endicott.

1891   GC founds the Stirchley Institute.

JC sees Free Education for All enacted by Salisbury's government.

1892   Austen Chamberlain elected MP for East Worcestershire.

1894   GC moves to The Manor.

Harcourt's Local Veto Bill.

1895   GC starts to purchase land and starts to build the first houses in Bournville Village.

JC becomes Colonial Secretary.

Three Bechuana chiefs visit Birmingham.

December – The Jameson Raid.

GC becomes the first President of the National Free Church Council.

1897   Parliamentary Inquiry into Jameson Raid exonerates JC.

JC sets out to establish University of Birmingham.

JC inspires the passage of the Workmen's Compensation Act.

Ebenezer Howard, founder of the Garden City movement, visits Bournville Village.

1898   GC helps fund a conference of the National Old Age Pensions League in Browning Hall, London.

GC initiates a gathering of trade unionists and others at Birmingham Town Hall to discuss compulsory arbitration of industrial disputes.

1899   Richard Cadbury dies; *Cadbury* becomes a limited company.

Boer War breaks out.

University of Birmingham becomes a reality.

1900   Khaki Election; Unionists win substantial majority.

Formation of the Labour Representation Committee (Labour Party).

Bournville Village Trust established.

GC persuaded to help fund the *Daily News*.

1901   Lloyd George nearly lynched at Birmingham Town Hall anti-Boer War meeting.

Cadbury directors first learn of use of slave labour in São Tomé and Príncipe.

1902 Balfour replaces Salisbury as Unionist Prime Minister.

Balfour Education Act prompts revival of militant Nonconformity.

End of Boer War; at end of the year Chamberlain embarks on a tour of conquered South Africa.

1903 On 15 May JC delivers his Tariff Reform speech in Birmingham.

September JC resigns from the Cabinet to be free to campaign against Free Trade.

Austen Chamberlain is appointed Chancellor of the Exchequer.

GC founds Woodbrooke Quaker College in Selly Oak.

1905 *Cadbury Dairy Milk* launched.

Balfour resigns; Unionist party riven by Tariff Reform divisions.

Henry Campbell-Bannerman (Liberal) becomes Prime Minister.

1906 January – stunning Liberal General Election victory. Only Chamberlain's Duchy resists the swing to Liberals and Labour.

JC's stroke ends his active and effective political career.

GC and the *Daily News* organise an exhibition to highlight Sweating. National Anti-Sweating League Conference funded by GC.

Bournville Cocoa launched.

1908 Old Age Pensions enacted by the Liberal government; GC and Edward Cadbury prominent in Old Age Pensions League.

1909 Trade Boards Act passed, legislating against sweating.

Cadbury v Standard libel trial in Birmingham over issue of slave-grown cocoa.

Lloyd George's People's Budget rejected by Lords.

1910 Two General Elections on issue of Lords' reform. Unionists make gains. Birmingham remains loyally Unionist.

1911 Neville Chamberlain and George Cadbury junior elected to Greater Birmingham City Council.

Austen Chamberlain fails to land the leadership of Unionist Party.

Elizabeth Cadbury chairs the Hygiene Committee of the Greater Birmingham Education Committee.

1912 Edward Cadbury publishes *Experiments in Industrial Organisation*.

1914 JC dies.

Mary Chamberlain starts the breaking-up of the Highbury household; Austen Chamberlain makes it available for use as a hospital for wounded soldiers.

First World War begins.

Elizabeth Cadbury chairs the Peace and International Relations Committee of the National Council of Women.

1915 Neville Chamberlain becomes Mayor of Birmingham.

Austen Chamberlain joins Asquith's Coalition War Cabinet.

George Cadbury junior publishes *Town Planning*.

1916   Mary Chamberlain re-marries.

1917   Austen Chamberlain resigns over the Kut debacle.

1918   First World War ends.
        Highbury sold.

1919   Elizabeth Cadbury elected to Birmingham Council for King's Norton ward.
        Visit of King George V and Queen Alexandra to Bournville Village.

1921   Austen Chamberlain becomes Leader of the Conservative and Unionist Party.

1922   GC dies.
        Lloyd George loses office; Austen Chamberlain is ousted in backbench coup.
        Neville Chamberlain becomes Minister of Housing.

1937   Neville Chamberlain becomes Prime Minister in May.

1951   Elizabeth Cadbury dies.

1953   The Cadbury family sells The Manor, Northfield to the University of Birmingham.

NOTES

Author's Note

[1] For recent biographies of Joseph Chamberlain see: Marsh, P., *Joseph Chamberlain – Entrepreneur in Politics* (New Haven/London, Yale University Press, 1997); Crosby, T., *Joseph Chamberlain – A Most Radical Imperialist* (London, I.B. Tauris, 2011); Ward, R., *The Chamberlains* (Croydon, Fonthill, 2015).

Introduction

[2] Hopkins, E., *Birmingham: the First Manufacturing Town in the World* (London, Weidenfeld and Nicolson, 1989).

[3] Reekes, A., *Speeches that Changed Britain* (Alcester, West Midlands History, 2015), pp. 10-51.

[4] Cannadine, D., 'The Chamberlain Tradition and Birmingham,' in: *In Churchill's Shadow* (London, Allen Lane, 2002), pp. 117-133.

[5] Report for BBC News by Dominic Casciani, 3 July 2003, *news.bbc.co.uk/3056286.stm*

[6] Charles Booth and Joseph Rowntree were English social reformers in the late nineteenth and early twentieth centuries whose pioneering investigative studies of poverty in London and York shaped government policy on poverty. Maud Pember Reeves, an Australian who came to London, published an influential study of poverty in Lambeth just before the outbreak of the First World War. See their respective entries in the *Oxford Dictionary of National Biography*.

Chapter 1: Birmingham Businessmen

[7] Alexander, H., *Richard Cadbury of Birmingham* (London, Hodder and Stoughton, 1906).

[8] Vernon, A., *A Quaker Businessman* (London, George Allen & Unwin, 1958).

[9] Marsh, P., *Joseph Chamberlain: Entrepreneur in Politics* (New Haven/London, Yale University Press, 1997), pp. 10-28.

[10] Ward, R., *The Chamberlains* (Croydon, Fonthill, 2015), p. 12.

[11] Ward, R., *op. cit.*, p. 13.

[12] Rowlinson, M.C., 'Cadbury's New Factory System 1879-1919', (unpublished Ph.D. thesis, University of Aston, September 1987), pp. 150-167.

[13] Jones, E., *The History of GKN* vol. I (Macmillan, London, 1987), pp. 146-153.

[14] Chamberlain, J., 'Manufacture of Iron Wood Screws' in *The Resources, Products and Industrial History of Birmingham and the Midlands Hardware District*, ed. Timmins, S., (Birmingham, 1866), pp. 604-608; and Hooper, A., 'Mid-Victorian Radicalism: Community and Class in Birmingham 1850-1880', (unpublished Ph.D. thesis, University of London, 1978), p. 19.

[15] Hooper, *op. cit.*, p. 200.

[16] Alexander, H., *op. cit.*, p. 193.

[17] Gardiner, A.G., *Life of George Cadbury* (London, Cassell and Co. Ltd., 1924), pp. 30-34; 73-84.

[18] Gardiner, *op. cit.*, p. 106.

[19] Williams, I., *The Firm of Cadbury, 1831-1931* (London, Constable, 1931), p. 54.

[20] Williams, *op. cit.*, p. 92.

[21] Jones, E., *op. cit.*, pp. 146-148.

[22] Jones, E., *op. cit.*, pp. 146-148.

[23] Jones, E., *op. cit.*, p.146.

[24] *Bournville Works Magazine*, no.1, vol. 1.

[25] Rowlinson, *op. cit.*, p. 90; Gardiner, *op. cit.*, p. 27.

[26] Vernon, *op. cit.*, p. 90. Rowntree christened the new unadulterated cocoa 'Elect', the name 'emphasizing its undiluted purity for elect was an adjective used in the druggists' trade to describe quality'.

[27] Minute Book – *Cadbury Bros*. Committee of Management Vol. No.5, entry for 21 March 1904.

[28] Othick, J., 'The Cocoa and Chocolate Industry in the Nineteenth Century', in *The Making of the British Diet*, ed. Oddy, D., and Miller, D. (London, Croom Helm, 1976), p. 88.

[29] Rowlinson, *op. cit.*, pp. 272-276.

[30] Rowlinson, *op. cit.*, pp. 167-174.

[31] William Cadbury in *Personal Reminiscences of 63 Men and Women from Bridge Street and Bournville, 1929* (Manuscript collection in *Cadbury* Archives).

[32] Marsh, *op. cit.*, p. 21.

[33] Jones, *op. cit.*, p. 152.

[34] Jones, *op. cit.*, p. 152.

35 Minute Book - *Cadbury Bros.*, Committee of Management Vol. 1, 1899, entry for 18 April.

36 Vernon, *op. cit.*, p. 173.

37 Marsh, *op. cit.*, pp. 44-46.

38 Jones, *op. cit.*, p. 157.

39 The *Daily News*, 15 November 1884.

40 Thompson, E.P., 'Time Work Discipline and Industrial Capitalism', *Past and Present*, Dec.1967, No.38, pp. 56-97.

41 Gardiner, *op. cit.*, pp. 71-100.

42 Marsh, *op. cit.*, pp. 62-63.

43 William Cadbury, *op. cit.*

44 Williams, I., *op. cit.*, p. 153.

45 Gardiner, *op. cit.*, p. 84.

46 Bailey, A, 'Constructing a Model Community – Institutions, Paternalism and Social Identities in Bournville, 1879-1939' (unpublished Ph.D. Thesis, University of Birmingham, 2002), p. 82.

47 Minute book – Committee of Management, *op. cit.*, entry for 25 August 1903.

48 Gardiner, *op. cit.*, p. 83.

49 Rowlinson, *op. cit.*, p. 199.

50 Chamberlain, J., in Timmins, S. *op. cit.*, p. 608.

51 Marsh, *op. cit.*, p. 28.

52 Quoted in Hooper, A., *op. cit.*, p. 499.

Chapter 2: A Zeal for Education

53 Gardner, P., 'Literacy, Learning and Education', *A Companion to Nineteenth Century Britain* ed. Williams, C., (London, Blackwell, 2004), pp. 355-362.

54 Gardiner, A.G., *op. cit.*, p. 46.

55 Chamberlain, J., Lecture on Education to the Mutual Improvement Society of the Church of the Messiah, 18 April 1870. JC 4/1/11.

56 Marsh, *op. cit.*, p. 51.

57 Extract from *The Woman at Home* 1900, JC 1/17/12.

58 Watts, R., 'Joseph Priestley and his influence on Education in Birmingham,' in: *Joseph Priestley and Birmingham*, ed. Dick, M., (Alcester, Brewin Books, 2005), pp. 48-64.

59 Camberwell newspaper 1912, JC1/17/4; memories of Charles Fellowes. *The Rt. Hon. Joseph Chamberlain as a Sunday school teacher* (1900) JC1/17/4.

60 Garvin, J. *op. cit.*, pp. 64-67.

61 Joseph Sturge (1793-1859) was a Birmingham Quaker, abolitionist, Chartist, and founder of the Complete Suffrage Union to unite middle and working classes in the fight for Parliamentary Reform.

62 Gardiner, *op. cit.*, p. 39.

63 Alexander, *op. cit.*, pp. 370-1.

64 Rose, J., *The Intellectual Life of the British Working Classes* (New Haven, Yale University Press, 2001).

65 Alexander, *op. cit.*, p. 375; Gardiner, *op. cit.*, p. 46.

66 Sam Mould, quoted in Charles Fellowes, *op. cit.*

67 Gardiner, *op. cit.*, pp. 41-45.

68 Marsh, *op. cit.*, p. 28.

69 Garvin, *op. cit.*, p. 66.

70 Hennock, *op. cit.*, p. 84.

71 Church of the Messiah Day Schools Meeting of Subscribers, 10 July 1867, Library of Birmingham, UC2/10/2/1.

72 Hennock, *op. cit.*, p. 95.

73 Gardiner, *op. cit.*, p. 38.

74 Gardiner, *op. cit.*, p. 45.

75 Hennock, *op. cit.*, p. 84.

76 Marsh, *op. cit.*, p. 36.

77 Garvin, *op. cit.*, p. 92.

78 JC 6/3/2/24.

79 Auspos, P., 'Radicalism, Pressure Groups and Party Politics', *Journal of British Studies* 20 (1980), pp. 184-204.

80 Garvin, *op. cit.*, p. 109.

81 Garvin, *op. cit.*, p. 111.

82 Letters JC to Dixon 26 February to 3 March 1870: JC 5/27/12-13.

83 Garvin, *op. cit.*, p. 125.

84 Garvin, *op. cit.*, p. 211.

85 JC School Board notebooks 1873 on JC 31/3; JC 31/5.

86 Marsh, *op. cit.*, p. 54.

87 Quoted by Garvin, *op. cit.*, p. 146.

88 Auspos, *op. cit.*, p. 198.

89 Speech at the Annual General Meeting of Severn Street Adult School, 30 November 1874, quoted in Boyd, C.W. ed. *Mr. Chamberlain's Speeches vol.i* (London, Constable, 1914), p. 55.

90 *The Dart*, 20 July 1878.

91 Bailey, A., *op. cit.*, p. 212.

92 Gardiner, *op. cit.*, pp. 145-6.

93 Bailey, A., *op. cit.*, p. 173.

94 *The Times*, 6 January 1885.

95 Lord Salisbury speaking at Nottingham, 26 November 1889. Quoted by Roberts, A., in *Salisbury – Victorian Titan* (London, Weidenfeld and Nicolson, 1999), p. 556.

96 Munson, J.E.B., 'The Unionist Coalition and Education, 1895-1902, *Historical Journal*, 20/3 (September 1977), pp. 607-45. The School Board elections gave each ratepayer the same number of votes as there were places on the Board. In Birmingham in 1870 that had been fifteen votes for each voter.

97 H.W. Lucy, *A Diary of the Unionist Parliament 1865 – 1900* (1901), quoted by Munson, *op. cit.*, p. 619.

98 Crosby, T., *Joseph Chamberlain – A Most Radical Imperialist*, (London, I.B. Tauris, 2011), pp. 158-160.

99 Crosby, *op. cit.*, p. 159.

100 JC letter to Lord Selborne, 7 November 1901, JC 11/32/19.

101 *The Times*, 11 October 1902.

102 JC letter to Devonshire, 26 October 1903, JC 18/18/48.

103 A note on university provision, 21 November 1898 JC/1/1/2.

104 Letter Haldane to JC August 1902, JC 12/1/1/34.

105 JC letter to Richard Cadbury, 13 January 1899, JCL Add.74.

106 Gardiner, *op. cit.*, pp. 69-70.

107 Day journal entry for 8 July 1909, Elizabeth Taylor Cadbury, MS 466 1/11.

108 Gardiner, *op. cit.*, p. 193.

109 Gardiner, *op. cit.*, p. 202.

Chapter 3: Projecting Values in Brick and Stone

110 Engels, F., *The Condition of the Working Class in England*, (first published in Germany in 1845, and translated and published in England in 1892).

111 Garvin, J., *op. cit.*, p. 148.

112 Garvin, J., *op. cit.*, p. 90.

113 Hennock, *op. cit.*, p. 139.

114 Hennock, *op. cit.*, p. 141.

115 Boyd., C.W., *Mr. Chamberlain's Speeches, Vol. ii* (London, Constable, 1914), pp. 58-65. Speech 'On the Sanitary Conditions of Large Towns', Birmingham, 13 January 1875.

116 Cadbury, E., 'Paper read on 29 September 1929 at the Jubilee Celebration of the removal of the works from Bridge Street to Bournville in 1879.' (*Cadbury* Archive 001407).

117 Williams, I., *The Firm of Cadbury* (London, Constable, 1931), pp. 218-219.

118 Gardiner, G., *The Life of George Cadbury* (London, Cassell, 1922), p. viii.

119 Deed of Foundation of the Bournville Village Trust, 14 December 1900, MS 1535, Library of Birmingham.

120 Hillman, J., *The Bournville Hallmark* (Studley, Brewin Books, 1994), pp. 13-15. Harrison, M., *Bournville: Model Village to Garden Suburb* (London, Phillimore & Co. Ltd., 1999).

121 Cannadine, D., *In Churchill's Shadow* (London, Allen Lane, 2002), pp. 120-124. Cannadine quotes Bunce who wrote an article on 'Art in the Community' in 1877, published in the *Fortnightly Review*.

122 Gardiner, *op. cit.*, p. 134.

123 Rowlinson, *op. cit.*, pp. 122 ff.

124 Howard, E., *Garden Cities of Tomorrow* (London, Swan Sonnenschein, 1902).

125 Rowlinson, *op. cit.*, p. 110.

126 Bailey, A.R. and Bryson, J.B., 'Stories of Suburbia (Bournville UK from Planning to People Tales)', *Social and Cultural Geography* vol. 7, no. 2, April 2006, pp. 179-198.

127 Correspondence of George Cadbury, BVT, MS 1536.

128 Hennock, *op. cit.*, pp. 142-143.

129 Boyd, *op. cit.*, pp. 72-73, quoting Chamberlain at a dinner given in his honour, 9 November 1876.

130 Quoted by Reekes, A.E., *Speeches That Changed Britain*, (Alcester, West Midlands History, 2015), p. 58.

131 The Woodman public house was in Easy Row and was closed in 1965 before eventual demolition.

132 Hennock, *op. cit.*, p. 177; for Leeds see Frazer, D., *Power and Authority in the Victorian City* (Oxford, Blackwell, 1979), pp. 51-77.

133 Rosenthal, L., 'Joseph Chamberlain and the Birmingham Town Council 1865-1880', *Midland History*, 41, no.1, 2016, pp. 71-95.

134 *Birmingham Council Proceedings 1873-4*; Medical Officer of Health's Report 19 August 1873 to the Sanitary Committee. (Library of Birmingham, BCC L34 3).

135 *Birmingham Council Proceedings 1873-1874*, *op. cit.*, entries for 25 November 1873; 2 December 1873; 10 February 1874.

136 Hennock, *op. cit.*, p. 119.

137 Hennock, *op. cit.*, p. 123.

138 Speech by Chamberlain to Council 4 December 1874, quoted by Garvin, *op. cit.*, p. 192.

139 *Birmingham Council Proceedings 1873-4*, *op. cit.*, 9 June 1874.

140 Boyd., *op. cit.*, p. 72.

141 Marsh, P. *Joseph Chamberlain: An Entrepreneur in Politics* (New Haven/London, Yale University Press, 1997), pp. 93-4.

142 Marsh, *op. cit.*, pp. 93-4.

143 Hennock, *op. cit.*, p. 125.

144 Letter Chamberlain to Collings, 12 March 1876 quoted by Garvin, *op. cit.*, p. 202.

145 Marsh, *op. cit.*, p. 78.

146 Hennock, *op. cit.*, p. 129, quoting from the *Proceedings on the Adoption by the Council of a Scheme for the Improvement of the Borough* (Birmingham 1875).

147 Ward, R., *City State and Nation* (Chichester, Phillimore, 2005), p. 77.

148 Speech in Birmingham 5 January 1885, quoted in Boyd, *op. cit.*, p. 138.

149 Speech in Warrington, 8 September 1885, quoted in Boyd, *op. cit.*, p. 190.

150 Speech in Birmingham 11 October 1894, Boyd, *op. cit.*, p. 356.

151 *The Birmingham Dart*, 3 August 1878.

152 Gardiner, *op. cit.*, p. 59.

153 Gardiner, *op. cit.*, p. 12.

154 Williams, I., *op. cit.*, pp. 218-219.

155 Gardiner, *op. cit.*, pp. 135-141.

156 Bailey, *op. cit.*, p. 122.

157 Harvey, W.A., *The Model Village and its Cottages: Bournville* (London, B.T. Batsford, 1906).

158 Constantine, S., 'Amateur Gardening and Popular Recreation in the Nineteenth and Twentieth Centuries', *Journal of Social History*, 1981, vol. 14, pp. 389-403.

159 Hillman, *op. cit.*, p. 7.

160 Williams, *op. cit.*, p. 121.

161 Constantine, *op. cit.*, pp. 389-403.

162 Harvey, W.A., *The Model Village and its Cottages: Bournville* (London, B.T. Batsford, 1906).

163 Bailey, *op. cit.*, pp. 124-136.

164 BV Council Year Book 1920, MS 1536/1, p. 39, Library of Birmingham.

165 'Minutes of the Committee', 16 March 1904, BVT Estate Office.

166 Marsh, *op. cit.*, p. 165.

167 Boyd, *op. cit.*, J. Chamberlain speech, 5 January 1885, p. 137.

168 Gardiner, *op. cit.*, p. 134.

169 Gardiner, *op. cit.*, p. 154.

Chapter 4: Social Preoccupations

170 Speech by Joseph Chamberlain in Birmingham, 11 October 1894 reported in *The Times* on 12 October 1894.

171 Kneale, J., 'The Place of Drink: Temperance and the Public, 1856-1914', *Social and Cultural Geography* (2001, 2:1), pp. 43-59.

172 Hoppen, K.T., *The Mid-Victorian Generation 1846-1886* (Oxford, OUP, 1998), p. 353; Searle, G.R., *A New England? 1886-1914* (Oxford, OUP, 2004), p. 538; Vernon, A., *A Quaker Business Man – The Life of Joseph Rowntree* (London, George Allen & Unwin, 1958), p. 138.

173 Hoppen, *op. cit.* p. 353.

174 Burn, W.L., *The Age of Equipoise* (London, George Allen & Unwin, 1964), pp. 281-283.

175 Harrison, B., *Drink and the Victorians: The Temperance Question in England 1815-1872* (London, Faber and Faber, 1971), p. 31.

176 Harrison, B., 'Religion and Recreation in Nineteenth Century England', *Past and Present*, No. 38, pp. 112-115.

177 Morley, J., *Life of W.E. Gladstone* (London, Macmillan, 1903), Book vi, ch. 14.
178 Shiman, L.L., 'Blue Ribbon Army: Gospel Temperance in England' *Historical Magazine of the Protestant Episcopal Church*, vol. 50, no. 4 (1981), pp. 391-407.
179 Lawrence, J., *Speaking for the People* (Cambridge, CUP, 1998), p. 107.
180 Sellars, I., *Nineteenth Century Nonconformity* (London, Arnold, 1977), p. 43.
181 Harrison, B., 'Religion and recreation in Nineteenth Century England, *Past and Present* No. 38, pp.112-115.
182 Alexander, H., *op. cit.*, p. 49, passim.
183 Bailey, *op. cit.*, p. 153.
184 *The Dart*, 3 August 1878; Hennock, *op. cit.*, p. 153.
185 Scott, R., *Elizabeth Cadbury 1858-1951* (London, George G. Harrap,1955), pp. 69-70.
186 Bailey, A., *op. cit.*, p. 150 quotes from a letter to Mr. J.W. Bridgeman from H.E. Johnston, 20 May 1895, Miscellaneous Items CWA 023/0032247.
187 Hillman, J., *op. cit.*, pp. 21-23.
188 Bailey, *op. cit.*, p. 154.
189 Quoted by Bailey, *op. cit.*, p. 154.
190 Gardiner, *op. cit.*, p. 286.
191 Speech by Joseph Chamberlain at the Annual General Meeting of Severn Street Adult School, 30 November 1874, reprinted in Boyd, C., *Speeches* Vol.1, p. 55.
192 Marsh, *op. cit.*, p. 69; he quotes from a letter of December 1873, JC to H.J. Wilson.
193 Boyd, *op. cit.*, pp. 73-75 quoting JC's speech of 13 March 1877.
194 Boyd, *op. cit.*, pp. 73-75 quoting JC's speech of 13 March 1877.
195 Speech of 11 October 1894 reported in *The Times*, 12 October 1894.
196 Readman, P., 'The 1895 General Election and Political Change in Late Victorian England,' *Historical Journal*, no. 42 (1999), pp. 467-493.
197 Quoted by Searle, *op. cit.*, p. 558.
198 Ward, R., *City State and Nation*, (Chichester, Phillimore, 2005), p. 168.
199 It was in defining a poverty line, and calling attention to the widespread prevalence of poverty – some 27% of York's population were described as poor – that Joseph and Seebohm Rowntree, and Charles Booth were of seminal importance. Old Age was a significant contributor to poverty. See Gazeley, I., *Poverty in Britain 1900 – 1965* (London, Palgrave Macmillan, 2003), p. 174.
200 *The Times*, 18 March 1891.
201 Marsh, P., *op. cit.*, pp. 327-350.
202 *The Times*, 19 June 1892 reporting Chamberlain's speech in Smethwick the previous day.
203 The 'Hungry Forties' was a popular epithet for the 1840s in England, a time of deep recession in the industrial Midlands and North, widespread hunger and sometimes widespread violent protest from thousands of Chartists demanding political reform.
204 Searle, *op. cit.*, p. 212.
205 *Op. cit.*, pp. 459-460.
206 Crosby, T., *Joseph Chamberlain: A Most Radical Imperialist* (London, I.B.Tauris, 2011), p. 158.
207 Searle, *op. cit.*, pp. 392-3.
208 Rowlinson, *op. cit.*, p. 195.
209 Gardiner, *op. cit.*, p. 95.
210 Clinton, A., *Trade Union Rank and File: Trade Councils in Britain 1900-1940* (Manchester, MUP, 1977), p. 45; Macnicol, J., *The Politics of Retirement in Britain, 1878 – 1948* (Cambridge, CUP, 2002), p. 134.
211 Letter from George Cadbury to Councillor Stevens quoted by Gardiner, A.G., *op. cit.*, pp. 112-113.
212 Watts, M., *The Dissenters Vol. III: The Crisis and Conscience of Nonconformity* (Oxford, OUP, 2015), pp. 317-320.
213 Gardiner, *op. cit.*, pp. 215-217.
214 Murdie-Smith, R., *Sweated Industries: being a handbook of the 'Daily News' exhibition* (*Daily News*, 1906).
215 Snowden, E., *Report on the Conference on National Minimum Wage, National Anti-Sweating League, 24 to 26 October* (London, 1907).
216 Marsh, *op. cit.*, p. 63; p. 328.
217 Gardiner, *op. cit.*, p. 66.
218 Crosby, *op. cit.*, p. 29.
219 Chamberlain, J., 'The Labour Question,' *Nineteenth Century*, XXXII (November 1892), pp. 671 and following. Mallalieu, W.C., 'Joseph Chamberlain and Workmen's Compensation,' *Journal of Economic History* (May 1950), vol.10, pp. 45-57.
220 Marsh, *op. cit.*, p. 398.
221 Marsh, *op. cit.*, p. 227.

Chapter 5: Differences over Party and Politics

222 Vincent, J., *The Formation of the British Liberal Party 1857-1868* (London, Constable, 1866), pp. 14-29.

223 Vincent, *op. cit.*, p. 74.

224 Speech by Chamberlain, J., on 21 April 1886 reprinted by Boyd, C.W., *Mr Chamberlain's Speeches, vol. i* (London, Constable, 1914), p. 256.

225 Rosenthal, *op. cit.*, p. 77.

226 Marsh, *op. cit.*, pp. 116-121; Auspos, P., 'Radicalism, pressure groups, and party politics: From the National Education League to the National Liberal Federation', *Journal of British Studies* 20, pp. 181-204; Crosby, *op. cit.*, p. 23.

227 Hurst, M.C., 'Joseph Chamberlain and West Midlands Politics, 1886-1895', *Dugdale Occasional Papers* No.15, 1962; Reekes, A.E., *Speeches Which Changed Britain – Oratory in Birmingham*, (Alcester, West Midlands History, 2015), chapter 5 'Joseph Chamberlain and political survival'; Ward, R., *City State and Nation* (Chichester, Phillimore, 2005), pp. 95-119; Cawood, I., *The Liberal Unionist Party: A History* (London, I.B. Tauris, 2012).

228 Gardiner, *op. cit.*, p. 60.

229 *The Dart*, 20 July 1878.

230 Wright, R.A., 'Liberal Party Organisation and Politics in Birmingham, Coventry and Wolverhampton 1886-1914', unpublished Ph.D. thesis from the University of Birmingham, 1977, pp. 11-15.

231 Gardiner, *op. cit.*, p. 61.

232 Morgan, K., *The Age of Lloyd George* (London, George Allen & Unwin, 1971), pp. 26-29.

233 Morgan, *op. cit.*, pp. 26-29.

234 Reekes, A.E., *The Rise of Labour* (London, Macmillan, 1994), pp. 1-4.

235 Gardiner, *op. cit.*, p. 62.

236 Pugh, M., *Speak for Britain: A New History of the Labour Party* (London, Bodley Head, 2010), p. 58.

237 Rowlinson, M., *op. cit.*, p. 146.

238 Pelling, H., *Origins of the Labour Party* (London, Macmillan, 1954), p. 221.

239 That telling, and memorable, phrase was coined by Henry Campbell-Bannerman in a speech in London in June 1901, quoted by J. Wilson in *A Life of Sir Henry Campbell-Bannerman* (London, Constable, 1973).

240 Speech made by Joseph Chamberlain in Birmingham Town Hall, 15 May 1903, quoted by Boyd, C.W., *Mr. Chamberlain's Speeches, vol. ii* (London, Constable, 1914), pp. 125-140.

241 Russell, A.K., *Liberal Landslide* (Newton Abbott, David & Charles, 1973), pp. 62-94.

242 Gardiner, *op. cit.*, p. 66.

243 Clarke, P.F., *Lancashire and the New Liberalism* (Cambridge, CUP, 1971), pp. 393-407.

244 Gardiner, *op. cit.*, p. 69.

245 Churchill, W.S., quoted in *Winston Churchill's Maxims and Reflections,* ed. Cooke, C., and Batchelor, D., (Boston, Houghton Mifflin, 1947), p. 64.

246 Webb, B., *Diaries*, LSE digital library, p. 142.

247 Reekes, A.E., *Speeches, op. cit.*, pp. 63-85.

248 JC 6/6/1C/3;JC 6/6/1F-38.

249 *Hansard*, 30/31 October 1884.

250 *Birmingham Daily Post* 19 December 1901–4 January 1902.

251 Gardiner, *op. cit.*, pp. 206-208.

252 Grigg, J., *The Young Lloyd George* (London, Eyre Methuen Ltd., 1973), p. 279. Quoting a Letter, Cadbury, G., to Lloyd George, D., 18 December 1900, National Library of Wales.

253 Letter Cadbury, G., to Scott, C.P., quoted by Gardiner, *op. cit.*, p. 212.

254 Gardiner, *op. cit.*, pp. 214.

255 Quoted by Gardiner, *op. cit.*, p. 224.

Chapter 6: Three Dividing Lines

256 See Foster, R.F., *Modern Ireland, 1600 – 1972*, (London, Allen Lane, 1988), pp. 289-430; Lyons, F.S.L., *Ireland Since the Famine*, (London, Weidenfeld and Nicolson, 1971), pp. 15-184.

257 Marsh, P., *op. cit.*, p. 192 ff.

258 Kimberley, J., *Journal of Kimberley*, 29 September 1886, quoted by Crosby, T., *op. cit.*, p. 209.

259 Speech by Chamberlain, J., 21 April 1886, quoted by Boyd, C.W., *op. cit.*, p. 259.

260 Speech by Chamberlain, J., 1 June 1886, House of Commons, reproduced in Boyd., *op. cit.*, pp. 248-254.

261 Matthew, H., *Gladstone 1875-1898* (Oxford, Clarendon Press, 1995), pp. 235-254.

262 Speech by Chamberlain, J., 12 October 1887 in Belfast, reproduced in Boyd, *op. cit.*, pp. 286-298.

263 Jenkins, R., *Gladstone* (London, Macmillan, 1995), p. 237.

264 Matthew, *op. cit.*, pp. 126-7.

265 Matthew, *op. cit.*, pp. 213.

266 Gardiner, *op. cit.*, p. 209.

267 Porter, A., 'The South African War: Context and Motive Reconsidered', *Journal of African History* 31 (1990), pp. 43-57; Hobsbawm, E., *Age of Empire 1875-1914* (London, Weidenfeld and Nicolson, 1987), p. 66; Ward, R., *The Chamberlains* (Croydon, Fonthill, 2015), p. 48.

268 Crosby, T., *Joseph Chamberlain, A Most Radical Imperialist* (London, I.B. Tauris, 2011), p. 147.

269 Speech by Chamberlain in the House of Commons, 11 October 1899, quoted by Boyd, *op. cit.*, pp. 20-26.

270 Marsh, *op. cit.*, p. 465.

271 Marsh, *op. cit.*, p. 479.

272 Speech by Chamberlain at the Grocers' Hall, 1 August 1902, quoted by Boyd, *op. cit.*, p. 70.

273 Speech by Chamberlain at the Fishmongers Hall, 21 October 1900, quoted by Crosby, *op. cit.*, p. 151.

274 Marsh, *op. cit.*, p. 498.

275 Grigg, J., *The Young Lloyd George* (London, Eyre Methuen Ltd., 1973), p. 275.

276 Marsh, *op. cit.*, p. 503.

277 Gardiner, *op. cit.*, p. 208.

278 Gardiner, *op. cit.*, p. 208.

279 Russell, A.K. *Liberal Landslide* (Newton Abbott, David & Charles, 1973), p. 106.

280 Gardiner, *op. cit.*, p. 209.

281 Bailey, 'Constructing a Model Community: Institutions, Paternalism and Social Identities in Bournville, 1879-1939' (unpublished University of Birmingham Ph.D. Thesis 2002), p. 171.

282 Gardiner, *op. cit.*, p. 309; Bailey, *op. cit.*, p. 171.

283 Lines from the *Economist*, December 1843 quoted by Amery, J., *Joseph Chamberlain and the Tariff Reform Campaign – the Life of Joseph Chamberlain, vol. 5, 1901–1903*, (London, Macmillan, 1969), p. 210.

284 Trentmann, F., *Free Trade Nation* (Oxford, OUP, 2008), pp. 35-87.

285 Wright, G.H., *Chronicles of the Birmingham Chamber of Commerce AD 1813–1913* (Birmingham 1913), pp. 308-311.

286 Quoted by Garvin, J.L., *Life of Joseph Chamberlain*, vol. ii (London, Macmillan, 1932), p. 121.

287 Boyd, vol. ii, *op. cit.*, Speech by Joseph Chamberlain, 4 November 1903.

288 Zebel, S.H., 'Joseph Chamberlain and the Genesis of Tariff Reform', *Journal of British Studies*, 1967, vol.7, No.1, pp. 131–157.

289 Russell, *op. cit.*, p. 57.

290 *Manchester Guardian*, 15 January 1906.

291 Sykes, *Tariff Reform in British Politics* (Oxford, OUP, 1979); Reekes, A.E., 'Birmingham Exceptionalism, Joseph Chamberlain and the 1906 General Election', unpublished M.Res. thesis, University of Birmingham, 2014.

292 Rowlinson, *op. cit.*, p. 172.

293 Orthik, J. 'The Cocoa and Chocolate Industry in the Nineteenth Century', in *The Making of the British Diet*, ed. Oddy, D., and Miller, D. (London, Croom Helm, 1976), p. 89–90.

294 Rowlinson, *op. cit.*, p. 156.

295 Gardiner, *op. cit.*, p. 65.

Chapter 7: Scandal

296 Hasian, M., 'The Cadbury Chocolate Scandals – Mediated Reputations and Modern Globalised Slavery', *Journal of Communication Inquiry*, Vol. 32 (3), 2008, p. 250.

297 Board minutes, 30 April 1901, MS 133, *Cadbury* Papers, Special Collections, University of Birmingham.

298 Higgs, C., 'Happiness and Work: Portuguese Peasants, British Labourers, African Contract Workers and the Case of São Tomé and Príncipe 1901-1909', *International Labour and Working-Class History*, No. 86, 2014, pp. 55.

299 Board Minutes, *op. cit.*, 5 July 1904.

300 MS 180/94 *Cadbury* Papers, Special Collections, University of Birmingham.

301 John, Angela, V., 'A New Slavery?' *History Today*, June 2002, 56:6, p. 34.

302 Hasian, *op. cit.*, p. 250.

303 Hasian, *op. cit.*, p. 250.

304 Higgs, *op. cit.*, p. 60.

305 Board Minutes for 15 November 1906, MS 133 *Cadbury* Papers, Special Collections, University of Birmingham.

306 Burtt, J., and Horton, W.C., 'Report on the Conditions of Coloured Labour on the Cocoa Plantations of São Tomé and Príncipe', July 1907, MS 198, *Cadbury* Papers, University of Birmingham.

307 Higgs, *op. cit.*, p. 65.

308 MS 180/477 Letter from Cadbury, George to Brailsford, H.N., 30 April 1907, *Cadbury* Papers.

309 MS 180/94 Board Minutes, *Cadbury* Papers, *op. cit.*

310 MS 180/477 *Cadbury* Papers, Special Collections, University of Birmingham.

311 MS 180/953 Letter WAC to Frys, June 1908, *Cadbury* Papers, *op. cit.*

312 MS 180/953 Letter WAC to Frys, June 1908, *Cadbury* Papers, *op. cit.*

313 MS 133 *op. cit.*

314 Satre, Lowell Joseph, *Chocolate on Trial; Slavery, Politics and the Ethics of Business*(Athens/Ohio, Ohio University Press, 2005), p. 149.

315 Hasian, *op. cit.*, p. 258.

316 Satre, *op. cit.*, p. 178.

317 For the trial: Satre, *op. cit.*, pp. 149-175; and Hasian, *op. cit.*, pp. 249-270.

318 A farthing = 1/4d

319 MS 179/ 1-86 *Cadbury* Papers, *op. cit.*

320 Crosby, T., *op. cit.*, p. 133.

321 Parsons, N., *King Khama, Emperor Joe and the Great White Queen* (Chicago, University of Chicago Press, 1998), p. 60.

322 Parsons, *op. cit.*, p. 122.

323 Parsons, *op. cit.*, p. 144.

324 Garvin, J., *The Life of Joseph Chamberlain*, vol. 3 (London, Macmillan, 1932), p. 39.

325 *Hansard*, 13 February 1896.

326 Marsh, P., *op. cit.*, p. 380.

327 Letter of 19 December 1895 from Fairfield to Chamberlain, JC 10/1/21.

328 Garvin, *op. cit.*, p. 79.

329 Letter Fairfield to Chamberlain, 28 December 1895, JC 10/1/22.

330 Marsh, *op. cit.*, pp. 391-2.

331 Report of the Select Committee of the House of Commons on British South Africa, 13 July 1897. JC10/1/93.

332 Holli, M.G., 'Joseph Chamberlain and the Jameson Raid: a Bibliographical Survey', *Journal of British Studies*, 3 (May 1964), pp. 152-166; Garvin, *op. cit.*, p. 125; Winkler, H.R., 'Joseph Chamberlain and the Jameson Raid', *The American History Review*, Vol. 54 No. 4, July 1949, pp. 841-849; Drus, E., 'The Question of Complicity in the Jameson Raid', *English Historical Review*, October 1953, Vol. 68 No. 269, pp. 582-593.

333 Telegram 2 August 1895, Harris to Rhodes, JC1/1/48.

334 JC 1/1/48

335 Winkler, *op. cit.*, p. 844.

336 Telegram Harris to Rhodes, 4 November 1895 quoted by Winkler, *op. cit.*, p. 844.

337 Judd, D., *Radical Joe, A Life of Joseph Chamberlain* (London, Faber, 1977), pp. 198-9.

338 Marsh, *op. cit.*, p. 380.

339 Letter Chamberlain to Fairfield, 17 December 1895 quoted by Marsh, *op. cit.*, p. 381; Letter Chamberlain to Meade, 18 December 1895, JC 10/1/20.

340 Winkler, *op. cit.*, p. 848.

341 Letter, Hawksley, B., to Fairfield, E., 20 August 1896, JC 10/1/60.

342 Drus, *op. cit.*, p. 589.

343 Crosby, *op. cit.*, p. 138.

344 Report of Select Committee on British South Africa, 13 July 1897, JC 10/1/93.

345 Drus, *op. cit.*, p. 583.

346 JC 10/1/48.

347 Garvin, *op. cit.*, p. 82.

348 Garvin, *op. cit.*, p. 38.

349 Garvin, *op. cit.*, p. 82.

Chapter 8: Private Passions

350 Gardiner, *op. cit.*, p. 48.

351 Gardiner, *op. cit.*, p. 170.

352 Sellars, I.A., *Nineteenth-Century Nonconformity* (London, Edward Arnold, 1977), pp. 92-94.

353 Marsh, *op. cit.*, pp. xii and 7.

354 Letter Chamberlain to Morley, J., 7 December 1875, JC 5/54/61.

355 *The Diaries of Beatrice Webb*, LSE Digital Library, http://digitallibrary.lse.ac.uk p. 366.

356 Marsh, *op. cit.*, p. 95.

357 Ballard, P., 'A Commercial and Industrial Elite: A Study of Birmingham's Upper Middle Class, 1780 -1914' (Unpublished Ph.D. Thesis), University of Reading, 1983, pp. 205-226.

358 Gardiner, *op. cit.*, p. 191.

359 Gardiner, *op. cit.*, pp. 179-203.

[360] Peacock, R., 'The 1892 Birmingham Religious Census' in *Religion in the Birmingham Area – Essays in the Sociology of Religion*, ed. Bryman, A., (Birmingham, University of Birmingham, 1977), pp. 12-28.

[361] Ballard, *op. cit.*, pp. 128-133.

[362] Burn, W.L., *The Age of Equipoise*, (London, George Allen & Unwin,1964), pp. 115-117.

[363] Gardiner, *op. cit.*, p. 105.

[364] Gardiner, *op. cit.*, p. 110.

[365] Chamberlain, J.C., *Fortnightly Review*, October 1874, quoted by Marsh, *op. cit.*, p. 107.

[366] Marsh, *op. cit.*, p. 321.

[367] Ballard, P., 'Rus in Urbe: Joseph Chamberlain's Gardens at Highbury, Moor Green in Birmingham, 1879-1914', *Garden History*, vol.14, No.1, Spring 1986, pp. 61-76; for the 1914 garden party see Marsh, *op. cit.*, pp. 664-5.

[368] Quotes by Constantine, S., 'Amateur Gardening and Popular Recreation in the 19th and 20th Centuries', *Journal of Social History*, vol.14, no.3, Spring 1981, pp. 387-406.

[369] Perrie, M., 'Hobby farming among the Birmingham bourgeoisie: the Cadburys and the Chamberlains on their suburban estates, *c.*1880-1914', *Agricultural History Review*, 61, I, pp. 111-134.

[370] Marsh, *op. cit.*, p. 362; Perrie, *op. cit.*, p. 115.

[371] Ballard, 'Rus in Urbe' in *Garden History, op. cit.*, p. 65.

[372] Alexander, H.A., *Richard Cadbury of Birmingham* (London, Hodder and Stoughton, 1906), p. 256.

[373] Scott, R., *Elizabeth Cadbury 1858 – 1951* (London, George G. Harrap, 1955), p. 55; Ballard, 'A Commercial and Industrial Elite', *op. cit.*, p. 769.

[374] Holyoak, J., 'J.H. Chamberlain' in Ballard, P., ed., *Birmingham's Victorian and Edwardian Architects* (London, The Victorian Society, 2009), pp. 153-181.

[375] Webb, B., *op. cit.*, diary entry for 28 February 1886, p. 354.

[376] Roberts, S., *Joseph Chamberlain's Highbury – A Very Public Private House* (Birmingham Biographies, 2015), p. 3.

[377] Marsh, *op. cit.*, p. 139.

[378] *Cassell's Family Magazine 1888*, p. 380 commented: 'Mr Chamberlain planned this supply of his own when the domestic use of electric light was in its infancy', JC 4/11-12.

[379] Letters Mary Chamberlain to Mrs Endicott: 27 December 1888 AC 4/3/47 and 8 February 1889, AC 4/3/57.

[380] 'Society in London', *Edgbastonia*, vol. V, May 1885, p. 69, quoted by Ballard, *op. cit.*, p. 381.

[381] Ballard, *op. cit.*, p. 732; Roberts, *op. cit.*, p. 9.

[382] Ballard, *op. cit.*, pp. 401-409.

[383] Roberts, *op. cit.*, p. 3.

[384] Ballard, *op. cit.*, pp. 340-352.

[385] Gardiner, *op. cit.*, p. 180.

[386] Gardiner, *op. cit.*, pp. 236-8.

[387] Gardiner, *op. cit.*, pp. 254-5.

[388] Perrie, *op. cit.*, p. 118 and p. 134.

[389] *The Times*, 'Mr Austen Chamberlain as a farmer,' 20 December 1894.

[390] Letter Austen to Neville, 21 December 1891, AC5/3/28.

[391] For the paragraphs on model farming of Austen Chamberlain and George Cadbury, Maureen Perrie's article already cited has been invaluable.

[392] Letter Harriet Kenrick to Mrs Chamberlain, 2 September 1861, AC 1/1/54.

[393] *New Penny Handbook* (1897), cited by Constantine, *op. cit.*, p. 389.

[394] Ballard, 'Rus in Urbe', *op. cit.*, p. 72.

[395] Ballard, 'A Commercial and Industrial Elite' *op. cit.*, pp. 883-899; 'Rus in Urbe,' *op. cit.*, p. 69; Marsh, *op. cit.*, p. 442.

[396] Ballard, 'Rus in Urbe,' *op. cit.*, p. 68.

[397] Ballard, 'Rus in Urbe,' *op. cit.*, p. 68.

[398] Ballard, P., *Highbury Park, Moseley, Birmingham. Historic Landscape Appraisal* (Birmingham, 2009), p. 25, quoted by Roberts, S., *op. cit.*, p. 12.

[399] Alexander, H.C., *op. cit.*, p. 55.

[400] Gardiner, *op. cit.*, p. 19.

[401] Bailey, *op. cit.*, pp. 123-125.

[402] Marsh, P., *The Chamberlain Litany* (London, Haus Publishing, 2010), p. 97.

[403] *Birmingham Mail*, 11 June 2015.

Chapter 9: Family and Dynasty

[404] Marsh, P., *op. cit.*, p. 90.

[405] Webb, B., *Diary*, entry for 18 March 1884.

[406] Bartley, P., *Votes for Women* (London, Hodder Murray, 2007), pp. 23-30.

407 JC 28/A1/22.

408 Quoted by Ward, R., *The Chamberlains* (Croydon, Fonthill, 2015), p. 75.

409 Marsh, *op. cit.*, p. 302.

410 Quoted by Marsh, *op. cit.*, p. 320.

411 Marsh, *op. cit.*, p. 302.

412 AC 4/3/1-124.

413 Ballard, *op. cit.*, p. 386 ff.

414 Marsh, P., *The Chamberlain Litany* (London, Haus Publishing, 2010), p. 97.

415 Scott, R., *Elizabeth Cadbury 1858-1951* (London, George G. Harrap, 1955), p. 75.

416 Scott, R., *op. cit.*, p. 59.

417 Scott, R., *op. cit.*, p. 74.

418 Smith, H.V., 'Elizabeth Taylor Cadbury: Religion, Maternalism and Social Reform in Birmingham, 1888-1914' (unpublished Ph.D. Thesis, University of Birmingham, 2012), pp. 24-27.

419 Scott, *op. cit.*, p. 118.

420 Smith, *op. cit.*, p. 56 and p. 231.

421 Scott, *op. cit.*, p. 90.

422 Bailey, A., and Bryon, J.R., 'A Quaker Experiment in Town Planning', *Quaker Studies*, No.1, 2006, p. 109; Bartley, P., 'Moral Regeneration: Women and the Civic Gospel in Birmingham, 1870-1914', *Midland History*, XXV (2000), pp. 143-158.

423 Smith, *op. cit.*, p. 68.

424 Quoted by Richenda Scott, *op. cit.*, p. 190.

425 Self, R., (ed)., *The Austen Chamberlain Diary Letters* (Cambridge, CUP, 1995), p. 5, quoting Dangerfield, G.

426 Self, R., *op. cit.*, p. 4.

427 Letter, AC to MC, 7th May 1911 in Chamberlain, A., *Politics from Inside* (London, Constable, 1936), p. 337.

428 Cannadine, D., 'The Chamberlain Tradition and Birmingham,' in Cannadine, D., *In Churchill's Shadow* (London, Allen Lane, 2002), p. 126.

429 Jenkins, R., *The Chancellors* (London, Macmillan, 1998), p. 112.

430 Ward, *op. cit.*, p. 71.

431 Self, *op. cit.*, p. 7.

432 Amery, L., *My Political Life* vol.1 (London, Hutchinson, 1953), p. 303 quoted by Self, *op. cit.*, p. 8.a

433 Quoted by Self, R., *Neville Chamberlain* (Aldershot, Ashgate, 2006), p. 41.

434 Quoted by Ward, R., *op. cit.*, p. 107.

435 Self, R., *Neville Chamberlain* (Aldershot, Ashgate, 2006), p. 114.

436 Ward, R. *op .cit.*, p. 124.

437 Self, R., *op. cit.*, p. 141.

438 Self, *op. cit.*, p. 167.

439 Self, *op. cit.*, pp. 42, 113, 134.a

440 *Hansard*, 4 February 1932.

441 Letter AC to NC 5 November 1931 quoted by Self.

442 Self, *op. cit.*, p. 298.

443 Webb, B., *op. cit.*, diary entry for 3 September 1939.

444 Williams, I., *op. cit.*, pp. 82-83.

445 See chapter 1 above.

446 Marks, W., *George Cadbury Junior 1878-1954* (Birmingham, 1970), pp. 14-23.

447 From a pamphlet on *The History of Avoncroft*, produced by the College in 1975.

448 Hillman, J., *The Bournville Hallmark* (Studley, Brewin Books, 1994), p. 11.

449 Cadbury, G., *Town Planning – with special reference to Birmingham schemes* (London, Longman, 1915).

450 NC1/20/1/78.

451 Gardiner, *op. cit.*, p. 224.

452 Cadbury, E., *Experiments in Industrial Organisation* (London, Longmans Green and Co., 1912), p. 244.

453 Rawlinson, *op. cit.*, pp. 201-228.

INDEX

Notes: GC = George Cadbury; JC = Joseph Chamberlain; italics indicate images; notes with additional information are indicated by page number, then reference number and 'n' (e.g. '135:239n').

Act of Union (1801) 73
Adult Schools 20–2, 26–7, 95, 113, 116, 123–4
agricultural workers 38–9, 123
alcohol see temperance
Alexander, H. 21
allotments and small holdings 39, 42, 60
Amery, Julian 81
Amery, Leo 118
Andros, Bahamas 120
Angola, slavery in 84, 85, 86
Anti-Sweating League 44, 60–1, 97
Artisans' and Labourers' Dwellings Improvement Act (1875) 32, 37, 38
Arts and Crafts movement 50, 99
Asquith, H.H. 58, 59, 66, 71, 119
Aston (constituency) 53, 57, 69
Attwood, Thomas 3
Australia, Cadbury's chocolates in 11, 14, 125
Avery, Thomas 38
Avoncroft, Offenham and Stoke Prior 123

Bailey, A. 55
Bakers (chocolate manufacturer) 14
Baldwin, Stanley 121
Balfour, Arthur 29, 64, 67, 119
Ballard, P.D. 112
Band of Hope, temperance group 54, 97
Bathoen (Bechuana chief) 90
Baths and Parks Committee 39
Beach, Hicks 81
Bechuanaland 90–2, 103
beer consumption 44, 55
Beerhouse Act (1830) 44
Bingley Hall, Birmingham 80
Birmingham 3–5; celebrations of JC and GC 4, *101, 106*; city development 4–5, 34, 37, 38, 42–3; establishment of Greater Birmingham 121, 124; map of *46; see also specific places*
Birmingham Artisans' Association 28
Birmingham Chamber of Commerce 17, 79–80
Birmingham Children's Hospital 97
Birmingham Cripples' Union 97
Birmingham Daily Post (newspaper) 34, 65, 89
Birmingham Education Society 23, 32
Birmingham Liberal Association 64
Birmingham Mail (newspaper) 19
Birmingham Museum and Art Gallery 34, 36, 42, 109
Birmingham Political Union 3
Birmingham Repertory Company 117
Birmingham Rowton House scheme 98
Birmingham School Board 4–5, 25, 27
Birmingham Screw Company (manufacturer) 16
Birmingham Small Arms (manufacturer) 78
Birmingham Symphony Orchestra 117

Birmingham Theatre 109
Birmingham Town Council 23, 27, 34, 124, 125; *Birmingham Council Proceedings, The* 35, 36;
    Council House 34, 42; Mayorship 10, 24, 26, 35–8, 121
Birmingham Town Hall Fountain *51*
Birmingham Union of Girls Clubs 116
Birmingham University 30–1, *46, 48*, 58
Birmingham West (constituency) 118
Blue Ribbon movement 18, 53, 54
Board Schools 22, 24–5, 27–9, 31, *48*, 67
Boer War ('Joe's War'; South African War) 4, 15, 29–31, 40, 58, 66, 69–70, 73, 76–80
Booth, Charles 57, 59
Booth, Richard 53, 54
Bournville Athletics Club 18
Bournville Cocoa 11, 14, 122
Bournville factory (Cadbury's chocolate) 10–13, 17–18, 33–4, 39, 41, *48*, 60, 122–3; *Bournville Works Magazine* 13, 14
Bournville Village 4, 5; architecture and design 14–15, 33–4, 39–41, 43, *50*, 99, 115–16; churches in 97;
    Garden City movement and 116, 124; gardens 41; maps of *46, 49*; Royal visit (1919) 4, 31, 41, *106*; rules 41, 55;
    schools in 27, 31, 116; temperance and 54–5, 57
Bournville Village Trust 33, 40, 55, 97, 117, 124; *Trust Deed* 55
Bower, G. 92
Brailsford, H.N. 86, 88
Bright, John 3, 11, 26, 65, 75, 100
Bristol Street, Birmingham 124
British Colonial Office 91–4
British Empire *see* Imperialism
British Foreign Office, slavery controversy 85–7, 89
British South Africa Company 89–93
Browning Hall, memorial tablet 59–60, 124
Bruce, H.A. 53
Bunce, J.T. 34, 65
Burns, John 66
Burtt, Joseph 85–6

Cadbury, Edward (son of GC) 13, 18, 58, 59, 71, *108*, 122–5
Cadbury, Elizabeth (née Taylor; second wife of GC) 27, 31, 33, 54, 100, *108*, 109, 113–18
Cadbury, George 3–5; Boer War and 15, 67, 73, 76, 78–9; in business 10–19, 31, 34, 59; character 18, 34, 39, 42, 69;
    copywriting skills 14–15; early employment 15; education and 20, 21–3, 26–7, 29–31; exercise and 55, 109;
    family of 114–19, 122–5; family values 18, 27, 33, 39; farming and 100, 110, 111; Free Trade and 73, 82–3;
    gardening and 33, 40–1, 55, 112–13; homes of 31, 98–100, *105*, 109, 111, 113, 116; honorary degree 31; housing
    and 12, 15, 17–18, 23, 26, 33–4, 39–43, 54–5; hunting and 110; images of *45, 105, 108*; Imperialism and 66, 67, 79;
    influences 34; Irish Home Rule and 73, 75, 78; land rights and reform 42, 68; leadership qualities 42; libel trial
    (1909) 84, 86, 87–9; music and 109; as National Free Church Council President 95, 97, 117; newspaper
    proprietary 15, 29, 59, 63, 69–71, 78–9, 86–9, 125; pacifism of 67, 75; pensions and 57, 58–60, 71; philanthropy 40,
    59, 97–8, 99; politics of 63, 65, 66–8, 71, 75; Privy Council and 68; Quaker faith 10, 15, 18, 21, 31, 43, 59, 75, 86,
    95–100, 109, 115; reading and 109; on sanitation 33; school building 27, 31; slave-grown cocoa controversy 84–9,
    94, *102*; smoking and 100; social life 100; as teacher 20, 21–2, 95, 116; temperance and 44, 53–5, 57, 90, 100, 109;
    University of Birmingham and 30–1; vegetarianism 41; wealth of 95–7, 100; welfare reform and 67–8; worker
    recreation and 22, 40; working conditions and anti-sweating 13, 15, 17–18, 60–2, 66, 71, 78–9; *see also* Bournville
    Village; Cadbury's (chocolate manufacturer)
Cadbury, George (son of GC) 14, *108*, 122–4; *Experiments in Industrial Organisation* 125; *Town Planning* 124
Cadbury, Henry (son of GC) 125
Cadbury, John (father of GC) 10, 16, 54
Cadbury, Laurence (son of GC) 109–10, 114
Cadbury, Mary (née Tylor; first wife of GC) 100, 114, 115
Cadbury, Richard (brother of GC) 10–13, 15, 17, 21, 30, 54, 56, 59, 97, 112–13; Uffculme home *46*, 90, 99, 109, 110
Cadbury, William (nephew of GC) 84–7
Cadbury Alexander, Helen (daughter of Richard Cadbury) 12, 54, 112
Cadbury Bros. (chocolate manufacturer) *see* Cadbury's (chocolate manufacturer)

Cadbury family 3, 54, 84, 99, *108*, 114–19, 122–5
Cadbury's (chocolate manufacturer; *earlier* Cadbury Bros.) 4; 'Absolutely Pure' marketing campaign
    14–15, 40, 41, 52, 79; Bechuana chiefs' visit 90; Boer War and 79; *Bournville Cocoa* 11, 14, 122; Bournville factory
    10–13, 17–18, 33–4, 39, 41, *48*, 60, 122–3; Bridge Street factory 10, 12, 33; Christmas parties 17; *Dairy Milk
    Chocolate* 11, 12, 14, 82, 122; distribution 123; early success 10; exports 11, 125; female employees 13, 18, 27, *48*;
    Free Trade and 82; gambling and 18; industrial action 18; industry partnerships 15; management of 122–3, 125;
    map of *46*; pension scheme 17, 58; piece work 18, 125; processes and machinery 11–14, 122; slave-grown cocoa
    84–9; temperance and 54, 55; worker education 17; working conditions 13–17, 60, 62, 125; working hours 16;
    Works Councils of 18, 123
Campbell-Bannerman, Henry 42, 66, 68, 71, 135:239n
Canada, trade agreements 80–1
Cannadine, David 120
Carey Hill College 31
Carr's Lane chapel, Birmingham 90
Carson, Sir Edward 87–9
Carter Lane Chapel, London 20
Catholic Church, Ireland 73, 75
Cecil, Hugh, 1st Baron Quickswood 81
Chamberlain, Arthur (brother of JC) 57, 77–8
Chamberlain, Austen (son of JC) 68, 78, 100, *107*, 109–11, 114–15, 118–20, 122, 125
Chamberlain, Beatrice (daughter of JC) *107*, 114, 115
Chamberlain, Florence (second wife of JC) 95
Chamberlain, Herbert (brother of JC) 78
Chamberlain, Ida (daughter of JC) 110, 111
Chamberlain, J.H. 99
Chamberlain, Joseph 3–5; art collection 109; on Birmingham Town Council 23, 26, 32, 35–6, 39, 56; Boer War and
    52, 58, 69, 73, 76–9, 80; in business 10–19, 20, 23, 25, 32, 44, 69, 79–80; character 15–16, 39, 68, 69, 74;
    city development 4–5, 34, 37, 38, 42–3; as Colonial Secretary 29; death 118; Duchy 65, 81, 120; education and
    17, 20–30, 31, 32, 58, 96; exercise and 109; faith of 10, 21, 95–6; family of 114–15, 118–22, 125; farming and 110;
    French language 15, 21; gardening and 20, 109, 111–12, 113; on gas supplies 35; homes of 98–100, *104*, 109–11,
    115, 118; as host 98, 100, 115; housing and 38–9, 42–3; hunting and 110; images of *45, 52, 101, 104, 107*;
    Imperialism of 13, 65, 74, 77, 78, 79, 80, 81; industrial disputes arbitration 61; influences 23, 35, 37;
    innovation and 99–100, 111–12; investments 120; Irish Home Rule and 73, 74–5; Jameson Raid (1895)
    controversy 84, 89–94; land reforms 42; leadership qualities 24, 35, 42; legislation and 17, 19, 96, 98; as Mayor of
    Birmingham 10, 24, 26, 35–8; oratory skill 35, 37, 64, 68, 74; party politics and 24–6, 29, 39, 63–9, 71–2, 74, 115,
    119–20; pensions and 57–9, 81; philanthropy 35, 98, 99, 109; political violence and 69; publicity of 68, 69;
    on sanitation 32–3, 35–8; as School Board Chairman 4–5, 24, 27; school building 22, 25, 31; smoking and
    100; stroke 31, 58, 111, 115; Tariff Reform and 67–8, 71–3, 79–83, 115; as teacher 20–2; temperance and 44, 53–4,
    56–7, 100; as Trade Board President 61; University of Birmingham and 30; wealth of 95, 98, 112; work ethic 15,
    25; worker recreation and 22; on working classes 19, 32; working conditions and anti-sweating 13, 16–19, 32,
    60–2; on working hours 16–17; writings of 11, 19, 23, 25, 57
Chamberlain, Mary (*née* Endicott; third wife of JC) 98, 100, *107*, 109, 114–15, 118
Chamberlain, Neville (son of JC) 78, 83, 100, *107*, 110, 115, 118, 120–2, 124–5
Chamberlain family 3, 24, *107*, 114–15, 118–22, 125
Chartism 3
Cheltenham, riots 53
Chester, Bishop of 56
Chinese slave-labour, South Africa 28, 53, 63, 71, 78–9, 87, 88
Church of England 3, 28, 53, 63, 73
Church of England schools (voluntary schools) 24, 28–9, 67
Church of England Temperance Society 54
Church of the Messiah 20, 22
Church of the Saviour 23, 35
Church Party, against school boards 25
Churchill, Winston 60, 67, 68, 70
Clarion (newspaper and vans) 82
Clarke, Peter 67
Class XIV, Severn Street School 21, 22, 95, 116

Clifford, John 29
Collings, Jesse 23, 38, 109
Colonial Nursing Association 115
Conservative Party 32, 42, 53, 56–7, 63–4, 68–9, 80
Coppersmith's Arms, Rea Street, Birmingham 22
Corporation Street, Birmingham 34, 37, 42, 54
Crosby, Travis 93
Cross, Richard 37

Daily Chronicle, The (newspaper) 70
Daily Graphic, The (newspaper) 86
Daily Mail, The (newspaper) 70
Daily News (newspaper of GC) 15, 29, 59–60, 70–1, 78–9, 124–5; slave-grown cocoa controversy and 86–9
Daily Telegraph, The (newspaper) 70
Dairy Milk Chocolate 11, 12, 14, 82, 122
Dart, The (satirical newspaper) 27, 39, 65
Davenport, Baron John 55
Dawson, George 23, 35
Devonshire, Spencer Cavendish, 8th Duke of (Lord Hartington) 30, 64, 75, 81, 100
Dilke, Sir Charles 60, 100
Disraeli, Benjamin 32
Dixson, George 23, 24, 32
'Drink question' *see* temperance
Drus, Ethel 94

East Worcestershire (constituency) 68, 118
Economist, The (magazine) 79
Edgbaston Debating Society 109, 120
Edgbaston High School 22
education 17, 20–3, 32, 123; GC and 20, 21–3, 26–7, 29–31; JC and 17, 20–30, 31, 32, 58, 96; legislation 22, 24–6, 28, 29, 30, 67, 123; of women 22, 27, 116; *see also* schools
Education Act (1902) 29, 30, 67
Education Act (1918) 123
Education Act (1944) 123
Edward VII, King of the United Kingdom 68
Edwardian era 11, 41, 82
Edwards, Thomas 14
Elementary Education Act (1870) 22, 24, 25, 26, 28, 29
Elliot's (manufacturer) 120
Employers' Liability Act (1880) 61
employment 71, 78–9, 82; *see also* working classes
Endicott Carnegie, Mary *see* Chamberlain, Mary (*née* Endicott; third wife of JC)
Engels, Frederick 32
exercise and health 18, 22, 55, 109
Exeter, riots 53
Exhibition of Sweated Industries (1906) 71

Factory Acts (1860s) 17
Fair Trade 79–80; *see also* Tariff Reform (Protection)
Fairfield, Edward 90–1, 92, 93
farming 100, 110, 111
Fircroft, Selly Oak 123, 124
Forster, W.E. 22, 24–6, 28, 29
Frampton-on-Severn, Cadbury factory 12
Free Trade 31, 67, 72–3, 79–83, 116
Frys of Bristol (chocolate manufacturer) 15, 85

gambling 18
Garden City movement 4, 34, 41, 116, 124
gardening 20, 33, 40–1, 55, 109, 112–13
Gardiner, A.G., *Life of George Cadbury* 12, 17, 18, 22, 27, 31, 33, 34, 39, 40, 55, 59, 65, 66, 67, 70, 71, 79, 86, 109, 110
Garvin, J.L. 21, 22, 23, 24, 32, 92, 94
gas supplies 27, 36, 41, 43, 67
George V, King of the United Kingdom 4, 31, 41, *106*
gin consumption 44
GKN (manufacturer) 10, 13, 16
Gladstone, William 24–6, 28, 53, 61, 63–5, 73–6, 97
Gore, Dr, Bishop of Birmingham 97
Gorst, John 29
Gospel Temperance 18, 53, 54
Gothenburg scheme, drink trade 56
Great Reform Act (1832) 3
Greater Birmingham, establishment of 121, 124
Greater Birmingham City Education Committee 117
Green Belt 124
Grey, Sir Edward 66, 85, 86, 87, 94

Hadley Castle, Shropshire 13
Harcourt, William 53, 56, 66
Hardie, Keir 67
Harper's Monthly Magazine 85
Harris, Frederick Rutherfoord 89, 90, 92, 94
Harris, William 64
Hartington, Lord (Spencer Cavendish, 8th Duke of Devonshire) 30, 64, 75, 81, 100
Harvey, Alexander 39, 41
Hawkins, John 15
Heath Street factory, Smethwick (Nettlefold and Chamberlain) 11, 13, 18, *46, 47*
Highbury, home of JC *46*, 90, 98–100, *104*, 109–13, 115, 118
Hill, Alfred 35–6
Hitler, Adolf 121
Hobsbawm, Eric 76
Home Rule *see* Irish Home Rule
Hoskins (manufacturer) 78, 120
housing conditions and reform 12, 14–18, 23, 26, 32–4, 37–44, 54–5, 66, 115–17, 120–1
Howard, Ebenezer, Garden Cities and 34, 124
'Hungry Forties, The' 58, 81, 134:203n
hunting 110
Huntley and Palmers (biscuit manufacturer) 58

Imperial Wire Company (manufacturer) 13
Imperialism 66, 74, 77–9, 81, 121–2
industrial disputes arbitration 61
industrial relations 18, 66
International Council of Women 116, 117
Ireland 73, 75
Irish Home Rule 64, 65, 73–6, 78, 122
Irish National Party 73
Isaacs, Sir Rufus 87

James and Avery (manufacturers) 15
Jameson Raid (1895) controversy 76, 84, 89–94, *103*
Jenkins, Roy 118
jingoism *see* Imperialism
Jones, E. 16

Kenrick, Florence (second wife of JC) 114, 118
Kenrick, Harriet (first wife of JC) 111, 118
Kenrick family (in-laws of JC) 109, 111
Khama (Bechuana chief) 90
Kimberley, John Wodehouse, 1st Earl of 74
Kingsmead College 31, 96–7
Knighton, Cadbury factory at 12
Kruger, Paul 76, 77, 91
Kynoch's (manufacturer) 77–8

Labour Party 66–7, 97
Labour Representation Committee (LRC) 66–7
land reform 42, 68
Lehmans (chocolate manufacturer) 14
Leighton Park, Quaker school 96, 97, 122
Leverhulme, William Lever, 1st Viscount of 34
Liberal Association of Birmingham 64
Liberal Party 4, 25–8, 30, 53, 58–61, 63–7, 71, 73–6, 78–9, 81, 116
Liberal Unionist Party 29–30, 56–7, 61, 64–5, 118, 120
licencing reform 44, 53, 56
Likey Hills, homes of Cadbury family 99, 124
Lindt and Sprüngli Ltd (chocolate manufacturers) 82
Livesey, Joseph 44, 54
Lloyd George, David 42, 58, 66–7, 69–71, 77–8, 119
Local Education Authorities (LEAs) 29
Local Government Bill (1880) 56
Local Veto Bill (1894) 53, 56
Long, Prof., Cirencester 110, 111
Lowe, Robert 22

Macdonald, Ramsay 67
Manchester Guardian (newspaper) 70, 81
manhood suffrage 3
Manor, The, Northfield, home of GC *46*, 60, 96, 99–100, 109, 111, 113
Marsh, Peter 37, 42, 78, 95
Martin, William 99
Mary of Teck, Queen of the United Kingdom 4, 31, 41, 79, 100, *106*
Mason, Josiah 16, 30, 97
Mason College 30, 120
Masterman, C.P. 70
Meade, Sir Robert 93
Menier (chocolate manufacturer) 14
Milner, Alfred 77, 78
minimum wage 60
Morley, John 66, 92, 95
Morning Leader (newspaper) 15
Morning Post (newspaper) 70
Moseley and King's Heath Journal 112
Mutual Improvement Society 20

Nation, The (newspaper) 15
National Anti-Sweating League 44, 60–1, 97
National Cash Register Company, The 14
National Council of Women 117
National Education League 23–4, 25, 26, 28, 29
National Free Church Council 95, 97, 117
National Liberal Federation (NLF) 26, 64, 65

National Old Age Pensions League 59, 124
National Peace Council 117
National Review (newspaper) 57
National Temperance League 44
National Union of Conservative Associations 57
Nettlefold and Chamberlain (manufacturer) 11–13, 15–18, 25, *46, 47*
Nettlefold family 24
Nettleford, John Sutton (brother-in-law of JC) 10, 11, 13
Neville, Lady Dorothy 111
Nevinson, H.W. (journalist) 85, 86–7, 88, *102*
New Penny Handbook (1897) 111
New Street, Birmingham 37
Newton, F. 92
Nightingale, A. 85
Nonconformism 3, 10–11, 20, 24–9, 44, 53–4, 63, 67, 95–7
North Worcestershire (constituency) 65, 66, 79
Northern Echo, The (newspaper) 15
Northfield, Birmingham 27, 116; The Manor, home of GC 46, 60, 96, 99–100, 109, 111, 113

Old Age Pensions 17, 44, 57–60, 71, 81, 124, 125, 134:199n
Old Age Pensions Act (1908) 59–60, 124
Othick, J. 14

Parents National Education Union 116
parks and public spaces 37
Parnell, Charles Stewart 73, 74
Parry, W.J. 71
Penrhyn, Edward Douglas-Pennant, 1st Baron, and the Penrhyn quarrymen 71
pensions 17, 44, 57–60, 71, 81, 124, 125, 134:199n
philanthropy 35, 40, 59, 97–9, 109, 117
piece work 18, 60, 125
Pitsani Strip, Bechuanaland 90–2, *103*
Pitt the Younger, William 73
Plimsoll, Samuel 61
Poor Laws 57, 58, 62
Portugal, West African slave labour 84–6, 88, *102*
Priestley, Joseph 10, 20
Prime Ministership 119, 121
Príncipe, Portuguese cocoa island 84, 85–7, *102*
prohibition 44, 53, 54, 56, 57
Protection *see* Tariff Reform (Protection)
Public Health Act (1872) 36
Public Health Act (1875) 40
public houses and publicans 44, 53–7

Quakers 10–11, 15, 18, 21, 27, 31, 54, 117; faith of GC 10, 15, 18, 21, 31, 43, 59, 75, 86, 95–100, 109, 115; influence of GC on 96–7, 100, 109; *The Quaker Position on the War* (circular) 15

Radical Unauthorised Programme 28, 38, 42
Radicals 1, 26, 63–6, 74, 75, 77
Rendel Harris Library 124
Rhodes, Cecil 76, 78, 89–94; British South Africa Company 89–93
Richardson, John 34
Ridley, Sir Matthew White 61
Robinson, Sir Hercules 90, 92–3, 94
Rosebery, Archibald Primrose, 5th Earl of 66, 89
Rowntree, Joseph 10, 14, 15, 44, 54, 130:26n
Rowntree family 54

Rowntree's (confectionary manufacturer) 15, 58, 88
Royal Commission on Children's Employment (1864) 11
Royal Commission on Depression of Trade and Industry (1885) 80
Royal Cripples Hospital 117
Royal visit (1919), Bournville 4, 31, 41, *106*
Ryder Street, Birmingham 38

Salisbury, Robert Gascoyne-Cecil, 3rd Marquess of (Lord) 28, 42, 56, 57, 68, 76, 77, 91
Salvation Army 97
sanitation 32–3, 35–8, 120
São Tomé, Portuguese cocoa island 84, 85–8, *102*, 125
Schnadhorst, Frank 64, 65
schools: Adult Schools 20–2, 26–7, 95, 113, 116, 123–4; Board Schools 22, 24–5, 27–9, 31, *48*, 67; building schemes
    22, 25, 27, 31; Church/voluntary schools 24, 28–9, 67; Quaker schools 96, 97, 122; *see also* education
Scott, C.P. 70
Sebele (Bechuana chief) 90
Second Reform Act (1867) 22
Selborne, William Palmer, 2nd Earl 30
Selly Oak, Birmingham 22, 27, 31, 33, 96, 97, 124; *see also* Bournville Village
Selly Oak Colleges 4, 5, 30, 31, 96–7, 120, 123, 124
Severn Street Adult School 21, 26, 123, 124; Class XIV of GC 21, 22, 95, 116
Shaw, Flora 93, 94
Shaw, George Bernard 118
Shiman, Lilian 53
slum areas 32, 33, 37, 38, 40, 54
small holdings and allotments 39, 42, 60
Smethwick Working Men's Club 22
Smethwick Working Men's Institute 21, 32
South Africa 78, 81; Boer War 15, 29–31, 40, 58, 66, 69–70, 73, 76–80; Chinese slave-labour 28, 53, 63, 71, 78–9, 87, 88;
    Jameson Raid (1895) 84, 89–93
Southbourne, home of JC *46*, 99
Staffordshire (constituency) 65
Standard, The (newspaper) 86–7, 88
Star, The (newspaper) 15
Stirchley Institute 27, 33, 54, 67, 97
Stollwerck Bros. (chocolate manufacturer) 14, 122
Sturge, Joseph 21, 131n61
suffragette movement 114, 116–17
Sunday at Home (magazine) 55
Sunday closing 56
sweated labour and anti-sweating movement 44, 60–1, 71, 97, 124–5
Swiss milk chocolate 82

Tariff Reform (Protection) 58, 67–8, 71–3, 79–83, 115–16, 118–19, 121
Tariff Reform Committee 120
Tariff Reform League 82
Taylor, Elizabeth *see* Cadbury, Elizabeth (*née* Taylor; second wife of GC)
temperance 16–18, 22, 40, 44, 51, 53–7, 90, 100, 109
Thorn Road school, Birmingham 27
Times, The (newspaper) 70, 93, 110
Timmins, Samuel 11
Town Planning Committee 124
Trade Boards 60–1
Trade Unions 42, 66, 78–9
Transvaal, South Africa 85, 87, 88–94, *103*
Tylor, Mary (first wife of GC) 100, 114, 115

Uffculme, home of Richard Cadbury *46*, 90, 99, 109, 110
Uitlander uprising 90–2, 94
UK Alliance 44, 53–4
Ulster 75
Union of Women Workers 116
Unionist Party 4, 67, 73, 74, 77, 78, 81, 83, 118–20
Unitarian Chapel, Birmingham 32
Unitarianism 10–11, 20, 22, 95–6
universal manhood suffrage 3
University of Birmingham 10, 30–1, *46*, *48*, 58

Van Houten (chocolate manufacturer) 89
Versailles Peace Conference 117
Victoria Law Courts 87
Victorian era 16, 20, 58, 63, 68
Villa Gardener, The (magazine) 98
Vincent, John 63
voluntary schools (Church of England schools) 24, 28–9, 67

Wakefield, Mr. 13
Ward, Edward 54
Warwickshire (constituency) 65
water infrastructure 27, 32, 35–7, 63, 96
Webb, Beatrice 68, 95–6, 99, 114, 122
welfare reforms 61, 67, 71
West Africa, slave labour controversy 84–9, *102*
West Hill College 31, 96–7
Whigs 64, 65, 74, 75
Whitehall Laing, Diana 115
Wilhelm II, Kaiser of Germany 91
Williams, Iolo, *The Firm of Cadbury, 1831-1931* 12, 17, 33, 41
Wilson, J.W. 66, 79
Winds Point, Malvern, home of GC 100, 109
Winkler, H. 92
women: education of 22, 27, 116; employment of 13, 18, 27, *48*, 60, 79, 125; housing for 117; pensions and 59; suffragette movement 114, 116–17; temperance and 54; views on role of 114–16, 118
Women's Adult School 116
Woodbrooke, home of GC 31, *46*, 96–9, *105*, 116
Woodbrooke College (Quaker College) 123, 124
Worcestershire (constituency) 65, 66, 68
Workers' Suggestions Committees 13
workhouses 57, 59, 134:199n
working classes: agricultural workers 38–9, 123; education for 20–3, 26–7, 32, 95, 113, 116, 123–4; employment and 71, 78–9, 82; housing for 23, 32, 37–44, 54, 66, 115–17, 120–1; party politics and 66; pensions and 57–9; religion and 97; Tariff Reform and 81–2; temperance and 16, 44, 53, 56–7; views of JC on 19, 32; working conditions 44, 60–1, 71, 97, 124–5
working hours 16–17, 62
Workmen's Compensation Act (1897) 61
Works Councils 18, 123
Workshop Act (1870) 17

Young Women's Christian Association (YWCA) 116